CONTEMPORARY CHILDREN'S THEATER

CONTEMPORARY CHILDREN'S THEATER

EDITED BY
BETTY JEAN LIFTON

EQUINOX BOOKS/PUBLISHED BY AVON

AVON BOOKS
A division of
The Hearst Corporation
959 Eighth Avenue
New York, New York 10019

ISBN 0-380-00145-4

Cover photograph of the production of PUNCH AND
JUDY by Aurand Harris, performed by students in the
Program in Educational Theatre, The School of Education,
New York University, May 1973.

First Equinox Printing, November, 1974.

EQUINOX TRADEMARK REG. U.S. PAT. OFF. AND IN OTHER
COUNTRIES, MARCA REGISTRADA, HECHO EN U.S.A.

Printed in the U.S.A.

ACKNOWLEDGMENTS

CONTENTS

For the
      PLAYWRIGHTS THEATER FOR CHILDREN
         which is still in its youth.

Saint Emil[?] What the man[?] ... ... the
a little prince who came from a distant island[?] ... ...

INTRODUCTION

A Matter of Consequence

"Ah, little prince, dear little prince! I love to hear that laughter!"

"That is my present. Just that. It will be as it was when we drank the water . . ."

"What are you trying to say?"

"All men have the stars," he answered, "but they are not the same things for different people. For some, who are travelers, the stars are guides. For others they are no more than little lights in the sky. For others, who are scholars, they are problems. For my businessman they were wealth. But all these stars are silent. You—you alone—will have the stars as no one else has them—"

The Little Prince
Antoine de Saint-Exupéry

Saint-Exupéry had the stars when he wrote about the little prince who came from a distant asteroid. I like to think that all of us who write seriously for the young have the stars—at least a small glimmer of them. For like Saint-Exupéry we believe that such a pursuit is "a matter of consequence."

And yet in America today it seems as if children's theater is of no consequence at all. In spite of the early work of pioneers like Winifred Ward, Charlotte Chorpenning and Clare Tree Major, and the present endeavors of a few dedicated community college and residential theaters, there is an absence of quality and professional rigor in the field. Somewhere along the line it has given up, stopped protesting its segregated status, settled for second best. The result is that children's theater is looked on with disdain by critics who do not review it, by actors and directors who use it only as a meal ticket in-between jobs in the "real" theater, and by writers who cannot hope for professional productions or, for that matter, financial recompense.

How can we escape from the vicious cycle that now exists? Until the critics care enough to expose them, hack writers will continue to fill the void; as long as the hacks are encouraged, there will be no scripts to attract serious actors and directors; as long as the public accepts the mediocrity it is offered, there will be no artistic standards for the field.

It doesn't have to be this way. England has its Young Vic growing up in pride alongside the Old Vic, and Canada has a generously subsidized theater for its youth. Both countries are commissioning writers to produce innovative scripts. But here in America, which is supposedly child oriented, we keep patching up our Little Red Riding Hoods, Cinderellas, and Jack and the Beanstalks, like hand-me-downs that will make do for the youngest generation.

Not that I am against fairy tales, for their truths have been distilled through the centuries and have the power to reveal us to ourselves. Rather, I am impatient with those who manipulate and distort them for a few easy laughs. One cannot help longing for original artists to breathe new vision into these classics, to release their powers and let them reflect the absurdity, the terror, and the wonder of the age we live in. Or better still, for a Tolkien, who, in creating *The Lord of the Rings*, did not so much adapt the old sagas as forage from them— one creature here, one plot there—until he had constructed his own tale on the foundations of the universal unconscious.

This anthology was born of such impatience and longing. Its purpose was to find and make available some original voices writing in English for children's theater today. It was not easy—there were times when the search itself threatened to take on mythic dimensions, like seeking out the golden apples of the sun. For, although some groups—like the American Educational Theater Association—are encouraging regional theater and compiling script catalogues, there is still little communication between writer and publisher, writer and theater troupes, writer and the public.

However, in cultural as well as political affairs, there is always an underground. The word was that there were serious writers at work, that there were good scripts to be had. And there were.

The eight playwrights in this collection—American, English, Canadian—have national as well as generational differences. Their styles range from the participation play, theater of the absurd, commedia dell'arte to the well-made three-act play. Yet they share in common a dedication to the field of children's theater and a refusal to recognize the artificially imposed boundaries between it and adult theater.

These writers know that their work grows out of the universal theater tradition, differentiated only by content, not by techniques or standards. They have respect for their audiences, recognizing them not as mindless consumers of pap, but as thoughtful inheritors of outer space, the atom bomb, the computer, and Vietnam. These writers are experimenting, crossing the old conventional boundaries, just as the young people they write for are crossing the boundaries of childhood as we once knew it.

Of course, in crossing boundaries one always takes risks. One's well-ordered universe might collapse; even worse, one might fail. But the artist lives with such risks, even thrives on them. The serious playwright tests *all* the boundaries, from the technical ones within his craft, to the more subjective ones within himself, to those ultimate ones between life and death, mortality and immortality.

Playwrights' Boundaries

One of the more interesting developments in children's

theater has been the evolution of the participation play—a form in which the audience not only takes part but may influence the action of the play. This kind of production, usually performed in an intimate environment, is concerned with breaking through the boundaries between actors and audience. Like avant-garde adult theater, it is also preoccupied with the use of empty space—in placing its young audiences in unorthodox arrangements that will sharpen their awareness and elicit their response.

In England Brian Way, one of the early pioneers in audience participation, did away with static seating in front of a proscenium stage, and choreographed the participation moments in his scripts as carefully as a ballet. Jack Stokes in *The Incredible Journey of Fenda Maria* seeks an intimate relationship with his audience in any available space, be it a gymnasium, lunchroom or outdoor playground. His actors create the illusions of time and place with their own bodies: "The grasp itself produces the cup which is grasped."

Unlike Way, who includes detailed notes to the actors in his scripts, Stokes sends a playful but purposeful letter to his future school audiences, explaining what will happen and what to expect. By appealing to the children in advance to participate in certain places within the action, he makes them accomplices to the success of the production.

My own *Kap the Kappa* was not originally written for participation, but went through many evolutions as I experimented with opening it up to audience response. In one version the action of the play took place on two floors, making it necessary for the children to move with the actors from the lower level in the river to the upper level of land. In another version I tried removing all the boundaries between playing space and audience, letting the children move freely with the actors from one area to another within the set. This proved not only exhilarating but overstimulating. When I reestablished the tensions of boundaries between the cast and the audience, the children were better able to concentrate on the images of the play and to enter more creatively into the moments when they were asked to take part. However, each participation play requires different types of boundaries, depending on the intent of the writer or group and the nature of the material.

James Reaney's *Names and Nicknames* has some audience participation, but it is only incidental to what he is about. He has really created a kind of transformation play for schoolchildren to perform in. A large chorus, ("where everyone gets a chance") not only chants the words that set the scene, but also transforms into the seasons, objects, animals, and people who are named. Its techniques are reminiscent of those Viola Spolin developed in her improvisation exercises and which her son, Paul Sills, brought to Broadway for both adults and children under the name of Story Theater.

Although their experiments are not represented here, it should be noted that some children's theater troupes (including my own) are beginning to explore the ensemble techniques of Joe Chaikin's "Open Theater," Jerzy Grotowski's "Polish Lab Theater," and the Becks' "Living Theater," in which there is a stress on physicalization of action to express emotion rather than words. Often beginning with a concept rather than a script, these experimenters in group process usually create a director's rather than a writer's theater. However, for the playwright fortunate enough to survive the shifting boundaries inherent in ensemble work, there is an exciting and profound challenge here. At its best, such a collaboration can fertilize and deepen the writer's imagination.

Playwright and the Double
One boundary that has always preoccupied the writer is that which divides his many selves—a concept often expressed in the theme of the double which runs through so much of mythology, fiction, and psychological writing.

Stokes has taken his use of the double from African folklore in shaping his *Fenda Maria*. He gives it a wit and clarity that makes it not only entertaining but accessible to his young audiences, who may not understand why they are so delighted when the noble and cowardly halves of Ngana are finally reunited, but will store something away for a later day.

The double runs through *Kap the Kappa*, too, in that Kap has a mortal form when he lives in an amnesiac state on land, and an immortal one when he finds his way back to his river home.

Schiller tells us that "all creatures born of our fantasy, in the last analysis, are nothing but ourselves." Children with their great capacity for multiple selves, which show up in their games and play, understand this well. Because they are shape shifters, they can easily identify with the split personalities of characters such as Ngana and Kap, as if they were their own doppelgängers going forth to test themselves in the world.

Nonsense and Absurdity

If there are boundaries between sense and nonsense, sensibility and absurdity, one won't find them in Aurand Harris' adaptation of *Punch and Judy*. For the nonsense of the commedia dell'arte style is deadly serious in dealing with the absurdity that runs through the most seemingly sensible of lives. And Punch, that raucous character, who has resisted the fate of other puppets in this country— banishment to the nursery where they are expected to behave with propriety—has emerged triumphant once again. Only this time in human form. For just as he evolved over the centuries from a marionette to a hand puppet (the better to clobber everyone), now Punch jumps off the stage into the audience (the better to scandalize the kids up close).

Punch is a rebel, and this is not lost on our rebellious young who dig his antics, any more than it was lost on the European adults who loved watching him fulfill their fantasies—giving the doctor a dose of his own medicine, hanging the hangman with his own noose. Much like the slapstick Japanese characters in Kyogen, that comic twin of the aristocratic Noh, Punch has always exposed the underbelly of society and defended the underdog.

Punch and Judy, as a play, also deals with issues of victimization and violence. But those adults who would find reason to squelch the irrepressible Punch for his uncontrollable temper, reasoning that violence whether in TV or in theater, is not good for children in these turbulent times, should remember that the artistic rendition of violence is not only cathartic but also illuminating. Children, as much as adults, require an artistic confrontation with their demons to understand and eventually transcend them.

One is reminded of the roguish Punch while reading about the mischievous and crafty Tyl in Jonathan Levy's *The Marvelous Adventures of Tyl*. Based on the legendary German folk character, Till Eulenspiegel, Levy has written a hilarious tale in commedia style about the practical joker whose first act of mockery is to interrupt his birth cries with a lusty laugh. Tyl is not so much flailing out against society as exposing its mercenary values and hypocrisy. By playing the fool, he is better able to outwit his opponents.

In *Names and Nicknames*, Reaney's form of absurdity resembles the early Ionesco. Reaney's idea for *Names* came from an old practical speller owned by his father, just as Ionesco's English-French conversation manual sparked off *The Bald Soprano*. Reaney, like Ionesco, is experimenting with language and getting the same dosage of nonsense and truth that underlies the banality of words and human relations. But unlike Ionesco, whose dry, distilled absurdity was aimed at bourgeois society, Reaney's humor radiates warmth as it probes the tragicomic world of childhood with its attraction and vulnerability to teasing.

Space and Myth

The two space plays included here—*Starman Jones*, an adaptation of the Robert Heinlein novel by Douglas Lieberman, and *The Riddle Machine*, by Beth Lambert —were chosen for their subject matter which gives us quick entry into the contemporary world. Both plays put children into orbit and deal with the young's struggle with infinity. Both also confer upon the child the dream of unlimited space and unlimited power.

The college underground, which shares the same heritage as the very young, long ago discovered that science-fiction writers were also involved in fantasies about outer space. One of these young men, Douglas Lieberman, went back to his childhood favorite, Heinlein's *Starman Jones*, when he was asked to put something meaningful on the stage at the Goodman Theater in Chicago. The play has all the elements of a Walter Mitty fantasy and a prophecy of the future.

Teen-ager Maximilian Jones, who has stowed away on the starship *Asgard,* has to take over when the captain suddenly dies. By succeeding where the adults had failed, the child emerges as scientist and space visionary.

Beth Lambert's *The Riddle Machine* is not so much about exploring outer as inner space. Working more within the realms of allegory than science fiction, this Canadian writer designed her own spaceship and inhabited it with children controlled by a Robot as they ride to a new world. In the course of their five-hundred-year journey they learn that the greatest riddle of all is not space or the universe, but the human being.

The ultimate boundaries are of mythic dimensions—between good and evil, natural and supernatural, mortality and immortality. All of these are at play in Mary Melwood's three-act play *Five Minutes to Morning.*

Fey and impractical Mrs. Vinney, a retired schoolteacher, is the symbol of the magical forces of good in a universe forever at battle with the dark forces, here embodied in hunter and trapper Tom Skinch, her once errant pupil. When the evil Skinch announces: "I shall be around in one shape or another . . . when the guns boom, the bombs burst—I am there," we are reminded of Camus' plague, which he tells us will come back someday in another form or another shape.

Melwood has created a kind of ghost sonata that slips through childhood, in and out of time with the equally immortal and invincible Mrs. Vinney: "A wood named after me. Why it may grow into a forest someday and I'll be part of it . . ."

In the end these plays must speak for themselves, as do the playwrights in their prefaces to their work. We are happy that we are no longer like the poet Po Chu-i madly singing in the mountains—that others can hear our song.

The Incredible Jungle Journey of Fenda Maria

A Play for Bare Stage for Children

by Jack Stokes

PREFACE

All theater is much too auditorium-bound. Children's theater, in particular, should free itself from the auditorium so that it can go where the children are.

I have no quarrel with elaborate sets, only with those that anchor theater to the auditorium. Theater ought to be prepared to climb into existing transportation this afternoon and go wherever children and adults can gather —gym floor or all-purpose room, cafeteria or parking lot. Time enough to construct the most complex sets once the play has arrived at the playing space.

The playwright is the designer, the actor, the chief carpenter of this set that is built by words, given shape and substance by the actor's speech and movement, lent grandeur by the music, and finished and decorated by the audience's imagination. How fearlessly do I erect and strike and reerect set after set!—now this dense jungle of trees that writhe, now the basket of that balloon in midair, now this plunge by parachute through cloud and blue to the surface of the ocean, and now at last the bottom of this sea with its smirking denizens swimming by. How epic the play that unfolds! The *Odyssey* itself, staged in front of the cafeteria steam-table, holds no terrors for a company whose actors prove to be such superb carpenters and technicians.

For it is the actor who, by his reaction to imagined scenery, produces the scenery. The grasp itself produces the cup which is grasped. The agony on the upturned face creates the ineffable sky-beast which has evoked that agony. The actor's tortured gait gives birth to the monster-infested swamp through which the actor slogs.

The lighting plot of such a play has a single requirement—that the audience be able to see; and ordinary daylight or overhead lighting satisfies this need. The costume plot requires only that the audience visualize; and a few shreds of cloth and some cardboard boxes and a feather or two—yes, even a circlet of colored paper spoken of as "crown"—effectively licenses the audience to start visualizing. In the hands of hard-working, competent (not necessarily superior) actors and directors, the transubstantiation of space that marks the sacred ritual of theater wherever it occurs is born of, and results in, a faith as substantial as any found in the auditorium.

Liberated, the play brushes past such notions as "esthetic distance" and moves in so close to the children that the very skirts of the costumes may brush the faces of the first row sitting on the floor. Story and characterization are barrier enough; but this is a barrier that must be insisted upon. Any attempts at an audience participation which sacrifices story and characterization to some notion of the therapeutic value of physically involving as many children as possible must fail as theater while sometimes succeeding (it must be granted) as games.

While we are about the business of liberation, let us consider:

1. The astounding possibility that children's theater may have as much right to original stories as adult plays (or even children's *books*) have. Oh, the old stories and characters are indeed grand, and no one will deny that well-known characters provide a practical shorthand to signal to the audiences the response which they are expected to make. But perhaps shorthand may deny exercise to faculties now atrophying from the 179th adaptation of everybody's old favorite.

2. The fearsome proposition that nonwriters are no better at writing children's programs than they are at writing adults'. If you are unable to write effectively for adults, what insolence born of resignation prompts you to think you will do any better for children?

3. The unsettling asseveration that, while there may be a narrow band of experience which only children can appreciate, and another narrow band which only adults can appreciate, there is a vast everyman's land in between where children and adults can appreciate together, though perhaps on different levels. After all, the great children's classics are those which both adults and children enjoy. (To those who protest that lists of children's classics are compiled by adults I must reply that I am still waiting to see the ones made up by children.)

4. The unsurprising probability that, finally, a script is justified by its workability and not by remarks like the foregoing which, like all credos, are written *after* a fact in order to justify that fact. "But," someone says, "aren't credos written to show where one should go?" "No," I respond, "to show where one has been."

JACK STOKES

PRODUCTION NOTES

Stage:

The play was written for bare stage, any open area where actors and audience can confront one another—a gym floor, a hall, a classroom, a playground, or a parking lot. It requires, at most, an exit right or up right, an exit left or up left, and an exit up center. If these exits can be provided by already existent openings, no other set is required. If they are not available, a small screen up left, a small screen up right, and a curtain up center (suspended by a piece of clothesline) are recommended. More elaborate scenery can be used, of course; but scenery which too specifically places the action or which would interrupt the action for the purpose of shifting is discouraged. The play is a play in one long, uninterrupted act.

Audience Seating:

The children can be seated on the floor in a semicircle, separated by four or five feet from the actors.

Lighting:

If the audience can see the action, no artificial lighting is required.

Makeup:

Except for those characterizations which require it (e.g., the Witches), makeup can be very light—for instance, a touch of lipstick or an eyebrow pencil to outline the eyes.

Costumes:

Costumes can be elaborate, but no particular style of costume is demanded. The original production dressed Maria in a flowing gown; Takaya in a red many-layered robe; the Doctor in a few pieces of fur and a head-dress; the Villagers in various kinds of robes and dresses; the Narrator in a medieval scholar's robe; the Tiger Man (who could as easily be Panther Man, Lion Man, Jaguar Man, Gorilla Man, etc.) in tiger-striped imitation fur.

Pantomime:

Much of the action is pantomimed—for example, the Chief Man's working in his "office"; Fenda Maria's crying and filling the jars of tears; the walking through the jungle and the confrontations with jungle vines, eye, and sky-beast.

Props:

Except for the Doctor's rattler and the medal, they are almost nonexistent. This is a play for touring.

NOTE ON SOURCE

This play was suggested by three entries in the *Standard Dictionary of Folklore, Mythology, and Legend,* Maria Leach, ed., published in New York by Funk and Wagnalls. The three entries are "Fenda Maria," "False or Substituted Bride," and "Act of Truth."

CHARACTERS

Narrator
Chief Man of the Village, a robust man in his prime who before
    our eyes grows old
Messenger, who can be doubled by the Narrator
Bird-Talker, who can be either male or female
Villagers (Chorus)
    Maria's Girl Friend
    Maria's Mother
    A Villager, who can be either male or female
    Additional Chorus Members, if desired
Fenda Maria, a beautiful girl in her teens
The Doctor, the local witch doctor, a foolish young man
Takaya, a witch
Horrenda, a witch
Uggl-Uggl, a witch
Tiger Man

SCENE

*The bare stage which, at the Narrator's behest, becomes
village square, jungle, and the clearing across the
jungle.*

TIME

*First, several years ago a week before most of you
were born; second, a week ago.*

A bare stage. One screen up left, one screen up right, and one screen or curtain up center. The NARRATOR *enters.*

Narrator.

Good afternoon. Today we are going to tell you a story. I'm the Narrator of this story—in other words, the storyteller. (*Pause.*) This is the story of what happened to a little village a long way from here. Now one day several years ago—in fact, one week before you were born—the Chief Man of the Village was in his office. (*As the* CHIEF MAN *comes out from screen up left.*) This is the Chief Man of the Village.

Chief Man.

(*A vigorous man in his prime, bowing.*) How do you do.

Narrator.

(*As the* CHIEF MAN *begins to pantomime some kind of work.*) The Chief Man of the Village was in his office working—when suddenly a messenger from across the jungle ran into his office.

Messenger.

(*Coming in from up right.*) Oh, sir, oh, sir.

Chief Man.

(*Continuing his work, hardly paying attention*). Yes?

Messenger.

Oh, sir, oh, sir, I greet you with terrible news!

Chief Man.

(*Continuing with his work.*) Well, give me the terrible news so that I can get on about my work.

Messenger.

Oh, sir, oh, sir, have you seen your son lately?

Chief Man.

My son Ngana the prince? No. I never see my son. He is a foolish cowardly young man, always giggling—hoo hoo ha ha—and he never works. He never comes home.

Messenger.

The terrible news, sir, is about your son.

Chief Man.

(*Suddenly disturbed, now paying attention.*) My son? What about my son?

Messenger.

On the other side of the jungle, as he was walking down a path, he met . . . a very bad witch—

Chief Man.

A witch?

Messenger.

She said to him, "You told me you were going to marry me!" And he said, "Get out of here, you bad witch!" And as he pushed her aside and walked on down the path, she raised her arm high into the air and—and—

Chief Man.

Yes, yes, go on!

Messenger.

She split him in two!

Chief Man.

She—

Messenger.

Yes—she split him into two different people!

Chief Man.

Oh, my poor son!

Narrator.

(*As both the* CHIEF MAN *and the* MESSENGER *freeze.*) Maybe you don't know this, but witches can do this—and a lot worse besides. You see, some people say that all of us have two different people inside us—one that's good and one that's bad. If you're lucky, the good one will get the best of the bad one. But poor Ngana, the prince—well, his bad person got the best of his good one. And so the witch was able to split him into two different people.

Chief Man.
But where is my son now?

Messenger.
One part of him—the good one—is lying asleep across the jungle. He may sleep forever!

Chief Man.
Oh! (*Pause.*) And the foolish cowardly one?

Messenger.
The foolish cowardly one is wandering somewhere on earth, doing foolish cowardly things, giggling hoo hoo ha ha; but no one knows where. He could come into this village and no one would recognize him.

Chief Man.
Oh, what are we going to do? (*Calling off left.*) Bird-Talker!

Narrator.
The Chief Man called the Bird-Talker of the Village. This was an old woman who talked to birds and knew things that most of us don't know; because most of us can't talk to birds. (*As the* BIRD-TALKER *comes in.*) This is the Bird-Talker.

Chief Man.
Bird-Talker, you must help me! What have the birds told you?

Bird-Talker.
The birds tell me—

Chief Man.
The birds tell you—

Bird-Talker.
            The birds tell me:
            Across the terrible jungle deep
            Your son Ngana lies asleep.
            The birds tell me.

Chief Man.
The birds tell you. But what can we do?

Bird-Talker.
The birds tell me—

Chief Man.

The birds tell you—

Bird-Talker.

The birds tell me—
A girl must cross the jungle deep
And when she reaches him must weep
More tears than one could weep in years!
For she must cry twelve jars of tears!
The birds tell me!

Chief Man.

The birds tell you. And then will Ngana awake?

Bird-Talker.

And then he will awake.

Chief Man.

But what if no young girl will cross the jungle?

Bird-Talker.

Then the village will remain sad. And Ngana will sleep forever! The birds tell me!

Chief Man.

The birds tell you. Messenger!

Messenger.

Yessir!

Chief Man.

Tell the village to come to me!

Narrator.

(*As the* VILLAGERS *come in and the* BIRD-TALKER *exits.*) And so the village came to the Chief Man. And the Chief Man told the village what was needed— that a young girl must cross the jungle and cry twelve jars of tears where Ngana was sleeping. Then the two parts of Ngana would come together—and the land would be happy again.

Chief Man.

(*To the* VILLAGERS.) Who will cross the terrible jungle?

Narrator.

No one spoke.

Chief Man.

Will no one cross?

Narrator.
No one spoke.
Chief Man.
No one will cross.
Narrator.
And then something terrible happened. Before the very
eyes of the villagers, the Chief Man of the Village
began to grow old. He began to shrivel up—and the
life began to go out of him.
Maria's Mother.
Chief Man, what is it? You look as if you are going
to die.
Chief Man.
(*An old man now, for he has grown old before our eyes.*)

> No . . . I cannot die!
> My spirit's weary,
> My body aches,
> But I cannot die
> Till Ngana wakes!

(*The* CHIEF MAN *goes out left, the* VILLAGERS
shrinking from him. Then the VILLAGERS *also go out.*)

Narrator.
And that is what happened one day a week before
you were born. And after that, the village was very
unhappy. Many years passed and the town was still
very sad. Then just last week—seven days ago—
something happened.
Fenda Maria.
(*Coming out, chanting.*) The land is bad, the land
is sad.
Maria's Mother.
(*Coming out, chanting.*) There's nothing here to make
us glad.
Narrator.
Nothing goes right.
A Villager.
(*Coming out, chanting.*) When it's light, it's night—
Maria's Girl Friend.
When it's night, it's bright—

Narrator.

Nothing goes right.

Villagers.

(*Including* MARIA, *moving about and murmuring.*)
Nothing goes right . . . nothing goes right . . . nothing
goes right.

Chief Man.

(*Coming out left, frightening the* VILLAGERS.) Ohh-
hhhh, who will help?

Fenda Maria.

(*As she and the others stop their pacing.*) It's the old
man—the old Chief Man of the Village!

Maria's Mother.

He refuses to die—until a young girl crosses the terrible jungle and cries twelve jars of tears.

Chief Man.

I cannot die!
My spirit's weary,
My body aches,
But I cannot sleep
Till Ngana wakes!
Who will go through the jungle to awaken Ngana?
(*To* MARIA'S MOTHER.) Will you?

Maria's Mother.

Not I!

Chief Man.

I cannot die!
Lame are my legs
And blind my eyes,
But I cannot sleep
Till Ngana rise!
Who will go through the jungle to awaken Ngana?
(*To* MARIA'S GIRL FRIEND.) Will you?

Maria's Girl Friend.

Not I!

Chief Man.

(*To audience.*)

Some young girl must go through the jungle,
And cry twelve jars of tears!

And then the sleeping Ngana will swallow the foolish
   cowardly Ngana
And then Ngana will awaken!
Who will it be?
(*To all onstage.*) Will it be you?

Chorus.

Not us!

Narrator.

(*As* CHIEF MAN *goes off and all onstage freeze.*)
No. No one wanted to cross the jungle. Who would
want to cross a jungle worse than anyone ever *dreamed*
of? Full of savage creatures that *no one* had ever
dreamed of. Vines that are hungry for human flesh and
reach out to seize you! (*Pause for reaction from*
CHORUS.) The great sky-beast that spits jelly fire down
at you that sticks to you and burns through to the
center of you! (*Pause for reaction from* CHORUS.)
And yet . . . on this day, ladies and gentlemen, boys
and girls, this day one week ago—one of the young
girls of the village was going to be chosen.

(*The crowd breaks up, scatters, talks.* FENDA MARIA
and her GIRL FRIEND *play catch with an imaginary ball.*
Squeals.)

Narrator.

Look at these people. One of them will be chosen. I
wonder if you can tell which. (*Letting the girls play a
bit before continuing.*) Do you know? Can you tell
yet? (*To a child in the audience.*) Do you know? If
you know, come here a minute. (*To the child when
he or she has reached the playing area.*) Do you see
this medal? Take this medal to the person you think
will be chosen. If the person you take it to turns away,
you'll know that that person will not be the one. Go
on to the next one. When one of them takes the medal,
come back here and take your seat.

(*The child takes the medal, offers it until* FENDA
MARIA *takes it, comes back to* NARRATOR.)

Narrator.

Now take your seat.

(FENDA MARIA *moves downstage, stricken.*)

Maria's Mother.

What is it? What did he give her?

Maria's Girl Friend.

Maria, what is it? Is it the—?

Fenda Maria.

(*Softly.*) Yes.

Maria's Mother.

What does it mean?

Maria's Girl Friend

(*Her eyes on* MARIA.) It means that she has been chosen to go through the jungle—

Maria's Mother.

Oh—I knew it, I knew it would happen! (*To* MARIA'S GIRL FRIEND.) Who gave her the medal?

Maria's Girl Friend.

(*Waving hand toward audience.*) Someone—from out there!

A Villager.

Is it you, Fenda Maria? Are you the one who will go through the jungle and save our village?

Fenda Maria.

(*To* NARRATOR.) Must I go?

Narrator.

Yes. You have been chosen.

Fenda Maria.

Why was I chosen?

Narrator.

Because you love the village, and the village loves you.

Fenda Maria.

But why is that a reason?

Narrator.

It is a terrible thing to be loved.

Chorus.

Fenda Maria, you've got to go—

Fenda Maria.
(*To* CHORUS.) Must I?
Chorus.
Fenda Maria, you've got to go—
Maria's Mother.
       Fenda Maria, Fenda Maria,
       It's you who must go—and none other.
       For this will all mean, dear,
       That you will be queen, dear,
       And I will become the queen's mother.
Chorus.
Fenda Maria, you've got to go.
A Villager.
       Fenda Maria, Fenda Maria,
       It's you who must go if you can, dear.
       We cannot conceal, dear,
       The pride we will feel, dear,
       When you become queen of this land, dear.
Chorus.
Fenda Maria, you've got to go.
Maria's Girl Friend.
       Fenda Maria, Fenda Maria,
       It's you who must go—you're the one, dear.
       You only can do it—we'd never get through it.
       And the thing, we agree, must be done, dear.
Chorus.
(*To climax.*)
       Fenda Maria, you've got to go.
       Fenda Maria, you've got to go.
       Fenda Maria, you've got to go.

(*They have come down upon her, and she cuts them off by throwing her arms into the air as she speaks.*)

Fenda Maria.
Yes, yes, I'll go!
A Villager.
(*As he and the* CHORUS *go up left.*) She'll go.
Maria's Mother.
My daughter will go.

Doctor.

(*Jumping in from up right, startling all.*) Hoo ha! (*Shaking his witch doctor's rattle and moving across the front of the audience.*) Hoo ha! (*Selecting various audience members to shake his rattle at.*) Hoo ha!

Narrator.

(*To audience.*) This is the village witch doctor. He does this daily.

Doctor.

(*Making his rounds of the* CHORUS.) Hoo ha! (*To the* VILLAGER, *who shrinks.*) Hoo ha! (*To* MARIA'S MOTHER, *who shrinks.*) Hoo ha! (*To* MARIA'S GIRL FRIEND, *who shrinks.*) Hoo ha! (*Down to* FENDA MARIA, *who is lost in thought and has paid no attention to the* DOCTOR'S *entrance.*) Hoo ha! Away, evil spirits! Hoo ha! (*Rattling his rattler up one side and down the other of* FENDA MARIA, *who still pays no attention.*) Hoo ha! Hoo ha! Hoo—(*After a pause.*) What's the matter?

A Villager.

Good Witch Doctor, Fenda Maria has been given the medal.

Doctor.

Hoo—(*Pause.*) What medal?

A Villager.

The medal that shows she has been chosen to make the incredible jungle journey to reach Ngana on the other side.

Doctor.

No, no, no. (*Rattling at the* VILLAGER *and then at* MARIA'S MOTHER.) Hoo ha!

Maria's Mother.

Don't hoo ha the mother of Fenda Maria!

Doctor.

There is no Ngana! No, no! It is evil spirits! This moment they are entering into you—that is why you are saying such things. Ha hoo! I mean—hoo ha!

Maria's Mother.

She has been chosen.

Doctor.
(*Somewhat subdued.*) No. Tell them, Fenda Maria, tell them you won't be crossing the jungle.

Fenda Maria.
(*Quietly resigned.*) I will go, good Doctor.

Doctor.
No!

Fenda Maria.
I will go, good Doctor.

Doctor.
(*Louder.*) No!

Fenda Maria.
I will go, good Doctor.

Doctor.
(*Crushed.*) No.

Fenda Maria.
I have been chosen.

Doctor.
(*Pitiful.*) You can't. You'll cross the jungle and you'll marry Ngana and become the princess and—what will become of me?

Maria's Mother.
What does it matter, foolish cowardly man, what happens to you?

Doctor.
There is no Ngana!

Maria's Mother.
Yes, there is! I know one who can talk to birds!

Doctor.
Sense-non! I mean—nonsense! No one can talk to birds! Hoo ha!

Maria's Mother.
Stop it! There she is now.

Doctor.
(*To* BIRD-TALKER, *who is emerging from up left.*) Get out of here, you silly thing with your talk of birds!

Maria's Mother.
Tell us, Bird-Talker, what did the birds tell you?

Bird-Talker.
The birds tell me—

Chorus.
The birds tell you—
Bird-Talker.
> The birds tell me
> That there is a jungle—
> A jungle never crossed by man—
> The birds tell me—

Chorus.
The birds tell you—
Bird-Talker.
> The birds tell me
> That there lives in the jungle
> Nothing but creatures escaped from the nightmares
> of men—

Chorus.
Oh . . .
Bird-Talker.
The birds tell me—
Doctor.
Shut up, shut up, shut up about birds—
Bird-Talker.
(*Turning on him.*) The birds tell me!
Doctor.
(*Intimidated, falling back.*) The birds tell you?
Bird-Talker.
> The birds tell me
> About creatures
> Not like ordinary jungle things scary
> Like tigers and spiders and other things hairy—

Chorus.
Oh . . . tigers and spiders and other things hairy—
Bird-Talker.
But yellow-green monsters with eyes glowing red—
Chorus.
Oh . . .
Bird-Talker.
Jelly-things dropping from trees on your head—
Maria's Mother.
On your head?

Bird-Talker.
   On your head.
Doctor.
   On my head?
Bird-Talker.
   On your head! (*Still looking at the* DOCTOR.)
      Long hairy arms reaching out as you walk—
      Stepping on soft squishy creatures that squawk.
Doctor.
   (*Scared.*) Oh . . .
Bird-Talker.
   (*Facing front again.*) That's what the birds told me.
Maria's Mother.
         And what did the birds tell you
         Is on the other side of the jungle?
Bird-Talker.
   The birds tell me—
Chorus.
   The birds tell you—
Bird-Talker.
      The birds tell me
      There's a bank of a river with no living breath.
      Nothing's alive there—
   (*Turning on the* DOCTOR *again.*) There's nothing but
   death!
Doctor.
   (*Shrinking.*) Oh, for sakeness' good!
Maria's Mother.
   And Ngana.
Bird-Talker.
   And Ngana.
Doctor.
   She's lying. (*To* BIRD-TALKER.) You're lying! You are
   full of evil spirits! (*Shaking his rattle at her.*) Hoo
   ha!

   (BIRD-TALKER *knocks the rattler from his hand.
   The* DOCTOR *is shocked.*)

Doctor.

Oh . . . she knocked the rattle from the hand *of* a doctor!

(BIRD-TALKER *goes out left.*)

Maria's Mother.

You should not have shaken it in the face of one who has talked to birds.

(*Sadly the* DOCTOR *picks up the rattler and goes up left center, his back to the audience.*)

A Villager.

Fenda Maria, you must go soon. But first you must choose one person in the village to go with you across the jungle.

Fenda Maria.

All right. I have one friend greater than all others. I choose the Doctor.

Doctor.

(*Pouting.*) No. I won't go. There is no Ngana—to be woke up and to marry Fenda Maria.

Fenda Maria.

I ask you to go, dear Doctor.

Doctor.

No—no.

Fenda Maria.

But, dear Doctor—

Doctor.

No.

Fenda Maria.

I want your protection.

Doctor.

Oh?

Fenda Maria.

I want you to work charms—

Doctor.

Oh.

Fenda Maria.

So that I won't be hurt.

Doctor.
(*Turning to her.*) Ah.

Fenda Maria.
Here—I want you to keep the medal for me.

Doctor.
You—?

Fenda Maria.
Perhaps you can cast a spell on it to make it more powerful.

Doctor.
You . . . want . . . me . . . to do that?

Fenda Maria.
Yes, Doctor.

Doctor.
(*His old self.*) Fenda Maria, be assured: this medal will be safe with the Doctor. No creature alive or dead will dare challenge the magic of this Doctor! No one shall get this medal from the Doctor!

(FENDA MARIA *fondly touches his arm and leaves the stage. The* CHORUS *also leave. The* DOCTOR *and the* NARRATOR *are alone.*)

Narrator.
What are you going to do with that medal, Doctor?

Doctor.
(*As though seeing him for the first time.*) And who, pray, are you?

Narrator.
I'm the Narrator.

Doctor.
The what?

Narrator.
I'm telling the story.

Doctor.
What story?

Narrator.
The one you're in.

Doctor.
Well, you're doing a very bad job. The idea of putting

in a creature that claims to talk to birds. Cockypop!
I mean—Poppycock!

Narrator.

But you claim to be able to talk to birds.

Doctor.

That is quite different. I'm a Doctor of Bird-Talk.
(*Cupping his mouth toward the sky.*) Hee—oooo! (*To*
NARRATOR.) That means: How's the weather up there,
bird friends? (*Cupping his ear, as though listening.*)
Ah yes, ah yes.

Narrator.

What did they say?

Doctor.

Oo ah oo ah ee.

Narrator.

What does that mean?

Doctor.

It means: fine, fine, thanks for asking.

Narrator.

You didn't tell me what you are going to do with that
medal.

Doctor.

I don't know that it is any of your business. However,
for the sake of being civil, I'll tell you this much:
I'm going to cast two or three of my best magic spells
on this medal.

Narrator.

Can you do that?

Doctor.

There are no limits to what a doctor can do.

Narrator.

Well, be careful. Fenda Maria may need that medal
to show who she is when she gets across the jungle.

Doctor.

I'll thank you, sir, not to advise me. Doctors advise
people, not the other way around.

Narrator.

But I only—

Doctor.

Silence! (*Rattling.*) Hoo ha!

Narrator.
Oh, very well.

Doctor.
You had better watch your tongue, sir. My magic can make tongues drop off.

Narrator.
You're a doctor of magic too?

Doctor.
Oh yes. Why . . . if I wanted to, I could snap my fingers like that! Click my heels like that! And suck in my breath like this—and you would disappear! And even you would wonder where you went.

Narrator.
I see. You're a doctor of disappearing too.

Doctor.
Don't be sarcastic. You're simply asking for it. All I have to do is turn myself briskly in a circle three or four times—four is better—and when I stop, you will be gone. (*As he sees the* NARRATOR'*s skeptical look.*) Yes, you *are* asking for it. All right, I'll do it. (*Turning briskly.*) Booga booga booga! (*Rattling.*) Whaaaag!

(*The* DOCTOR *ends up, facing upstage away from the* NARRATOR.)

You see! You're gone! Nowhere to be seen! (*Turning downstage toward audience.*) Now, boys and girls, for my next trick—(*Seeing the* NARRATOR.) When did *you* get back?

Narrator.
I haven't been gone.

Doctor.
Sticklefids!

Narrator.
Sticklefids?

Doctor.
I mean ficklestids. That is, stiddleficks. I mean—kiddlestiffs. Stifflekids. Kifflestids—

Narrator.
Kifflestids?

Doctor.

Stiddlekiffs. Some secret witch has made you reappear.
Kistelfids! (*Perhaps trying to straighten his mouth.*)
Be careful, sir: Next time it won't be so easy to return.
(*To audience.*) Now—I'm going to take this medal
and go over there in a corner and work such powerful
magic that bad creatures like Takaya won't dare to
steal it away from Fenda Maria.

(*The* DOCTOR *goes to up left corner and, with his
back to the audience, appears to be doing things with
the medal.*)

Narrator.

(*To audience.*) Takaya! The name has been spoken.
Are you ready? Because Takaya, the witch, is about
to enter. She has been watching all this, and she ought
to be coming out of there about—now!

(*The* NARRATOR *turns and directs the audience's attention to one of the stage entrances. While all eyes are
trained on this entrance,* TAKAYA *pops up elsewhere—
perhaps at the back of the auditorium.*)

Takaya.

Haw! Here I am, honey! Here I am, back here with
Mr. ———, the principal. We've been having the
nicest talk. Right, Mr. ———? Oh, I do like men with
curly hair—

(*Here* TAKAYA *can mention one or two of Mr.
———'s characteristics [from among those which he
would not be embarrassed by]; or she can simply say,*
"Oh, I do like handsome men!")

Takaya.

How about a yummy kiss, Mr. ———?

(*Mr. ———, the principal, may or may not give
her a yummy kiss. In any case,* TAKAYA *shrieks with
laughter and comes forward to the stage.*)

Takaya.

Yessiree, I'm the witch in this story. As a matter of

fact, I've got a group: The Three Hags Full. Haw!
You'll meet the others in a moment. (*Seeing the*
NARRATOR.) Who are you, honey?

Narrator.

I'm the Narrator.

Takaya.

Don't tell me you're the storyteller.

Narrator.

That's right.

Takaya.

Sweetie, you're doing a rotten-lousy job of it, putting
in silly old goofy-nutties like that Doctor there.

Narrator.

We don't speak about doctors like that.

Takaya.

He can't do magic. I can do real magic. I can—by a
wave of my hand—make people invisible.

Narrator.

Can you really?

Takaya.

Didn't I say so, doll? And by the opposite sign—
(*Demonstrating.*)—make them visible again.

Narrator.

Remarkable!

Takaya.

Don't get carried away, wise boy. And by another
wave—(*Demonstrating a different gesture.*)—I can
make people inaudible.

Narrator.

Inaudible?

Takaya.

You know—so you can't hear them.

Narrator.

Oh . . . so you can't hear them.

Takaya.

There an echo in here? And by the opposite sign,
make 'em audible again.

Narrator.

I've heard you have some *remarkable* powers.

Takaya.
Don't get sickening, sweetheart. Watch.

(TAKAYA *makes the "invisible" sign over the audience, then backs up right.*)

Doctor.
(*Turning back to the audience.*) Oh yes, I'm putting
some excellent spells on this—(*Finding the audience
invisible.*) Oh—now where did they go? (*Coming
down center and looking out.*) They *are* gone! But no
—I hear some giggling—(*Feeling around with his
hands over the heads of the children in front.*) But I
can't see anyone. Maybe my magic has worked. All
right. You can come back now.

(*Behind him,* TAKAYA *makes the "visible" sign to
the audience.*)

Doctor.
There you are! You're back. Oh, I can hardly wait to
tell Fenda Maria that my magic is working again.

(*The* DOCTOR *goes back to his corner.*)

Takaya.
(*To* NARRATOR.) You see? My magic works.
Narrator.
I see that it does. (*Slyly.*) I'll bet you could also split
people in two.
Takaya.
(*Eyes slit.*) Maybe I could.
Narrator.
How about trying that on the Doctor?
Takaya.
(*For a moment, very cautious.*) No. I couldn't do that
on him. For a very good reason. (*Attacking.*) But you
mess around with me, laddie, and I'll try it on you.
Narrator.
Oh—please . . .
Takaya.
Watch yourself then. Now—what have you got planned
for me?

Narrator.
What do you mean?

Takaya.
In this story. What do I do?

Narrator.
Well, I thought that you might—

Takaya.
(*Harsh.*) Forget it, Buster! It's out of your hands now. You brought me into this story—and nothing you can do is going to stop me now.

Narrator.
Stop you from what?

Takaya.
Guess.

Narrator.
(*Suddenly realizing.*) You're going to try to stop Fenda Maria from getting through the jungle.

Takaya.
You're bright, honey.

Narrator.
But why?

Takaya.
Well—the main reason is I'm wicked.

Narrator.
Wicked?

Takaya.
You know—evil. Dirty. Low down. That kind of thing.

Narrator.
But why should that make you want to stop Fenda Maria?

Takaya.
Because I want this town to stay unhappy-sad.

Narrator.
I think the real reason is you want to become the bride of Ngana.

Takaya.
Well, why shouldn't I? (*Dreamily.*) I'm more beautiful-pretty than Fenda Maria.

Narrator.
Well . . .

Takaya.
Does Fenda Maria have eyes that glow in the dark?
Narrator.
No.
Takaya.
I do. Does Fenda Maria have a nose that quivers in the moonlight?
Narrator.
No.
Takaya.
I do. Teeth that grow sharper after midnight?
Narrator.
No.
Takaya.
I do. Nails like claws?
Narrator.
No.
Takaya.
I do. (*Caressing her arms.*) Skin like a cat's?
Narrator.
No.
Takaya.
I do. Finally, isn't Fenda Maria's hair made out of hair?
Narrator.
Why, of course.
Takaya.
Mine's made of snakes. Haw!
Narrator.
Real ones?
Takaya.
Whadja think? Plastic? Yes, indeed, I wouldn't mind being a beautiful-lovely princess—especially if it means keeping this town miserable-wretched.
Narrator.
Well, what are you going to do?
Takaya.
First, I'm going to get that medal away from the Doctor. So Fenda Maria can't prove who she is. (*To audience.*) And one of these nice little boys and girls is

going to help me. Who wants to? (*Pointing to one.*)
You? All right, honey, come up here. Now, little one,
I'll tell you what I'm going to do. I'm going to turn you
into a water fountain! How do you like that? Then I
am going to make the Doctor thirsty. Then he'll come
and get a drink from you. And when he lays the medal
down, you'll pick it up. And when I ask you for it,
you'll give it to me. You see? Good. All right. (*Making a sign.*) You are a water fountain! And this—
(*Taking the child's fist in her hand.*)—is the handle.
I just turn this handle—and water—(*Watching it
come up from the child's head.*)—comes up! (*Taking
a drink.*) Ah—delicious water! Watch it—water fountains don't giggle. (*To audience.*) Now—I'll make
the Doctor thirsty. (*Running toward the* DOCTOR,
who still has his back to everyone.) You are thirsty!

(TAKAYA *goes to the side.*)

Doctor.
(*Straightening up and turning around.*) Hm. I'm
thirsty. Working charms certainly is thirsty. Ah—
there's a water fountain. I'll get a drink. (*Going to
the child and taking the "handle."*) What's this—a
water fountain that giggles! What won't they think of
next! I'll just lay my medal down here—(*Putting the
medal either on the child's head or on the floor next
to him.*)—and have a drink. (*Drinking and then turning away from the fountain to address the audience.*)
Ah yes. Most bracing!
Takaya.
(*From where she is hiding.*) All right, honey, take the
medal in your hand.
Doctor.
(*Turning back to the fountain.*) Now . . . where did I
put that medal? Where did I—? (*The possibility dawning on him.*) Is it possible—? Is it possible that my
magic spells have made it disappear? Oh, wonderful,
wonderf—(*Realizing.*) But no! Fenda Maria needs
that medal! She must have it to show that she really
is the one who has been chosen. I'll work my magic

to make it come back. (*Moving about with his back
to the fountain.*)

                    Medal, medal, do you hear?
                    Do you hear me? Reappear!

(*The* DOCTOR *repeats this several times with appropriate gestures—long enough to give* TAKAYA *a chance
to go to the fountain, take the medal, and return the
child to his seat. Then the* DOCTOR *turns back to the
fountain.*)

Doctor.

Oh no! My magic is getting better and better! *Now*
I've made the water fountain disappear! Oh, this
is terrible! My magic is getting out of control! (*Suddenly becoming aware of the audience.*) Did you see
who has my medal?

(*As the children begin to speak and to point out*
TAKAYA, TAKAYA *makes her "inaudible" gesture.*)

Doctor.

What? You're moving your mouths, but I can't hear
you. I'll tell you what: point to whoever has the
medal.

(TAKAYA *makes her "invisible" sign.*)

Doctor.

Huh? Where did they go? Oh dear—I'm making
everything disappear! (*Turning away, despairing.*)
Oh dear—where is poor Fenda Maria's medal? What
will I do?

Fenda Maria.

(*Reentering.*) What's the matter, dear Doctor?

Doctor.

You won't call me dear when you hear what's happened.

Fenda Maria.

What's happened?

Doctor.

(*Pretending joy.*) Oh, I have wonderful news! Fenda
Maria, my dear, I have made your medal disappear!

Fenda Maria.

I'm so happy, Doctor. Your magic is working again.

Doctor.

Yes. Isn't it wonderful! I knew you'd be pleased.

Fenda Maria.

Where is it now?

Doctor.

Where is what?

Fenda Maria.

My medal.

Doctor.

Oh—your medal! It's—well, it's disappeared.

Fenda Maria.

Well, it's time for us to leave. So make it reappear.

Doctor.

Do we—uh—really need it?

Fenda Maria.

I think so. It's to protect—and to show that I am really the girl chosen.

Doctor.

(*Despairing.*) Oh, I know! What will I do?

Fenda Maria.

Can't you make it reappear, Doctor?

Doctor.

I don't know what happened to it.

Fenda Maria.

(*A bit aggrieved.*) But you said you would keep it for me. (*Softening as she sees the* DOCTOR *pouting.*) Well, never mind. Come on, we have to be leaving, Doctor. (*Pause, as the* DOCTOR *remains silent.*) Doctor? (*Pause, as the* DOCTOR *looks up at her.*) I can't go without you, Doctor.

Doctor.

Well, all right . . . if you want me to.

Fenda Maria.

I want you to, Doctor.

(*The* CHORUS OF VILLAGERS *comes out, the* CHIEF MAN *among them.*)

Chief Man.

Fenda Maria!

Fenda Maria.

Yes, old man.

Chief Man.

Fenda Maria, the time is here!

Fenda Maria.

I know, old man.

Chief Man.

Now go. And we in the village will stand here and be with you in spirit as you go through the jungle. You will not be able to see us—and we will not be able to see you. But we will be with you. Now go!

Narrator.

And with that—(*As* FENDA MARIA *and the* DOCTOR *join hands and face the audience from about center stage.*)—Fenda Maria and the Doctor stepped—

(FENDA MARIA *and the* DOCTOR *pantomime, in unison, an elaborate step.*)

—into the jungle . . . Ladies and gentlemen, boys and girls: the incredible jungle journey of Fenda Maria!

(*The* CHORUS *never leaves the stage during the journey, remaining in the up left corner in front of the screen.* FENDA MARIA *and the* DOCTOR *move through the jungle by facing the audience at center stage, joining hands, and, to the accompaniment of the* CHORUS's *chant, making step movements in place, which can be as dancelike as the director feels appropriate.*)

Chorus.

(*Beginning immediately after* NARRATOR's *last speech.*)

Walk . . . walk . . . walking through the jungle,
Walking through the jungle of a very bad dream!
Walk . . . walk . . . walking through the jungle,
Walking through the jungle of a very bad very bad
Very bad dream!

Narrator.

(*As* FENDA MARIA *and the* DOCTOR *freeze.*) Yes. A jungle. A jungle that is only dreamed of. A jungle like a very bad dream.

Chorus.

(*As* FENDA MARIA *and the* DOCTOR *resume their movement.*)

Walk . . . walk . . . walking through the jungle,
Walking through the jungle of a very bad dream.
Walk . . . walk . . . walking through the jungle,
Walking through the jungle of a very bad very bad
Very bad dream!

Narrator.

(*As* FENDA MARIA *and the* DOCTOR *either freeze or move to the* NARRATOR'*s particular beat.*)

Have you ever been lost in a dream, in a dream?
Have you ever been lost in a dream?
Have you ever woke up and discovered at dawn
The dream you were dreaming is still going on?
And the terrible shapes you were certain had fled
Are grinning their grins at the foot of your bed?

Chorus.

Walk . . . walk . . . walking through the jungle,
Walking through the jungle of a very bad dream.
Walk . . . walk . . . walking through the jungle,
Walking through the jungle of a very bad very bad
Very bad dream!

Narrator.

(*As* FENDA MARIA, *the* DOCTOR, *and the* CHORUS *freeze until further notice.*) The journey continued. But Takaya, the witch, was busy every moment.

Takaya.

(*Coming out from up right, sweetly singing it.*) Where *are* you? Come out, you devil's darlings, wherever you are!

Horrenda.

(*Sticking her head out from behind one of the screens.*) Harkalarkalark! Who calls with silvery voice?

Takaya.

It is Takaya, calling her sweet companions in horror.
Come out, come out, my dumplings!

Horrenda.

Here we are, Takaya.

Uggl-Uggl.

(*Sticking her head out, giggling.*) Here we are, Takaya.

(*Each* WITCH *successively sounds the note of a
chord. Then, together, they jump into the air. As they
hit the floor, the sound of the chord stops.*)

Takaya.

There they are—the ineffable Horrenda and the unbelievable Uggl-Uggl! What superb hags!

Horrenda.

You're a doll, Takaya. All we ask is the chance to
serve you in these underhanded undertakings.

Takaya.

These shady shenanigans!

Uggl-Uggl.

These odious operations!

Takaya.

These murderous machinations!

(*Again they do their chord.*)

Uggl-Uggl.

Yes, my dear Takaya, where would we be without
you?

Takaya.

True, my lovelies! You walk around today only because I cared enough to put you together out of rusty
razor blades, poison rattails, and venomous snake
fangs!

Horrenda.

You forgot the dried pumpkin seeds.

Uggl-Uggl.

Yes, and the smelly onion rinds!

Takaya.

Indeed, I did—two of the most important ingredients.

Horrenda.
Why did you hale us here today, Takaya?

Takaya.
We have important business. Do you see these travelers?

Horrenda.
Yes, who are they?

Takaya.
The girl is Fenda Maria.

Horrenda.
What a disgusting face! They ought to make her cover it!

Uggl-Uggl.
Not everybody has your charm, Horrenda.

Takaya.
Try to control your feelings, Horrenda.

Horrenda.
I may be sick.

Uggl-Uggl.
(*Who has been examining the* DOCTOR.) And what do you call this, Takaya?

Takaya.
That, Uggl-Uggl, is called a man.

Uggl-Uggl.
I want one for myself.

Takaya.
Sorry, Uggl-Uggl. You're a witch.

Uggl-Uggl.
Oh, does that mean—?

Takaya.
That's what it means.

Uggl-Uggl.
Oh dear. I so like the way his horns grow out of his head.

Takaya.
They aren't real horns, Uggl, dear—like so much about him.

Uggl-Uggl.
I like them anyway.

Horrenda.

Are these travelers dead, Takaya?

Takaya.

No, no, Horrenda. It is just that we are moving so fast it looks as if they are standing still. Actually they are busy walking through the jungle at this very moment.

Horrenda.

Why are they going through the jungle, Takaya?

Takaya.

Fenda Maria intends to awaken Ngana.

Horrenda.

Oh, she must not be allowed to do that.

Takaya.

Exactly. Now—my question is: What do you have, in your malevolent repertory, that will prevent her from arriving at her destination?

Uggl-Uggl.

Let me see. *I* know—I'll cause a vine to be formed at the side of the path and make it reach out and—and—and—

Takaya.

(*Excited.*) Yes, yes, yes—

Uggl-Uggl.

And—tickle them!

Horrenda.

Uggl!

Takaya.

Uggl, I'm afraid you're going to need more job training. Look—make that vine a man-eating, strangling, asphyxiating, crushing vine—and I'll buy it.

Uggl-Uggl.

(*Disturbed.*) Oh . . . Takaya.

Takaya.

Now you, Horrenda.

Horrenda.

Let me see, let me see. Yes, I have it!

A giant eye

Which will hang in the sky

And look down at her, look through her eyes into
her soul
And see everything a young girl wants to keep secret
from the world!

Takaya.

(*Jumping with joy.*) Excellent, excellent, Horrenda!
She will die of shame!

Horrenda.

And what will you provide, Takaya?

Takaya.

I've been saving this. If these two fail, I shall call
upon the All-Evil to send the indescribable sky-
beast—

Uggl-Uggl.

(*Horrified.*) Oh, Takaya.

Takaya.

Yes, the abominable sky-beast that hovers on poisonous wings above us and spits jelly-fire down upon the
unsuspecting!

Uggl-Uggl.

Jelly-fire, Takaya?

Takaya.

Jelly-fire, Uggl. Jelly-fire that clings to the skin and
burns through into the very center of you.

Uggl-Uggl.

Ohhhh.

Horrenda.

You are truly nasty, Takaya.

Takaya.

And you are truly kind to say it. I know you're sincere.
Now—to work!

(*The* WITCHES *sound their chord and withdraw upstage.*)

Narrator.

The journey continued.

Chorus.

Walk . . . walk . . . walking through the jungle,
Walking through the jungle of a very bad dream.
Walk . . . walk . . . walking through the jungle,

>Walking through the jungle of a very bad very bad
>Very bad dream!

Narrator.

>(*As* CHORUS *advances, their arms imitating vines.*)
>Something to the left—

Fenda Maria.

>Oh, what can it be?

Narrator.

>Something to the right—

Doctor.

>Oh, I wish I could see.

Narrator.

>>Something to the back of us—
>>Front of us—
>>Left of us—
>>Something to the right!

Fenda Maria.

>Nothing but night!

Narrator.

>(*As the arms begin to encircle the travelers.*)

>Oh, what are these arms?
>What are these arms that are trying to harm?
>What are these hands?
>What are these hands that encircle like bands?
>What are these vines that entwine round the spine
> with design most malign—
>(*As the* CHORUS'*s arms form bars across the travelers.*)
>What are these bars!

Fenda Maria.

>Help me, help me!

Chorus.

>(*As vines.*) Turn back, turn back, look back, look
>back.

Fenda Maria.

>I can't.

Narrator.

>She has to go forward; help her, someone help her!

>(*The vines have concentrated on* FENDA MARIA,
>*and now she sinks to the ground, enveloped.*)

Narrator.
Help her, Doctor!

Doctor.
I know. I'll work my magic! (*Rattling.*) Hoo ha!
(*When there is no effect, rattling again.*) Hoo ha!
(*When there is still no effect.*) Why won't it work—
why won't my magic work?

Narrator.
Pull the vines off her—pull the vines away from her,
Doctor!

Doctor.
But—they're so frightening.

Narrator.
Do not be foolish, Doctor. Do not be a coward,
Doctor. It's the only way you can help Fenda Maria!

Doctor.
Yes, yes, I'm coming to help!

(*The* DOCTOR *wades into the vines, but they turn
on him and pull him down.*)

Doctor.
Help, help!

(FENDA MARIA *is unconscious.*)

Uggl-Uggl.
(*Feeling pity.*) Oh, Takaya.

Takaya.
Shut up and watch the show.

Uggl-Uggl.
But in a little while the vines will eat him up.

Takaya.
It's your trick, Uggl.

Uggl-Uggl.
But—

(*After only a moment of hesitation, she runs
toward the encircled figure of the* DOCTOR.)

Takaya.
Uggl, what are you doing?

Uggl-Uggl.

(*Intoning.*)

Vines and branches that surround,
Back into the poisonous ground!

(*The vines fall away and the* CHORUS *goes back to its place.*)

Takaya.

Uggl, you'll pay for this.

Uggl-Uggl.

Oh, Takaya, I couldn't let it happen. I so like the way he jumps around, rattles his rattle, and goes hoo ha!

Doctor.

(*Weakly, from the ground.*) Hooo haaa . . . (*Getting up slowly.*) What happened? Did my magic work? Come, Fenda Maria.

(*He helps her up.*)

Narrator.

And the journey continued.

Chorus.

Walk . . . walk . . . walking through the jungle,
Walking through the jungle of a very bad dream.
Walk . . . walk . . . walking through the jungle,
Walking through the jungle of a very bad very bad
Very bad dream!

Narrator.

What are those forms?
What are those forms that are moving like swarms
In the jungle beside us?

Chorus.

Oh, darkness hide us!

Narrator.

What is that shape?
What is that shape that resembles an ape?

(*Looking up, as* FENDA MARIA, *the* DOCTOR, CHORUS, *and* WITCHES *do also.*)

What is that Eye?
What is that Eye that's alive in the sky?

That is looking inside us?
What is that Eye?

Fenda Maria.
(*As all stare up with her.*) Oh . . . no . . . no . . . don't
look into me like that! Please! Someone stop it!

(FENDA MARIA *covers her eyes with her fingers.*)

Narrator.
But it was no use. The Eye can burn through fingers
and into the eyes and the very soul. Someone had to
stop it before Fenda Maria died of shame!

Takaya.
Turn back! You can escape the eye by turning back!

Fenda Maria.
Oh, it sees everything! I can't stand it!

Narrator.
Doctor, help her!

Doctor.
(*At first indecisive, then.*) Hoo ha!

Narrator.
Come, Doctor!

Doctor.
But what can I do?

Narrator.
You can stand in front of her—protect her from the
Eye—let the eye burn into you!

Doctor.
Into me!

Narrator.
Into you!

Doctor.
But—I have so many things to hide. How can I live
if the Eye sees everything?

Narrator.
You must save Fenda Maria.

Doctor.
(*As a last resort.*) Fenda Maria, please turn back.
Give up your plan to cross the jungle and waken
Ngana.

Fenda Maria.

(*Faintly, now on her knees.*) No . . . no . . .

Narrator.

She will soon be gone—dead of shame.

Doctor.

(*Indecisive.*) Oh . . .

Narrator.

One more moment. Young girls can die of shame.

Doctor.

(*Making up his mind.*) Oh . . . very well!

(*The* DOCTOR *jumps in front of* FENDA MARIA. *The impact from the Eye makes him reel.*)

Doctor.

Oh no!

Narrator.

And the Eye burned into the Doctor, seeing all that was inside—all that was foolish and cowardly!

Doctor.

Oh, it sees everything!

Takaya.

Blast that Doctor!

Uggl-Uggl.

Will he die, Takaya?

Takaya.

No, he won't die. He will be covered with shame, but he won't die. Only young girls die of shame.

Doctor.

(*One last gasp.*) Ohhhh.

(*The* DOCTOR *falls to the ground, alongside* FENDA MARIA.)

Narrator.

All the Doctor's secrets were known.

Takaya.

(*Approaching the* DOCTOR.) So, Doctor, everyone knows now.

Doctor.

(*Softly.*) Yes, yes.

Takaya.

Knows that you have no real magic.

Doctor.

(*A bit louder.*) Yes, yes.

Takaya.

Knows that you are foolish and cowardly.

Doctor.

(*Louder.*) Yes, yes. Call me all kinds of bad things.

Takaya.

The Eye showed you to be stupid.

Doctor.

Yes, yes.

Takaya.

A stupid silly.

Doctor.

Yes, yes.

Takaya.

A goofy nutty.

Doctor.

Yes, yes.

Takaya.

A dumb ugly!

Doctor.

(*For whom this is too much.*) What!

Takaya.

A dumb ugly!

Doctor.

(*Jumping to his feet, with the old indignation.*) Watch out or I'll make you disappear with a flick of my hand!

Takaya.

You! Remember what the Eye showed us: you have no magic.

Doctor.

(*Deflated.*) Oh dear. That's right.

Takaya.

(*Starting another build that is climaxed by the* DOCTOR's *exit.*) You have Fenda Maria to thank for this.

Doctor.

For what?

Takaya.
For showing what you are.
Doctor.
But how?
Takaya.
By insisting on going through the jungle and awakening Ngana.
Doctor.
(*Realizing.*) Yes. That's right.
Takaya.
If she had not insisted on going through the jungle, you could have lived the rest of your life in the village fooling people.
Doctor.
That's true!
Takaya.
You must show her!
Doctor.
Yes! How can she dare!
Takaya.
Leave her! Leave her now! If she wants to go through the jungle and marry Ngana, then let her!
Doctor.
That's what I'll do.
Takaya.
After what she has done to you, she should expect no help from you!
Doctor.
I'll show her!
Takaya.
She's kind to you only because she pities you!
Doctor.
(*The last straw.*) Pities! Me—the Doctor! I'm leaving. Good-bye, Fenda Maria! (*But as she continues to lie motionless.*) She'll—be all right?
Fenda Maria.
(*Only partly conscious, trying to reach a hand up to him.*) Doc . . . tor . . .
Doctor.
No. No more, Fenda Maria. I'm—leaving!

(*The* DOCTOR *goes out up left.*)

Fenda Maria.
(*Rising.*) Doctor, where are you? (*To* NARRATOR.)
Where is the Doctor?
Narrator.
He's—gone back—
Fenda Maria.
Oh no! Doctor!
Narrator.
He's gone, Fenda Maria. You must continue your
journey.
Fenda Maria.
Without the Doctor?
Narrator.
You must.
Fenda Maria.
All right.
Narrator.
And the journey continued.
Chorus.
Walk . . . walk . . .walking through the jungle,
Walking through the jungle of a very bad dream.
Walk . . . walk . . . walking through the jungle,
Walking through the jungle of a very bad very bad
Very bad dream!
Narrator.
(*Pointing up, as all look up.*)
Oh, what are those things?
What are those things that are spreading their wings
In the sky up above us?
Chorus.
Heaven protect us!
Narrator.
The sky-beast!
Fenda Maria.
What . . . is it?
Narrator.
And now the sky-beast began spitting down its jelly-
fire—

Fenda Maria.

(*As a piece hits her arm.*) Oh . . . (*As another hits her.*) Oh . . . (*As pieces continue to hit her.*) Oh . . . oh . . . oh . . .

Narrator.

And poor Fenda Maria sank to her knees . . . But still the relentless sky-beast pumped its fire downward—little pieces of jelly-fire that stuck to arms and legs and burnt through, through, through to the center of her!

Fenda Maria.

(*Falling unconscious.*) Oh . . .

Narrator.

At last, it seemed, the vengeful Takaya had won.

Takaya.

(*Standing over* FENDA MARIA, *with the quiet dignity of the victor.*) Now, dear lady, lie there with the fire of the jelly-fire burning through your skin. It will not be long before it is coursing through your veins and will have reached the center of you—and you will be no more. (*To* HORRENDA *and* UGGL-UGGL.) Come, my companions, let us go on to the clearing which is only a few yards away—there to meet Ngana!

(*The three* WITCHES *sound their chord and then exeunt up right.*)

Narrator.

Is she dead? Soon she will be—for the longer we wait, the more fiercely the jelly-fire burns into her. Quick—we must have someone—someone who can pluck the jelly-fire from her. The Doctor! (*Then realizing.*) But no—the Doctor has left. If only I could call him. (*Calling out.*) Doc-tor! Doc-tor! (*After a pause.*) It's no use. I'm only the storyteller and I can't shout loud enough. (*A sudden idea.*) But all of us—all of us together—perhaps *we* could be heard. Let's all shout. Come on, all together now. (*Directing the audience.*) Doc-tor! Doc-tor! Doc-tor!

(*The* NARRATOR *and the audience will continue until the* DOCTOR *pokes his head out from behind the screen.*)

Doctor.

Did someone call? Fenda Maria, wherever you are, I'll forgive you if you really want me to. Fenda Maria? Oh, where has she gone? Oh, why did I have to leave her? (*Almost stumbling over her.*) What—? Oh, Fenda Maria, is it you? (*Kneeling beside her.*) What can I do? (*Starting to touch her.*) Oh no—the jelly-fire!

Narrator.

Don't shrink back, Doctor.

Doctor.

But it's the jelly-fire!

Narrator.

You must pick it off, piece by piece.

Doctor.

Oh no—it burns!

Narrator.

But to save your Fenda Maria!

Doctor.

It would burn through me and—

Narrator.

(*Sarcastic.*) Then work your magic!

Doctor.

(*Turning away.*) You're making fun of me. You and the whole world know that I have no magic.

Narrator.

Then there is nothing to do.

Fenda Maria.

(*Weakly.*) Doc . . . tor . . .

Doctor.

She speaks. Fenda Maria, are you still alive?

Narrator.

Yes, Doctor. But not for long . . . unless the jelly-fire is picked off.

Doctor.

I'll save you, Fenda Maria! (*Picking off a piece, then pulling back.*) Oh . . .

Narrator.

Go on. Pick it off.

Doctor.

It's so hot.

Narrator.

It's the only way.

Doctor.

All right.

(*The* DOCTOR *picks off a piece, then dances with pain; picks off another piece, then dances; and so on.*)

Narrator.

Is it all off?

Doctor.

(*Continuing to dance.*) Yes.

Uggl-Uggl.

(*Peeping out from behind the up right screen.*) Look at him. I so like the way he dances.

Horrenda.

(*Behind her.*) Come on, Uggl. Takaya is waiting for us.

Uggl-Uggl.

But what's the matter with him? He seems to be growing weaker.

Horrenda.

Come on, Uggl. The jelly-fire is on him, and he'll soon be gone.

(*The* DOCTOR *has collapsed.*)

Uggl-Uggl.

Oh no.

(UGGL-UGGL *runs to him, starts picking off the jelly-fire.*)

Horrenda.

Uggl, what are you doing!

Uggl-Uggl.

I'm going to pick this jelly-fire off him.

Horrenda.

Takaya won't like it.

Uggl-Uggl.

She won't care. After all, it's Fenda Maria she wants to stop.

Horrenda.

I don't know.

Takaya.

(*Entering from up right.*) What are you girls waiting for? Come on. (*Seeing* UGGL-UGGL *picking off the jelly-fire.*) Uggl, what are you doing?

Uggl-Uggl.

Oh, hello, Takaya, I'm taking the jelly-fire off this poor Doctor here.

Takaya.

But why?

Uggl-Uggl.

Oh, I think he's nice. And besides there is no reason why *he* should have to suffer.

Takaya.

Wrong, Uggl! There *is* a reason! The reason is: he helped Fenda Maria. If you do someone a favor, it ought to cost you something. It was costing *him pain!* (*Pause.*) Now, Uggl, you are doing *him* a favor. Don't you think it ought to cost *you* something?

Uggl-Uggl.

(*Pausing, hands full of jelly-fire.*) What do you mean, Takaya?

Takaya.

Don't you feel any pain, Uggl?

Uggl-Uggl.

No. I'm a witch, Takaya, and jelly-fire hurts only people.

Takaya.

Uggl, haven't you sometimes wished you were a human being so that you might have the Doctor for a friend?

Uggl-Uggl.

Oh yes. He's so nice.

Takaya.
You have taken the first step to becoming a human being when you volunteered to take the jelly-fire off.
Uggl-Uggl.
(*Pleased.*) Oh.
Takaya.
But remember, Uggl, human beings feel the pain of jelly-fire. And you have it all over your hands. (*Pause.*) Do you feel anything?

(UGGL-UGGL *looks at her hands, begins to tremble; then, pathetically.*)

Uggl-Uggl.
Oh, Takaya.
Takaya.
I'm sorry, Uggl-Uggl.
Horrenda.
(*Sadly.*) Have you taken it all off him, Uggl?
Uggl-Uggl.
One last piece. (*Taking it off, feeling some pain.*) Now—it's all in my hands.
Horrenda.
Is it beginning to hurt?
Uggl-Uggl.
(*Softly.*) Yes, Horrenda. It hurts.
Takaya.
Uggl-Uggl, you will have to go into the deepest part of the jungle—and there come to your terrible end.
Uggl-Uggl.
Yes, Takaya. In a moment. (*Looking at the* DOCTOR.) I think he's reviving.
Doctor.
(*Not seeing anyone yet.*) Wh—what am I?
Uggl-Uggl.
You're a man, dear.
Doctor.
(*Still not looking at her.*) Where am I?
Uggl-Uggl.
Next to me, dear.

Doctor.

(*Looking up at her.*) Who are you? (*Seeing her.*)
Yeow! (*Scrambling to his feet, retreating to the left,
and rattling his rattler.*) Hoo ha!

Uggl-Uggl.

(*Clasping her hands.*) Oh did you see? I think he likes
me too. Did you see the way he screamed with delight
and rattled his rattle at me? He *does* like me. Good-
bye, dear.

(UGGL-UGGL *throws a kiss.*)

Doctor.

(*Horrified.*) Hoo ha!

Uggl-Uggl.

(*Feeling the pain.*) Oh . . . (*Pitifully.*) Oh, Takaya . . .

Takaya.

Good-bye, Uggl.

Horrenda.

(*With sympathy.*) Good-bye, Uggl.

Uggl-Uggl.

(*As she goes behind the screen up right.*) Good-bye
. . . oh . . . good-bye . . . good-bye . . .

Horrenda.

Takaya, can't you do something?

Takaya.

No. It was her choice. I am sorry, for we had some
good bad-times together. But it can't be helped.

Horrenda.

Poor Uggl.

Takaya.

Stop it, or you may end up the same way.

Horrenda.

All right. What do we do about Fenda Maria?

Takaya.

I'll think of something. Come on.

(*The two remaining* WITCHES *try sounding their
chord, but the harmony is off.* TAKAYA *snorts and
goes out up right.*)

Horrenda.

(*In response to the poor harmony of the chord.*) Oh,
Takaya . . .

(HORRENDA *goes out up right.*)

Doctor.

What were all those—those things?

Narrator.

Creatures of the jungle. What are you going to do
now?

Doctor.

As soon as Fenda Maria revives, we'll start our journey again.

Narrator.

Are you going to stay with her?

Doctor.

Yes.

Narrator.

To defend her?

Doctor.

You're laughing at me.

Narrator.

No. But you have only your love to defend her against
further terrors.

Doctor.

(*Failing a bit.*) What other terrors are in store for us?

Narrator.

You'll have to wait and see.

Doctor.

But—some hint?

Narrator.

One other terror, perhaps, before it's over.

Doctor.

Oh dear.

Narrator.

Perhaps the worst of all—

Doctor.

Oh dear oh dear.

Narrator.

But I can't tell you what. I'll say this, however: dig

down deep into the deepest dream you ever had and think of the most horrible creature that ever came at you in your dreams—

Doctor.
Let me see.

Narrator.
When he comes at you in a dream, you are lucky if you can wake up before—

Doctor.
I can think of only one such creature—

Narrator.
There *is* only one—

Doctor.
Striped, hugely clawed, and horribly fanged—

Narrator.
Yes?

Doctor.
The Tiger Man! (*As* NARRATOR *says nothing.*) Is it the Tiger Man? Must we face the Tiger Man?

Narrator.
(*Turning his back to the* DOCTOR.) I'm only the Narrator.

Doctor.
But the Tiger Man comes to tear you apart when you have sworn you are something you are not.

Narrator.
That's right.

Doctor.
But Fenda Maria *is* Fenda Maria!

Narrator.
But can she prove it?

Doctor.
Yes. With the tears she will cry for Ngana.

Narrator.
But suppose someone else claims the tears.

Doctor.
Then she can show the medal—the medal that the Messenger from—(*Waving over the audience.*)—Out There brought to her.

Narrator.

(*Turning to him.*) The medal, Doctor?

Doctor.

(*Remembering.*) Oh no. The medal was stolen.

Narrator.

That's true.

Doctor.

Oh, what can I do?

Narrator.

No one can do anything—unless help can be gotten from someone who saw the medal stolen.

Doctor.

You?

Narrator.

I'm only the Narrator.

Doctor.

But who?

Narrator.

Think.

Doctor.

(*Thinking.*) Someone here, besides you, who saw the medal stolen.

Narrator.

Keep thinking, Doctor.

(*The* DOCTOR *freezes in an attitude of thinking as the* CHORUS *comes alive.*)

Maria's Mother.

Oh, the Tiger Man comes when you tell a lie.

Chorus.

Oh, oh, the Tiger Man comes.

Maria's Mother.

The Tiger Man comes and he's ten feet high.

Chorus.

Oh, oh, the Tiger Man comes.

Maria's Mother.

When you cross your heart and hope to die
And still go make the treetops sigh
And the heavens cry with your terrible lie—
Then—the Tiger Man comes!

Chorus.

Watch out for the Tiger Man!

Tiger Man, Tiger Man, who has seen the Tiger Man?

(*Fading.*)

Tiger Man, Tiger Man, who has seen the Tiger Man?

(*The* CHORUS *freezes.*)

Narrator.

It was time to resume the journey.

Doctor.

(*Bending over* FENDA MARIA.) Fenda Maria, are you all right?

Fenda Maria.

(*Taking his hand and rising.*) Yes, dear Doctor. I'm so glad you're back.

Narrator.

And the journey continued. They had not far to go. No sooner had they started to walk again—

Chorus.

Walk . . . walk . . . walking through the jungle,

Walking through the jungle of a very bad dream.

Walk . . . walk . . . walking through the jungle,

Walking through the jungle of a very bad very bad Very bad dream!

Narrator.

—than—

Fenda Maria.

Doctor, look! I think we're here—I think we're in the clearing across the jungle!

Narrator.

They were indeed!

Fenda Maria.

But where—where is the sleeping prince?

Narrator.

(*Moving up center to the curtained area.*) Behold, Fenda Maria, the sleeping place of the prince!

Fenda Maria.

(*Going to the curtain and placing her hand on it.*)
Leave me now, Doctor.

Doctor.

(*Reluctant.*) Do I have to?

Fenda Maria.

Yes. I must cry my tears alone.

Doctor.

(*After a pause.*) All right. Good-bye, Fenda Maria.

(*The* DOCTOR *goes out behind the curtained area.*
FENDA MARIA *kneels before the area and pantomimes
crying.*)

Narrator.

(*To audience.*) And so the crying began:
How many jars of tears can you cry?
How many tears can you cry?
If you'd saved all the tears you have cried since your
birth,
Is it possible you would have twelve jars' worth?
How many tears can you cry, can you cry?
How many tears?
The crying continued.

Takaya.

(*Entering angrily from up right,* HORRENDA *behind.*)
There she is!

Horrenda.

Let's leave, Takaya. Let's go try to find Uggl.

Takaya.

Get away from me.

Narrator.

Give up, Takaya. Fenda Maria has won at last!

Takaya.

No. At some point she will hesitate. And when she
does, I'll have her!

Horrenda.

(*Going off up right.*) Oh, Takaya . . .

Takaya.

(*Hiding herself behind* NARRATOR, *stage right.*) I'll
just hide myself here—and wait.

Narrator.

The crying continued—until at last she had filled twelve jars with her tears ... Have you finished, Fenda Maria?

Fenda Maria.

(*Rising.*) Yes.

Narrator.

The tears have been cried!

Chorus.

The tears have been cried!

Narrator.

Now the people of the village arrived at the clearing; for now that Fenda Maria had crossed the jungle and cried the tears, all people could cross the jungle.

Chief Man.

Fenda Maria!

Maria's Mother.

It's the old Chief Man—the old Chief Man of the Jungle.

Chief Man.

Fenda Maria,
The tears have been cried.
Say the words that will awaken Ngana.

Fenda Maria.

What must I say?

Chief Man.

Say: My lord Ngana, for our sake,
Sleep no more—my lord, awake!

Fenda Maria.

(*Facing the curtained area.*) My lord Ngana—

Chief Man.

Go on.

Fenda Maria.

My lord—No. I must wait.

Narrator.

(*With a glance at* TAKAYA *behind him.*) Fenda Maria, you must do it now!

Fenda Maria.

I must rest first. (*Looking about.*) Where's the Doctor?

Narrator.

I beg you.

Fenda Maria.

I'll wait till the Doctor comes back—

Maria's Mother.

Fenda Maria!

Fenda Maria.

I'll wait for the Doctor.

(FENDA MARIA *lies down at stage left. The* CHORUS *make a protective circle around her, their backs to the audience, and freeze.*)

Takaya.

(*Coming out from behind the* NARRATOR.) Haw! Just what I needed.

Narrator.

Takaya, what are you going to do now?

Takaya.

Never you mind, you're just the Narrator.

Narrator.

Since I *am* the storyteller, I'll just leave you out of the rest of the story.

Takaya.

You wouldn't dare! I've become too important!

Narrator.

(*A bit at a loss.*) I'll—Next time I'll leave you out.

Takaya.

Who cares? If my scheme works out, I won't need to be in another story.

Horrenda.

(*Emerging.*) Takaya, what are you going to do?

Takaya.

As if you didn't know. (*Pretending to weep.*) Oh . . . oh . . .

Horrenda.

(*Going out up right, shaking her head.*) Takaya, Takaya . . .

Takaya.

(*Continuing to weep.*) Oh . . . oh . . .

Narrator.
What's the matter?
Takaya.
(*Under her breath.*) Shut up. (*Weeping again.*) Oh
. . . oh . . .
Fenda Maria.
(*Rousing.*) What's the matter? What is it?

(*The* CHORUS *open up to let* FENDA MARIA *face*
TAKAYA.)

Takaya.
(*Shrinking from the* NARRATOR.) Oh, dear lady, help
me! Help me!
Fenda Maria.
But what's the matter?
Takaya.
This terrible man! He is beating me!
Narrator.
Me?
Fenda Maria.
But why?
Takaya.
Because I'm his servant—
Fenda Maria.
That's terrible.
Narrator.
I didn't beat her.
Takaya.
He says he can treat me anyway he likes.
Narrator.
Well, yes, in a way, but—
Fenda Maria.
Shame on you. Poor little thing, how can I rescue you
from this cruel master?
Takaya.
A jar of tears will buy me. You have tears for every-
one else. You must have some tears for me.
Fenda Maria.
Of course. (*Pantomimes picking up a jar of tears from
in front of the curtained area.*) Here.

Narrator.

(*Taking the "jar," but protesting.*) But—

Takaya.

(*Under her breath to the* NARRATOR.) Shut up and play your part. (*To* FENDA MARIA.) Oh, thank you, dear lady, you are so kind.

Fenda Maria.

Come with me. I now have eleven jars of tears. After I rest and the Doctor comes back, I will cry one more. Will you watch the tears while I sleep?

Takaya.

Anything for you, dear lady.

Narrator.

Fenda Maria, you must cry the twelfth jar now and say the words which will awaken Ngana.

Fenda Maria.

I can't.

Narrator.

But why?

Fenda Maria.

I . . . don't know. (*Looking about.*) Where's the Doctor?

Maria's Mother.

Never mind him. You must awaken Ngana now.

Fenda Maria.

I'll wait till the Doctor returns.

(FENDA MARIA *lies down again with the* CHORUS *around her. They freeze.*)

Takaya.

Haw! She is mine!

Narrator.

One jar to go! She will awaken, cry the twelfth jar, and it will be all over for you!

Takaya.

One jar to go! You're crazy-mad! She has already cried the twelfth jar!

Narrator.

But she gave one to me to buy you.

Takaya.

Yes, didn't she? (*Seizing the "jar" from the* NARRA-
TOR.) Give me that jar of tears!

Narrator.

You can't do that!

Takaya.

Watch me, know-it-all! (*Going to the curtained area
and placing the jar next to the others.*) My lord Ngana
—for our sake—

Narrator.

Fenda Maria, wake up!

(*The* CHORUS *turn toward them, and* FENDA MARIA
awakens.)

Takaya.

Too late!

My lord Ngana—for our sake—
Sleep no more—my lord, awake!

(*As all freeze, the curtain is parted, and* NGANA *is
revealed in his glory. He is robed and veiled, standing
in a sleeping pose, his arms crossed on his chest. Slowly
he awakens and steps forward from the alcove.*)

Ngana.

The voice that called Ngana—let it speak again!

Takaya.

It was my voice!

Ngana.

Then, my bride, come to me!

(TAKAYA *goes to* NGANA. *He embraces her and
wraps his robe around her. They begin to go back
into the alcove.*)

Maria's Mother.

Fenda Maria, tell him you are the true bride! (*But
as* FENDA MARIA *turns away.*) My lord Ngana, wait!
That is a false bride!

Ngana.

What is this?

Takaya.

Pay no attention to the silly old nutty!

Maria's Mother.

My daughter, tell him you are the true bride!

Fenda Maria.

No.

Maria's Mother.

What?

Chorus.

What?

Fenda Maria.

I don't want to marry Ngana.

A Villager.

But you have to marry Ngana. You were chosen to cross the jungle and cry the tears.

Fenda Maria.

I have crossed the jungle and cried the tears. But I don't want to marry Ngana.

Maria's Mother.

You—must!

Fenda Maria.

I won't.

Maria's Mother.

So that you can be queen.

Fenda Maria.

I don't want to be queen.

A Villager.

But why?

Fenda Maria.

All through that dangerous jungle, someone held my hand the entire way. I want to marry that man! I want to marry the Doctor!

Maria's Mother.

The Doctor! That foolish coward!

Fenda Maria.

He is not foolish anymore. He is not a coward anymore. The Eye burned out his foolishness. His love conquered his cowardliness.

Maria's Mother.

The Doctor!

Fenda Maria.
Now . . . someone bring the doctor back to me! (*When no one moves.*) Then I'll go find him!

Chief Man.
(*As* FENDA MARIA *starts to go offstage.*) Fenda Maria!

Fenda Maria.
Yes?

Chief Man.
No one can ever bring the Doctor back to you.

Fenda Maria.
What do you mean?

Chief Man.
The Doctor will not come back again. He has been—swallowed up!

Fenda Maria.
Swallowed up! (*Hysterical.*) I must go to him. I must find the Doctor! (*Starts out, but is restrained by a gesture and a look from the* CHIEF MAN.) Let me go.

Chief Man.
You cannot go to the Doctor! There is only one way you can have the Doctor for a friend again!

Fenda Maria.
There's a way I can save the Doctor?

Chief Man.
There's a way you can have him for a friend again.

Fenda Maria.
(*Going to* CHIEF MAN.) Oh, Chief Man, tell me how!

Cihef Man.
One way only: You—must—marry—Ngana.

Fenda Maria.
Marry—Ngana!

Chief Man.
Marry Ngana.

Fenda Maria.
I can't. *She* is going to marry Ngana.

Chief Man.
Then you must try to prove that you are the true bride.

Fenda Maria.
All right. If that will bring the Doctor back. (*Turning*

to NGANA.) My lord Ngana, that woman is a false bride! I am the true bride!

Takaya.

She's full of jungle bananas!

Ngana.

You say you are the true bride?

Fenda Maria.

Yes.

Ngana.

Who awakened me?

Takaya.

I did.

Ngana.

(*To* FENDA MARIA.) Is that true, lady? (*As* FENDA MARIA *turns away*.) You will not answer? Very well.

(NGANA *starts to go into the alcove with* TAKAYA.)

Fenda Maria.

(*Stopping him*.) But it was I who cried the tears!

Ngana.

Who saw you cry the tears? (*As* FENDA MARIA *turns away again*.) You will not answer? Very well.

(NGANA *starts to leave again*.)

Fenda Maria.

(*Stopping him again*.) But it was I who was given the medal!

Ngana.

Show me the medal. (*As* FENDA MARIA *turns away again*.) You will not answer. Lady, you have spoken three times—and three times you have refused to show us the truth of what you have spoken. How you have escaped the Tiger Man this long, I cannot understand. Come, my bride.

(NGANA *and* TAKAYA *once again begin to move into the alcove*.)

Narrator.

Do something, Fenda Maria! You must save the Doctor!

Fenda Maria.

Yes . . . yes . . . (*Desperately.*) Wait! (*Then as* NGANA *and* TAKAYA *turn to her.*) All right—(*Taking a deep breath.*)—let the Tiger Man come then!

Chorus.

Oh.

Ngana.

You call upon the Tiger Man?

Fenda Maria.

Yes. To prove me the true bride.

Ngana.

You will die. You admitted you did not awaken me.

Fenda Maria.

If I am not the true bride,

Then—

Let the Tiger Man come to me and tear me to pieces!

Takaya.

Don't listen to her. The Tiger Man never comes.

Ngana.

In the jungle he always comes. In the villages you may call upon the Tiger Man—and sleep that night, safely surrounded by your lies. But in the jungle of very bad dreams, where the Tiger Man lives, the Tiger Man always comes.

Fenda Maria.

(*Softly, but with determination.*) I am the true bride.

Ngana.

Already he has come down from his tree at the center of the jungle—and is coming this way. Listen!

Chorus.

(*Which, in the interests of speeding matters, may speak only the first stanza.*)

Shhh . . .

Someone is coming,

Someone or something is coming, is coming,

Someone or something that lives at the heart of the jungle

Leaps down from his tree

And is coming this way.

(*Pause, perhaps as a distant drum beat sounds.*)

Someone is coming,
Someone or something is coming, is coming,
Someone or something is baring its claws at the
    heart of the jungle
And is coming this way,
And is coming this way.

(*Pause.*)

Someone is coming,
Someone or something is coming, is coming,
Someone or something steps huge through the jungle
And is coming, is coming—
Someone is coming—
S o m e o n e   i s   h e r e !

(*Then as* TIGER MAN *appears and advances, perhaps from the rear of the theater, repeats again and again under the dialogue.*)

Tiger Man comes, Tiger Man comes . . .
Narrator.
Listen! Did anyone see Fenda Maria get the medal? Did anyone see her go through the jungle? Did anyone see her cry the tears?
Horrenda.
(*Emerging.*) *I* saw the medal stolen!
I saw her cross the jungle!
I saw her cry the tears!
Takaya.
Horrenda!
Horrenda.
(*Pointing to the audience.*) And so did all these people here!
Narrator.
Then only they can save her!
Horrenda.
Yes. If some of them were to come up here and make a ring around Fenda Maria, the Tiger Man could not hurt her.

Narrator.
Would the Tiger Man hurt *them?*

Horrenda.
The Tiger Man cannot hurt them.

Narrator.
But they wouldn't come up here, would they?

Horrenda.
Is there anyone here who would come up here and make a ring around Fenda Maria?

(*Some of the audience will volunteer. If too many volunteer,* HORRENDA *and the* NARRATOR *can choose the ones they want.*)

Horrenda.
She should be the true bride, Tiger Man!

(*Now as the* TIGER MAN *moves about the circle, unable to break through it to* FENDA MARIA, HORREN-DA *leads the audience in a chant.*)

Horrenda.
Go 'way, Tiger Man,
Go 'way, Tiger Man.

(*The chant is continued until the rhythm begins to affect the* TIGER MAN. *He begins to dance, and at last dances off the stage. Cheers. Then as the cheers die down,* NGANA *turns his head slowly toward* TAKAYA, *she does the equivalent of a witch's gulp, and he pushes her aside.*)

Ngana.
(*To* FENDA MARIA.) Come to me, my true bride!

(NGANA *enfolds* FENDA MARIA *in his robe and begins to draw her into the alcove.*)

Fenda Maria.
Wait! They told me that if I married Ngana I would save the Doctor. Where is the Doctor?

Narrator.
Don't you know, Fenda Maria? Does anyone know where the Doctor is?

(Well, of course, most of the audience will know and will volunteer the information. But FENDA MARIA, *perhaps too close to the action, will have to have it explained to her.)*

Remember, Fenda Maria: Many years ago, a week before these people were born, a bad witch split Ngana into two different people!

Fenda Maria.

Yes, I remember.

Narrator.

There was a brave wise person and a foolish cowardly person. And the brave person was Ngana, who has been sleeping all these years.

Fenda Maria.

Yes, but—who was the foolish cowardly person?

Narrator.

Remember how, shortly after that, the Doctor came, a stranger, to your village, looking for work as a witch doctor?

Fenda Maria.

Oh yes. I liked him immediately.

Narrator.

The Doctor was the foolish cowardly part.

Fenda Maria.

Oh?

Narrator.

Now you have crossed the jungle, and the Doctor and Ngana have swallowed one another up. Ngana and the Doctor are the same person!

Fenda Maria.

(Looking at NGANA *with new eyes.)* You . . . the Doctor?

Ngana.

I am Ngana.

Fenda Maria.

(Looking closer, perhaps removing the veil.) Yes— you *are* the Doctor. Come with me, Doctor!

(She starts to lead him away.)

Ngana.
I am Ngana. I know no Doctor. I—

(*At that moment,* NGANA *sees the* DOCTOR's *rattler, which the* DOCTOR *left with the* NARRATOR *when he made his last exit. Curious, he takes it.*)

Ngana.
What's this? Hm, very interesting.

(*He looks at it, then is overcome by the power of it, and suddenly:*)

Ngana.
Hoo ha!
Fenda Maria.
That's my Doctor!
Ngana.
(*Puzzled.*) Now why did I do that?

(NGANA *holds it out to the* NARRATOR; *but before the* NARRATOR *can take it,* NGANA *is overcome again.*)

Ngana.
Hoo ha!
Fenda Maria.
(*Taking the rattler.*) Here, my Doctor. (*Handing it to the* NARRATOR.) That's all behind us. Come.

(*Together, they go into the alcove,* NGANA *a bit puzzled.*)

Narrator.
And that is the story of Fenda Maria and her incredible jungle journey!
Takaya.
Horrenda! You're disgusting! You're as bad as Uggl-Uggl! What got into you?
Horrenda.
(*Crossing to the* NARRATOR *and perhaps taking his arm.*) I don't want to go with you anymore, Takaya. Not after what happened to Uggl.

Takaya.

Aren't you ridiculous—making friends with the Narrator. I'll get even with both of you.

Narrator.

No, you won't. I'll leave you out of all my stories.

Takaya.

I'll get in them one way or another. You can't keep
me out! And when I do, I'll get even! (*Pause.*) If I
don't get even with you—why, let the Tiger Man come
and claw me to pieces!

Chorus.

Shhhh . . .

Takaya.

Huh?

Chorus.

Someone is coming . . .

Takaya.

Who comin'?

Chorus.

Someone or something is coming, is coming.

Takaya.

(*Disgusted with herself.*) Me and my big mouth!

Narrator.

Run, Takaya!

(*And now* TAKAYA *runs, the* TIGER MAN *behind her,
making the rounds of the auditorium. Occasionally*
TAKAYA *stops to chat with a teacher or a pupil, then
looks back to see the* TIGER MAN *gaining on her, and
takes off again. At last,* TAKAYA *and the* TIGER MAN
*return to the stage and join the rest of the company for
bows.*)

END OF PLAY

A LETTER TO THE AUDIENCE

A copy of the following letter (altered to suit the circumstances) can be sent a week or two in advance of the performance to each teacher supervising students who will see the play.

Dear Teacher:

Will you share some or all of the following information with the pupils in your room who are going to be seeing the play *The Incredible Jungle Journey of Fenda Maria* when the [Name of Producing Group] production visits your school?

To the Pupil

The cast, the crew, and the directors of the [Name of Producing Group] play *The Incredible Jungle Journey of Fenda Maria* are eagerly looking forward to visiting your school.

First, I want to assure you that Takaya, the witch, who is one of the chief characters in the play, has promised that she won't cast any horrible spells on your teacher when she visits your school. But, of course, you know how witches are; and the minute she sees your teacher or your principal, she may change her mind.

But even if she does promise to behave toward you and your teachers, I know she is going to be just as wicked as ever toward the other characters in the play. She has several unbelievable spells ready to cast on Fenda Maria herself; and I know that she will think of something particularly terrifying to do to the poor Witch Doctor. (The Witch Doctor thinks he can cast spells too, but he can't; the last time he tried to change somebody into something, he ended up changing himself into a duck.) Takaya is also pretty good at making people invisible and inaudible; and she'll probably give you a demonstration of her powers when she visits your school.

You see, what really makes Takaya angry is this: Several years ago—well, actually, it was one week before you were born—a young prince named Ngana was split in two. He became two different people—a good one, the prince, who went to sleep in a clearing across a terrible jungle, and would not awake; and a bad one, a foolish cowardly man, who wandered all over the earth doing foolish cowardly things. No one knew where the bad person was living.

The Bird-Talker of the Village, an old woman who could talk to birds and knew many things which most of us don't know (since most of us cannot talk to birds) told the villagers, "There is only one way to make the two different people come together and to make Ngana awake. You of the village must choose a young girl to go across the terrible jungle, cry twelve jars of tears at the place where Ngana is sleeping, and say the mysterious words which will awaken Ngana." At last Fenda Maria was chosen.

So, at the present time, this is the situation: Fenda Maria plans to make her journey across the jungle, cry twelve jars of tears, and awaken the prince. But Takaya is determined that Fenda Maria will not get across the jungle. With her two assistant witches, the stupefying Horrenda and the unbelievable Uggl-Uggl, she plans some vicious tricks to stop her: Jungle vines hungry for human flesh; a great Eye in the sky that looks into you and sees all your secrets and makes you die of shame; and, though I hate to say it, the abominable sky-beast that spits down jelly-fire on the unsuspecting. Then, if none of these work, there is always the Tiger Man.

Accompanying Fenda Maria across the jungle will be her good friend, the Witch Doctor of the village. Unfortunately the Witch Doctor gets scared easily, and we don't know yet just how much help he will be to the young girl.

Now there are some things which you pupils can do to help the story along. If you are sitting up near the front, you may be asked to go to the stage once in a while and help one of the characters. You must not be afraid to go onto the stage if you are asked to do so; since you are members of the audience, nothing can happen to you. (Your teacher may go up in a puff of smoke, however.)

Also there will be times when you can actually help by speaking. For example, as the travelers (Fenda Maria and the Doctor) travel through the jungle, the villagers speak in order to help them along. They will say:

Walk . . . walk . . . walking through the jungle,
Walking through the jungle of a very bad dream.
Walk . . . walk . . . walking through the jungle,
Walking through the jungle of a very bad very bad
Very bad dream!

The villagers will be saying this again and again as
Fenda Maria and the Doctor go through the jungle. If you
want to join in with them, to help Fenda Maria along, feel
free to do so. But as soon as the villagers stop speaking,
you will want to stop too; because the story will be continuing and you will want to hear what they are saying.

If the Tiger Man does come (and I don't know whether
I want him to come or not), one of the characters in the
play may try to get him to go away by saying over and over,
"Go 'way, Tiger Man. Go 'way, Tiger Man." You may want
to join in the chanting.

It is possible that there will be another point in the story
where the Witch Doctor may leave Fenda Maria alone in
the jungle. If that happens, and if the sky-beast starts attacking her, we may want to bring the Doctor back to help
her. Therefore, if one of the characters in the play asks you
to shout, "Doctor . . . Doctor . . . Doctor," don't hesitate
to join in.

Here is some of the verse that will be found in the play.
Maybe hearing it now will help you understand it better
when you see the play.

Have you ever been lost in a dream, in a dream?
Have you ever been lost in a dream?
Have you ever woke up and discovered at dawn
The dream you were dreaming is still going on?
And the terrible shapes you were certain had fled
Are grinning their grins at the foot of your bed?

Here's some more:

How many jars of tears can you cry?
How many tears can you cry?
If you'd saved all the tears you have cried
     since your birth,
Is it possible you would have twelve jars' worth?
How many tears can you cry, can you cry?
How many tears?

Someone in the play mentions the Tiger Man, who comes
when someone swears to something that he knows is not
true:

> Oh, the Tiger Man comes when you tell a lie.
> Oh, oh, the Tiger Man comes.
> The Tiger Man comes and he's ten feet high.
> Oh, oh, the Tiger Man comes!
> When you cross your heart and hope to die,
> And still go make the treetops sigh
> And the heavens cry with your terrible lie—
> Then—the Tiger Man comes!
> Watch out for the Tiger Man!

The Bird-Talker tells of creatures in the jungle:

> Not like ordinary jungle things scary
> Like tigers and spiders and other things hairy—
> But yellow-green monsters with eyes glowing red—
> Jelly-things dropping from trees on your head—
> Long, hairy arms reaching out as you walk,
> Stepping on soft squishy creatures that squawk!

If the vines try to get Fenda Maria, the Narrator will try to describe them for you like this:

> Oh, what are these arms?
> What are these arms that are trying to harm?
> What are these hands?
> What are these hands that encircle like bands?
> What are these vines that entwine round the spine
>   with design most malign?

Finally, I regret to say that the Witch Doctor gets his words mixed up sometimes. For example, when he tries to say, "Fiddlesticks," it sometimes comes out "Sticklefids" or "Ficklestids." You may want to help him by telling him the correct pronunciation.

You may be interested in learning something about some of the words used in connection with the play:

1. playwright (why is the author of a play called a "playwright" instead of a "playwriter"?)
2. director
3. producer
4. designer
5. technical director
6. set
7. rehearsal
8. narrator
9. incredible
10. Fenda Maria ("Fenda" means "lady")

We hope that after the play has been performed and you have gone back to your rooms, your teacher will allow one or two of the actors or actresses to come to your room in their costumes. Perhaps you can spend some time during the next few days thinking of some questions you would like to ask these actors and actresses about the play, the costumes, rehearsal, and touring the play.

This has been a long letter, but we want to help you enjoy the play as much as we do. We look forward to seeing you.

Sincerely,

Kap the Kappa

*An Original Play for Children
and Kappas*

by Betty Jean Lifton

PREFACE

I thought I had given theater up forever when I abandoned aspirations to act after college. Until a few years ago I have been preoccupied with writing books for the young and working as a free-lance journalist in the Far East.

However, in the summer of 1969 when an Off-Off Broadway troupe operating out of Provincetown, Mass., asked me for children's scripts, I became addicted to theater for the young. Not a very practical addiction. But, alas, I didn't know it then.

It was the time of the first moon landing. After sitting up all night watching our astronauts take their one small step for man on a surreal TV stage, I took my small step, writing *Moon Walk*, about the first children to go to the moon. It was also my first step toward audience participation—children were encouraged to moon walk with the cast and hunt for moonstones, which were rock candy carefully planted before the show.

The eager response of the audience that summer to the various scripts I wrote was more immediate than anything I had experienced with books. In New York the following winter I couldn't resist the chance to put *Moon Walk* on at the Electric Circus, adding rock music and media. Watching kids from all walks of life respond to the environment we were creating (and most poignantly, the invited groups of mentally retarded and emotionally disturbed), I knew that media was the language of this visually oriented generation, and that theater, to keep faith with them, must somehow incorporate it. The problem was how to get the funding to experiment so that it could become an integral part of the piece rather than just a decorative backdrop.

Another problem was that New York with its lack of innovative producing companies for the young (in spite of the energy of Off and Off-Off Broadway in adult theater) offers little chance for experimentation. Out of desperation I formed my own company, The Jugglers, which was dedicated to exploring participation, transformation and media within a dramatic form.

Kap the Kappa, an adaptation of my picture book about the mischievous water elves who inhabit the rivers of Japan, was produced with our first foundation grant. Like the Japanese, I am possessed by kappas: Ryunosuke Akutagawa (of *Rashomon* fame) immortalized them in his satiric novel *Kappa*, and Usen Ogawa left haunting portraits of those elfin creatures brooding like tormented poets on the riverbanks.

However, as a producer I soon found that my artistic concerns were overshadowed by financial ones. The struggle for a writer to keep a troupe going in New York City is too tortuous to go into here. I recommend it to no one interested in the contemplative life. Yet it is essential for a playwright to have access to a troupe of dedicated actors to develop his/her craft. Recently I joined with a few other writers to form The Playwrights Theater for Children. Our hope is to create a professional unit that will produce our plays and eventually those of other writers who are encouraged to enter the field.

In the meantime, I am deep in a book about dolphins, who, being clever as well as mischievous creatures, have managed to surface into a play.

BETTY JEAN LIFTON

PRODUCTION NOTES

Kappas:

Kappas (pronounced *cop*pas) are authentic folk creatures who inhabit the rivers of Japan. They are to the Japanese what the leprechaun is to the Irish. Kappas have a shell like a turtle on their backs, webbed hands and feet, and a bowl full of water in the tops of their heads. When the water is there, they are well and strong, but should it spill out while they are on land, they become very weak and could even die. They are gay and mischievous, and move in an agile, elflike way. Their dancing has a springy froglike quality. Human beings are fond of kappas, but they are also wary of them because they play tricks on people, steal cucumbers, and challenge them to wrestling matches.

Setting:

Arena style with children seated in brightly demarcated spots around the playing areas. In one production we used two floors of an old brownstone that had been renovated for media. The lower floor was the underwater world and the second floor was land. When Kap was captured by the fishermen, the audience swam upstream (up the stairs) to follow him. This script has been written for one playing space.

Style:

The Japanese element should only be suggested through the conventions of the hooded Property Man and the Musician who plays to one side of the stage. Costumes should be spare, perhaps leotards with accessories to suggest character. We used "happi" coats for the human children, and green leotards with shells on the back for the kappas. The water in the head was suggested by a hood attached to the leotard, with hair fringe around a bright blue cloth patch on the top.

Media:

We used media in our two productions of *Kap the Kappa*. A cyclorama was set up at one end of the curved playing area for projections of slides and film. However, effects can also be achieved through Japanese stage conventions—the moon can be a large disc on a pole held by the Property Man, the river can be a long blue cloth, etc.

CHARACTERS

Minstrel, dressed as minstrel figure in white face, acts as narrator and carries humorous instruments on body

Musician, plays music on minstrel's cues and sound effects

Kap, a young river elf

Kappa King ⎫ Kap's parents
Kappa Queen ⎭

Carpy, a young red carp

Michio, a boy

Taro, a boy

Yukiko, a girl

Michio's mother ⎫ can be played by Kappa King and Queen
Michio's father ⎭

Property Man (one or two), dressed in black with black hood; they sit to one side when not setting props

*As audience is coming in, media effects of under-
river world on cyclorama.*

MUSICIAN *plays music to "Kappa Is Lord of the
River."*

When he is finished, MINSTREL *enters from rear,
goes through the audience climbing over children,
making some move to let him through.*

Minstrel.
Excuse me . . . pardon me . . . do you mind moving so
that I can get through. Thank you so much. I'm in
such a hurry . . . I'm sure I shall be late . . . I'm on my
way to the Kappa Kingdom. I'm the court musician
and tonight there is to be the Full Moon Ball in the
Pearl-White Palace. I always play for the kappas on
the night of the full moon. Kappas love good music,
you know. You do know? You know what kappas
are? You don't? Where have you been all your lives?
Oh, of course, here in New York . . . on land. And
kappas live in the rivers of Japan. I don't know if
there are any in the Hudson or the East River. Have
you seen any there?

Well, if you should be swimming in a river and you
see a small creature with a shell on his back, and
webbed hands and feet and a bowl of water in his
head . . . if you see him swimming by . . . that's a
kappa. But be careful because kappas like to play
tricks almost as much as dancing. Dancing! Oh, I
shall be late to the Ball. I must swim down to the

Pearl-White Palace immediately. Would you like to go with me? You would! All right, come quickly through or we shall be late.

(*Sings "Kappa Is Lord of the River" as they all swim down to the Pearl-White Palace. Media goes into underwater effects.*)

Kappa is lord of the river,
Lord of the riverbed,
When the moon shines down on kappa land,
The water glows in his head.

Kappa is lord of the river,
With a water bowl in his head.
When the water's there, he's well and he's strong,
But without the water, he's dead.

Kappa is lord of the river,
He'll dance when the moon is bright.
Kappas dance by the light of the moon,
Dance and play tricks through the night.

(*Pearl-White Palace appears on screen—then film of* KAP *swimming.*)

Minstrel.
We're almost there . . . There's the Pearl-White Palace . . . and there's Kap, the prince of the kappas, swimming toward us. Be quiet now because kappas are shy of people . . . we don't want to scare him away, Kap is just about your age, I think. He's the only son of the Kappa King and Queen . . . and the prince of the riverbed. Pardon me while I speak to him in kappa language.

(KAP *appears from behind cyclorama eating a cucumber.*)

Minstrel.
Quock. Quock.
Kap.
Quock, quock.

Minstrel.

(*To audience.*) That's a kappa greeting. (*To* KAP.)
Quock, quock, quock, cleek, clerk, quock, quock.

Kap.

Quock, quock, blurk, urk, quock.

Minstrel.

Could you understand that? I asked him if we're late
to the ball and he said the moon is not full yet. There's
plenty of time. What a relief. Now listen carefully
. . . it's an easy language. If you concentrate, it will
soon sound just like English to you. Quock, quock.
Ock, qlock, qlock . . . I brought my friends down with
me. They want to come to the Ball.

Kap.

Quock, quock, querk, blerk, quock. Have a bite of
cucumber. (*He offers it around.*) What, you don't
like cucumber?

Children.

No.

Kap.

I've never heard of anyone not liking cucumber. What
do you like?

(*Children tell of things they like.*)

Kap.

Candy . . . ugh. Ice Cream . . . sounds terrible. What
strange fish you are. You are fish, aren't you?
(*Children call out* "No.")

Kap.

Not fish. Are you sure?

Children.

Not fish.

Kap.

If you're not fish, what are you?

Children.

Boys and girls.

Kap.

You're boys and girls? What's that?

(Children explain.)

Kap.

And where are you from?

Children.

Land.

Kap.

Land! You never know what you'll find in the river these days. Do you like to play tricks?

Children.

Yes.

Kap.

You do. Well, maybe I'll try being a boy or a girl too. I get tired of being a kappa all the time. I have no brothers or sisters and I get lonely swimming around by myself. Maybe I'll go back to land with you after the Ball.

Minstrel.

Don't say such things, Kap. You know the King and Queen would never let you leave the riverbed. Why . . . why you might spill the water from your head.

Kap.

That's true. They would never let me go. They're always saying, don't do this, and don't do that. Be careful of this, be careful of that. Always worried about something. Are human parents that way too?

Children.

Yes.

Kap.

Then I might as well stay a kappa.

Minstrel.

Oh, here come the King and Queen now.

(KING *and* QUEEN *enter. They exchange polite quocks with the* MINSTREL *and then notice* KAP.)

Queen.

Where have you been, Kap? I've been looking all over for you. I was so worried you were caught in a lily pad or lost in an underwater cave.

King.

You must not worry your mother like this, Kap. She

hasn't been able to eat a bite of cucumber the whole time she's been searching for you.

Kap.

There's nothing to worry about. I've been around here all the time. Have a bite of cucumber.

Queen.

(*Takes a bite.*) Oh, quock, that does make me feel better.

King.

(*Takes a bite.*) Quock, quock . . . Nothing like a cucumber to make one's cares disappear.

Queen.

Have a bite, too, Minstrel. You're going to be up very late tonight . . . until the moon sets.

Minstrel.

(*Takes a bite.*) I've been resting up for this since the last full moon.

Queen.

Oh, what fun the Ball is going to be. I've even invented some new dance steps.

King.

You must show me, my dear. I've been so busy with affairs in the river, I haven't had a chance to practice.

(*They do a few steps together.*)

Queen.

(*Remembering* KAP.) Kap, are you all ready for the Ball tonight? Turn around, let me see if your shell is shined.

Kap.

It's fine, Mother.

(*He turns around quickly.*)

Queen.

Just as I thought. You haven't shined your shell. It's dull and muddy. Come sit down right here and let me do it for you.

(KING *and* QUEEN *sit on their thrones.* KAP *sits at their feet.*)

Queen.

What will our subjects think if your shell is dull?
Musician, please play some shell-shining music.

QUEEN'S SONG
Little kappa, prince of grace,
Shell of turtle, monkey face,
The river you will rule one day,
Until then, just swim and play.

But outside the riverbed,
Guard the water in your head.
Should the water splash and flow,
From your body life will go.

Remember always what I've said.
Guard the water in your head.

King.

That's right, son. Always remember, never leave the
riverbed and guard the water in your head.

Kap.

(*Running off.*) I'll try to remember not to forget.

Queen.

Where are you going?

Kap.

Just for a little swim.

Queen.

Well, don't get your shell dirty.

King.

And don't be late!

King and Queen.

And don't forget!

Kap.

I told you . . . I'll try to remember not to forget.

(KING *and* QUEEN *go out.*)

Kap.

(*To children.*) Are human parents like that? Do you
have to shine your shells? (*They respond.*) Well, I do
love to dance so I won't be late. (*He does some dance
steps.*)

(CARPY *swims by.*)

Carpy.

Hi, Kap.

Kap.

(*Swimming to him.*) Oh, Carpy, let's go for a swim.

Carpy.

I can't, Kap. I have to go to school.

Kap.

School? At this hour?

Carpy.

A young carp is in a school of fish at all hours. (*To audience.*) That's why I'm such a *bright* red.

Kap.

What about that time you and I swam upstream?

Carpy.

I got into a lot of trouble for being gone so long, Kap. I had to swim after school.

Kap.

So get in trouble again. Come on, Carpy.

Carpy.

I can't today, Kap. We're having a test.

Kap.

What kind of test?

Carpy.

Jumping up waterfalls.

Kap.

Jumping waterfalls. Oh, teach me, Carpy.

Carpy.

Kappas don't jump up waterfalls.

Kap.

Then I'll pretend to be a carp. Come on, show me how you jump a waterfall.

(PROPERTY MAN *waves blue cloth or else lights flicker like a waterfall.*)

Carpy.

Oh, all right. But just for a few minutes. You jump like this. (*He jumps with fins in swimming motion.*)

Kap.
Like this?
Carpy.
Like that.
Kap.
Like that?
Carpy.
Like this.
Minstrel.

(*Sings song over their jumping.*)

I wish I was a red carp
With fin and gill and all,
Then I could swim and leap upstream
And jump a waterfall.

I wish I was a red carp
Living in the riverbed,
But I cannot be a red carp so
I'll be a kappa instead.

Carpy.
(*Stopping.*) I have to go now, Kap. They'll think I've
been caught by a fisherman or something.
Kap.
What's a fisherman? Some kind of fish?
Carpy.
No, they're humans who stand on shore and fish with
worms for fish.
Kap.
Ugh, I hate worms. But it would be great to see what
a fisherman looks like.
Carpy.
Stay away from them, Kap! If you know what's good
for you, you won't go searching around for fishermen.
Bye now, I'm on my way.
Kap.
Please stay, Carpy. I'll give you ten cucumbers.
Carpy.
(*Going out.*) I *hate* cucumbers.
Kap.
(*To children.*) What's the good of being a prince if

you've no one to play with. Well, I'll just swim along on my own for a while . . . and maybe if I'm lucky, I'll spot one of those fishermen on shore.

(KAP *swims.*)

Minstrel.

> Kappa prince, watch where you are,
> You are swimming much too far,
> Kappa prince, beware, beware,
> There is danger over there,
> Fishermen with lots of bait . . .
> Turn back, turn back,
> Before it is too late.

(*Lights up on fishing scene:* MICHIO *and his* FATHER.)

Father.

Now, son, we're ready for your first fishing lesson. We'll tie the string from the pole like this . . . and you're all set. For a beginner this kind of line will do. Someday, when you get to be as good as I am, I'll make you a stronger pole.

Michio.

I'm going to catch something today. I just know it.

Father.

Don't expect too much the first time, son. It will take many years to become as good as I am.

Michio.

I could never hope to be as good as you are, Father. But I'm going to try to catch just a tiny baby fish . . . just to show Taro and Yukiko.

Father.

Now your line is ready to go. All but the bait. I don't want to waste a good worm on you, so we'll just put this green lure on instead. The color may attract something and we won't have lost a valuable worm.

Michio.

Anything you say, Father.

Father.

Now, we're ready. You stand like this.

Michio.

Like this?

Father.

Like that. And drop your line like this.

Michio.

Like this?

Father.

Like that. In a few years you may look almost as grace-
ful as I do.

Michio.

I could never hope to look as good as you, Father.

Father.

And now comes the easy part. You just sit and wait.

Michio.

Like this?

Father.

Like that.

(*They both squat on shore.*)

Kap.

(*Swimming more slowly now.*) Oh, I'm getting tired.
And hungry. I'd give anything for something to eat . . .
like a juicy green cucumber. (*Sees end of fishing line.*)
What's that? Something green. Could it be . . . is it
possible it is a cucumber? I'll swim closer and see. I
think it is.

(*He swims up to it and is hooked.*)

Kap.

Oh, quock! Quock, quock! I'm stuck. Something's got
me. Help, quock, help!

Michio.

I think I've got something, Father.

Father.

Impossible.

Michio.

No, I feel something pulling.

Father.

Maybe an eel . . . pull it in.

Michio.

(*Trying frantically.*) I can't. It's too heavy. It feels
like a . . . whale!

Father.

You couldn't have gotten a fish . . . not the first time. I
can't believe it. (*He grabs rod.*) Saaaah, in all my
years I have never felt anything like this on the end
of my line.

(*There is a struggle between* FATHER *and* KAP *as
he is being pulled in. Everyone gets tangled in the
line.* KAP *loses the water from his head as he is being
dragged in and lies unconscious on the ground.*)

Michio.

What kind of fish is it, Father?

Father.

Saaaah, is it possible? A kappa! I've never seen one
before.

Michio.

A real kappa? Wait till the kids hear about this. I
caught a kappa. I caught a kappa.

Father.

It's a young one. And all the water has spilled from
its head so it can't run away. Let's take him home to
your mother so she can see him too.

(*They carry* KAP *to home area.*)

Father.

Wife, wife, come and help us!

Mother.

What did Michio catch?

Father.

You'll never guess.

Mother.

Michio caught this?

Father.

Well, I really caught it on his line.

Mother.

Of course, he could never catch such a thing by himself. But what is it? It's not a dragon . . . it has no tail.

It's got a shell, but it's not a turtle. (*To audience.*)
Do you know what it is?

Children.

(*Calling out.*) A kappa!

Mother.

A what?

Children.

A kappa.

Mother.

No, it couldn't be. Impossible.

Children.

It is!

Father.

(*Proudly.*) It is a kappa. See the place for the water
in its head.

Mother.

You're right, it is a kappa. But look, the water's almost
all spilled out. Michio, hurry and get some water or
it will die. They say a kappa cannot live without its
water.

(PROPERTY MAN *hands a small wooden bucket of
water to* MICHIO.)

Mother.

I'll prop its head up on this cushion. And try a little
at a time. (*She pours water.*)

Michio.

He's not waking.

Mother.

He will. He's lost so much water, it will probably take
a long time for him to wake up. He may even have
lost his memory and not know who or where he is.

Michio.

Poor kappa.

Mother.

He is cute, isn't he?

Michio.

(*Encouraged by her interest.*) Can we keep him?

Father.

(*Exploding.*) Keep him! I've never heard such non-sense.

Mother.

But, husband, maybe it's not a bad idea. We've been praying to the river god for another son. Perhaps he is the answer to our prayers.

Father.

Impossible. I'm throwing him back.

Mother.

But perhaps he was sent to us by the river god.

Michio.

That's right, Father. Please let us keep him.

Father.

Don't you know how dangerous kappas are? Why . . . they play tricks on people.

Michio.

Please . . .

Father.

My father told me that a kappa once stole all the cucumbers from his field.

Mother.

He's so young. He's probably harmless. He could be our new son.

Michio.

He could be my brother. Let us keep him.

Father.

Impossible. The other villagers would never agree to our keeping a kappa here. People are afraid of them. You'd have to disguise him . . . cover his shell . . .

Mother.

What a wonderful idea, husband. We could put Michio's jacket over his shell . . .

Michio.

And keep a hat on his head . . .

Mother.

And no one will ever know. You are so clever, husband, to think of this.

Father.

I always was rather inventive. Even as a boy.

Mother.

No one but you could have thought of disguising him as a human child.

Father.

But if we do this, we'll have to keep it secret. (*To audience.*) That means you too. You can't tell anyone he's a kappa, or the villagers will send him away. You must promise, Michio.

Michio.

I promise. I won't even tell Taro and Yukiko, my best friends.

Father.

Well, in that case, since it was my idea . . . I guess we can keep him.

Mother.

I have a new son.

Michio.

I have a brother.

Father.

(*Still worried.*) Wait a minute. What if he doesn't want to stay with us?

Mother.

He will, I just know it. He may not even remember who he was when he wakes up . . . he may believe he is really our son.

Michio.

When will he wake up!

Mother.

I'll put a little more water in his head and maybe he'll open his eyes. (*She sings as she pours.*)

> Little kappa, prince of joy,
> You will be my little boy.
> Michio's clothes will hide your shell,
> A cap will hide your water well.
> No longer will you roam the river wild,
> Now you will wake a human child.

(*They pause and wait.*)

Michio.

He didn't wake.

Mother.

He may need more time.

Father.

But we don't have more time. We have to finish the harvest in the fields. Come along, wife. We can't waste any more time on kappas.

Mother.

(*Jumping up at her husband's command.*) You stay with him while we finish up in the fields, Michio. Watch over him until he awakes.

Michio.

I won't leave his side.

(MOTHER *and* FATHER *go out.* MICHIO *sits by* KAP.)

Michio.

> Little kappa, my new brother,
> I want you and no other,
> Share my clothes to hide your shell,
> Share our secret . . . never tell.
> Forget the kappa you used to be.
> Oh wake, and be a boy like me!

(*At end of song,* KAP *stirs. Opens eyes, sits up and looks around confused. Sees* MICHIO *and tenses up as if to escape.*)

Michio.

Don't be frightened. You're safe.

Kap.

Safe . . . where?

Michio.

On land, in my house.

Kap.

Land? House? Who are you?

Michio.

My name is Michio. What's yours?

Kap.

I . . . I think it's Kap. But I can't remember how I got here. Or where I came from.

Michio.

Don't worry about that. You're going to be my adopted brother.

Kap.

I am? What's an adopted brother?

Michio.

Someone who's chosen to be part of the family—someone to play with.

Kap.

That sounds like fun ... to always have someone to play with. I'm an adopted brother! (*Pause.*) But I don't look like you.

Michio.

You will when you put some clothes on. You'll look like a real human boy.

Kap.

That's all it takes to be human ... just wearing clothes?

Michio.

It's a first step. Here, you can wear my best jacket.

(PROPERTY MAN *brings in jacket and hat.* KAP *gets into happi coat backward.*)

Michio.

No, like this. There. And a hat. You must never take it off. Don't forget.

Kap.

I'll try to remember not to forget.

(*They do a mirror routine.*)

Kap.

I'm a real boy.

Michio.

Come on, I want you to meet Taro and Yukiko. You'll really like them.

(*They go into outside area.*
TARO *and* YUKIKO *come in.* TARO *chases* YUKIKO *playfully with sword.*)

Michio.

There they are. Taro! Yukiko! What's that?

Taro.

A new sword made out of bamboo. It could cut your head off.

Michio.

Well, I have a *new* brother.

Yukiko.

A new brother!

Taro.

(*Suspiciously.*) A *new* brother. How did you suddenly get a brother?

Michio.

Oh, we adopted him from another village. Isn't that right, Kap?

(KAP *nods head.*)

Yukiko.

He doesn't look like you.

Michio.

Brothers don't always look alike.

Taro.

(*Impatiently.*) Never mind what he *looks* like. What can he do? (*To* KAP.) You might as well understand that I'm the leader around here. I'm the best jumper, the best wrestler, the best everything there is. Can you do anything?

Kap.

I don't know.

Taro.

(*Scornfully.*) You don't know.

Kap.

I can try.

Taro.

Well, you'll have to try pretty hard to keep up with me. No one can jump farther than me. I'll show you. (*To* YUKIKO.) Hold my sword. (*He gets into position and takes a big jump.*) There, can you beat that?

Michio.

(*Nervously.*) Maybe he should practice first.

Kap.
That's all right, Michio. I'll do my best. (*He takes a jump past where* TARO *was.*)

Yukiko.
Saaaah, he jumps just like a *frog*.

Michio.
(*Nervously.*) He jumps like a *boy* who jumps like a frog.

Taro.
Well, he may jump like a frog, but frogs can't wrestle. No one has ever beaten me at wrestling. Come on now, I challenge you to wrestle.

Michio.
I think we'd better go now, Kap.

Kap.
It sounds like fun, Michio.

Michio.
Some other time. We've got to get home.

Kap.
Oh, come on, Michio.

Taro.
Chicken, huh?

Michio.
He's not afraid. He's just tired.

Kap.
But I'm not tired at all. I want to wrestle to make Taro happy.

Michio.
Well, for a little while. We can't stay too long or Mother will worry.

(*They get set as if they are in a sumo wrestling ring.* TARO *grunts and puffs as he assumes positions.* KAP *easily defeats* TARO. *Looks puzzled that he has done so.*)

Yukiko.
Saaaah, he wrestles just like a kappa.

Kap.
A what?

Michio.

(*Nervously.*) He wrestles like a boy who wrestles like a kappa.

Kap.

What's a kappa?

Taro.

(*Superiorly.*) You don't know what a kappa is?

Kap.

I never heard of one.

Taro.

You may be good at jumping and wrestling, but you're pretty stupid not to know what a kappa is.

Yukiko.

A kappa has a shell on its back and walks like this. (*She walks around.*) And it says quock, quock, quock. (*She circles around saying* "Quock.") And it has to hold its head up straight because it has water in its head it can't spill.

Taro.

I'll bet I could make a better kappa. (*He walks around saying* "Quock.")

Yukiko.

You don't look like a kappa.

Taro.

Oh, don't I? . . . Well, I'm not done yet. I'm going to put a pillow on my back and a bowl on my head.

Yukiko.

That sounds like fun. Why don't we all dress up like kappas. I'll go get something.

Taro.

Copycat. Well, I'll still make the best one.

(YUKIKO *goes out.*)

Michio.

Come on, Kap, I don't like this.

Taro.

What, are you scared you won't look as good as me?

Kap.

It sounds like fun, Michio. Dressing up and pretending to be something else.

(YUKIKO *comes in with bowls and pillows.*)

Yukiko.

Come on, everyone. Let's see who can be the funniest kappa.

Taro.

My kappa is going to carry a sword and be very frightening.

Yukiko.

Mine is going to be very cute . . . a girl kappa. What's yours going to be, Kap?

Kap.

I don't know.

Michio.

His will be my brother.

(*As they dress, each actor takes a different stanza.* PROPERTY MAN *can help them tie pillows on their backs and paper bowls on their heads.*)

Yukiko.

I'm going to be a kappa girl
Living in the riverbed.
I'll put a pillow on my back,
And a bowl on my head.

Taro.

I'll look just like a kappa boy,
And wrestle like one, too.
And I'll play tricks on everyone . . .
And tease and torment you.

Michio.

I'm going to be a kappa boy,
Although I'd rather not.
I'd like to get Kap out of here,
Before things get too hot.

Kap.

I'm going to be a kappa now,
That's what they say to be.
But how I wish that I could know
Just what is really me.

(*They pretend to swim like kappas around the stage.*
MINSTREL *sings over them.*)

Minstrel.

> Kappa boys and kappa girl
> Swimming in the riverbed,
> Don't you know that one of you
> Has water in his head.
>
> Kappa boys and kappa girl
> All dress up for the part,
> Don't you know that one of you
> Is a true kappa at heart.

Taro.
Now let's see who is the best kappa . . . him or me.
Yukiko.
Saaaah, Kap looks just like a kappa.
Taro.
I look more like a kappa than he does.
Yukiko.
No, you don't. Kap looks best.
Taro.
(*To audience.*) Who looks more like a kappa, him or
me?

(*Children point to* KAP.)

Michio.
(*Nervously.*) You both look like kappas.
Taro.
You're all on his side. This game isn't fun anymore.
I'm going home. (*Takes off his things.*)
Kap.
Don't go, Taro.
Yukiko.
Oh, just when we were having fun.
Michio.
(*Eager to leave.*) We have to go, too. (*He and* KAP
take off things.)
Yukiko.
Can't you stay, Kap?

Kap.

I . . . I have to go with Michio.

Michio.

We have to hurry.

Taro.

Come on, Yukiko.

Yukiko.

(*Going off with* TARO.) Oh, Taro, you always ruin everything!

Taro.

There's something fishy about that boy! (*Exits.*)

Kap.

It was fun being a kappa. I'm hungry.

Michio.

Mother will have something waiting for us. Let's hurry, we were supposed to be back long ago.

(*They walk back into house area. Michio doesn't notice as* KAP *runs into audience and hides among children.*)

Michio.

Mother, Father, we're back!

Mother.

Oh, Michio, where were you? I was so worried. Where is, is . . .

Michio.

. . . Kap. He's right here. I took him out to met Taro and Yukiko. Kap . . . Kap! Where are you?

(MICHIO *searches for* KAP. *Asks children if they've seen him. When he finds him, leads* KAP *home.*)

Mother.

Kap. Welcome home, son. I am your new mother.

Father.

And I am your new father.

Kap.

I am glad to meet you, new Mother and Father.

Mother.

You must be tired after all that's happened to you today.

Kap.

No, I feel wide awake.

Michio.

He's just hungry.

Mother.

Hungry . . . Oh, come and sit down here. I have some rice balls for you and cucumbers.

Kap.

Cucumbers? I want to try cucumbers.

Mother.

Here's a nice big one. See if you like it.

Kap.

It's delicious. (*He gobbles it down.*) I'll have another. (*Gobbles.*) And another. (*Gobbles.*) And another.

Mother.

I'm afraid there are no more cucumbers. Anyway, you shouldn't eat too many. You'll get a stomachache.

Michio.

Kap beat Taro at jumping and wrestling.

Mother.

Oh, Michio, you should be careful.

Michio.

It was all right, Mother.

Kap.

And we dressed up as kappas.

Father.

(*Exploding.*) You what?

Michio.

It's all right, Father. We were just playing.

Mother.

It sounds like you've had *too* busy a day. You'd better go to bed right away because tomorrow is the harvest festival. And you don't want to be tired for that. What are you looking at, Kap?

(KAP *is looking up at the moon. It is a light projection or held on pole by* PROPERTY MAN.)

Kap.

(*As if mesmerized.*) The moon is full tonight.

Mother.
Yes, tonight is the thirteenth of the month when the
moon is at its fullest.

Kap.
How beautiful it is. It seems so close.

Mother.
It will protect you both while you sleep. (MOTHER *or*
PROPERTY MAN *puts down straw mats.*) Come now,
into bed, both of you. I'll sing you a moon lullaby to
help you sleep.

Michio.
Good night, Kap.

Kap.
Good night, Michio.

MOTHER'S SONG
(*To melody of Japanese song "Akatombo."*)

> Oh, moon that shines on my sons,
> Keep them safe from harm.
> Hold them close in your gentle beams
> Till the morning comes.
>
> Oh, moon that shines on my sons,
> I beseech you,
> Keep them safe from all evil ones,
> For the whole night through.

(*She tiptoes out with* FATHER *when finished. Flute
under . . . moon comes closer.*)

Kap.
(*Sits up slowly, as if in a trance.*) I feel so strange. I
don't know why. It's as if the moon is shining through
me. I want to throw off my clothes and dance in the
moonlight. But I mustn't. I'm sure real boys don't do
things like that. Real boys are sleeping now like
Michio. I must go back to sleep.

(*He lies down and tries to sleep.*)

Kap.
Quock! (*Like a burp . . . he sits up startled.*) Quock!

Quock! What are you trying to tell me, moon? What? Come out and dance? That's what you want? You want me to dance. Quock. All right, I'm coming, Moon, I'm coming.

(*He rises, throws off clothes and tiptoes out of room.*)

Kap.
(*On roof.*) Quock. I'm here, moon. How cool you feel on my body . . . You are part of me. I want to dance, Moon. Quock, quock, quock. I want to dance!

(KAP *does a solo to music.*)

Kap.
(*At end.*) Quock, quock. That was wonderful. I'm hungry now. Cucumbers, that's what I want. Quock, I'll just go out to the fields and see if there are any left. No one would mind if I borrowed one . . . Or maybe two . . . or three.

(*Cucumbers are flashed on cyclorama now. They could also be held on a pole by* PROPERTY MAN. *They disappear as* KAP *takes them. At the end, there are no cucumbers left.*)

Kap.
Oh, quock. There aren't any left anywhere. Maybe no one will miss them. Quock. That was good. I'd better get out of here. I'll just tiptoe quietly past everyone's door so no one will notice me.

(*As he tiptoes by, doors of the village appear on the cyclorama.*)

Kap.
Quock. Wouldn't it be fun to knock on all these doors and hide. Taro's. Yukiko's. Everyone's but my own. What a trick it will be. Quock. Quock.

(KAP *runs about knocking on doors.*)

Voices of Villagers.
Who's there?
Who's there?

Who's there?

Kap.

Oh, quock. They didn't see me. I tricked them all.
And now to steal silently to bed.

(*He goes back to house scene and into bed beside*
MICHIO.)

Minstrel.

> Hurry, Kap, back to your bed,
> Lest someone sees it's you.
> The villagers are very scared,
> And wondering what to do.

> So hurry, Kap, back in your clothes,
> Forget that it was you.
> Forget the things you've done tonight,
> And start the day anew.

(*Lights up for morning. Boys are sleeping. Loud
knock on door.* TARO *and* YUKIKO *come bounding in.*)

Taro.

Wake up, you two. Have you heard the news? An evil
spirit was in the village last night.

Michio.

An evil spirit! How do you know?

Taro.

He knocked on our door.

Yukiko.

And my door, too.

Taro.

And he stole all the cucumbers from our field.

Yukiko.

And he stole all of our cucumbers, too.

Michio.

You must have been dreaming. I didn't hear or see
anyone.

Taro.

Some dream. Everyone in the village heard him. And
some saw him dancing in the moonlight.

Yukiko.

But he got away when they opened their doors.

Taro.
He's a sly one, all right. And fast.

Michio.
I never heard of an evil spirit dancing . . . or liking cucumbers.

Taro.
This one did.

Yukiko.
It must be huge to eat so many cucumbers.

Taro.
Don't worry . . . I'll wrestle with it even if it's 10 feet high.

Yukiko.
Oh, Taro, you couldn't even beat Kap.

Taro.
Watch what you say, Yukiko.

Yukiko.
I'm sorry, but I don't want you to get hurt.

Taro.
Don't worry about me, Yukiko. I'm not afraid of any evil spirit. I'm staying with the grown-ups tonight to catch it.

Yukiko.
Everyone's going to stay up tonight to catch it, Michio. Oh, isn't it exciting?

Michio.
Why do they want to catch it?

Taro.
Why? It might take our rice next! Our whole harvest!

Yukiko.
Or our horse. Even the children will be allowed to stay up late.

Taro.
I always stay up late so that's nothing for me.

Yukiko.
And everyone will listen for him together. And when we hear him prowl about, we'll run out and catch him.

Taro.

I'll probably be the one to catch him.

Yukiko.

You may need Kap's help. Isn't it exciting, Kap?

Kap.

Quock! I . . . I think I have a stomach ache.

Taro.

Something you ate last night, maybe?

Kap.

I don't know. Quock! (*He hides mouth as if a burp.*)

Yukiko.

Oh, you can't have a stomach ache now, Kap. The harvest festival is in a few hours and we're all going to dance and sing and have such a good time.

Taro.

Yeah, you've got to be well for the festival, Kap. Come on, Yukiko! We have to go on to the other houses now and spread the word about the evil spirit.

Yukiko.

See you later, Kap. Good-bye, Michio.

Kap.

Quock!

(TARO *and* YUKIKO *run off.*)

Michio.

We're supposed to be stacking the rice before the festival, Kap. Do you feel up to it?

Kap.

I never stacked rice before.

Michio.

It's easy. I've been doing it since I was a little boy.

(*They start walking to the fields.*
PROPERTY MAN *scatters dry stalks on floor.*
They arrive in the fields.)

Michio.

Here we are. Now watch me. You do it like this. (*He bends over and piles a few together.*)

Kap.

Like this?

Michio.

Like that. Careful how you bend over. Like this.

Kap.

Like this?

Michio.

You've got it. You can finish these and I'll do those over there.

(*He walks a little way and turns his back on* KAP *as they work.*)

Kap.

Oh, my stomach hurts. I must have eaten something that boys shouldn't eat. And I want so much to be a real boy.

Kap.

(*Speaks the song.*)

I'm going to be a real boy now,
And do what real boys do.
Stack rice in straight little rows
And sleep the night through.

I'm going to be a real boy now,
That's what I want to be,
But how I wish that I could know
Just what is really me.

(*To audience.*)

Sometimes, I feel that I'm just about to
remember what I was before I became human.
But just as I am about to remember, I forget.
I try to remember not to forget. And then
I forget.

I'm going to be a real boy now.
I will! I will be!
But how I wish that I could know
Just what is really me.

(*He wakes from reverie and starts stacking frantically.*

MINSTREL *comes running in through audience.*)

Minstrel.

Excuse me . . . pardon me . . . do you mind moving so that I can get through. Thank you so much. I'm in such a hurry. I'm sure to be late. I'm on my way to the harvest festival. I'm the village musician and today there is a celebration for the harvest of the rice. Everyone will give thanks for this year's good crops. There will be dancing and singing and eating and drinking. And everyone, young and old, will have fun.

(MINSTREL *takes* KAP *and* MICHIO *by the arm.*)

Minstrel.

So come to the festival . . . the harvest festival
Now it's about to begin.
Forget your troubles,
Forget your cares,
Look at our jugglers,
Look at our wares.
Come to the festival, everyone . . .
Come to the festival and have fun!

(TARO *and* YUKIKO *run in carrying baskets or they bring in lanterns and string them up.* MICHIO *and* KAP *run in. They all talk and laugh together. They try juggling and drop things and laugh. The* MINSTREL *joins them in this.*
Bright carnival scenes flash on the cyclorama.
Flash paper is lit. MUSICIAN *plays drums as someone brings out lion mask with long cloth attached. The young people all get under cloth and do dance through audience shouting "Washoi, washoi."*
This scene can be as fanciful or spare as director choses.
MINSTREL *hits gong and goes into Tanka Bushi festival dance.*)

Minstrel.
The Tanka Bushi!
Yukiko.
Come on, Kap, we'll show you our harvest dance.

(MOTHER *and* FATHER *and* CHILDREN *get in a circle and dance the traditional Tanka Bushi.*

KAP *tries to imitate them and then gives up and goes into his own abandoned dance. He leaps about joyously and* TARO *and* YUKIKO *join him.* MICHIO *gets nervous that* KAP *will reveal his true identity.*)

Michio.
Stop!

(*Everything stops.*)

Michio.
Come on, Kap. Let's get home before it gets dark.

(YUKIKO *and* TARO *run over to see why they're leaving.*)

Taro.
Where are you going?
Michio.
Home. It's getting late.
Taro.
Aren't you going to wait up for the evil spirit with us tonight?
Michio.
No, I'm tired. I'm going to sleep.
Yukiko.
How about you, Kap?
Kap.
(*Uncertain.*) I should go with Michio.
Taro.
Well, if you two aren't going to come, we're going to need more help. (*To audience.*) How about you? Will you wait up with us tonight?

(*Audience calls back they will.*)

Yukiko.
Yes, please wait up with us. It's fun staying up late. And maybe we'll catch a fierce goblin or monster.
Taro.
There's a good hiding place over there. (*He hides in audience.*)

Yukiko.

(*Finds a place in audience.*) He'll never see me here. (*To audience.*) Everybody crouch down.

Taro.

(*From his hiding place to audience while* KAP *and* MICHIO *return to house section and lie down to sleep.*) Everyone stay quiet. And watch carefully. The moon is beginning to rise. The evil spirit may be coming around soon. Don't let him see you. And don't call out until you see him dancing. We want to catch him before he gets away.

Michio.

I'm tired from the festival, aren't you?

Kap.

No, I could have gone on doing the Tanka Bushi all night.

Michio.

You do love to dance, don't you?

Kap.

I don't know why. But I do.

Michio.

Kap . . .

Kap.

Yes, Michio . . .

Michio.

Don't go back out there tonight . . . no matter what happens.

Kap.

I wasn't going to, Michio. Why do you say that?

Michio.

I don't know. With the evil spirit roaming around and everyone waiting up, I think we're better off right here.

Kap.

Sure, Michio. I want to do whatever you do.

Michio.

Well, I'm going to sleep right now. Good night, Kap.

Kap.

Good night, Michio.

(*They both lie down as if sleeping.*
Flute under.
The moon moves in near KAP's *bed.*
KAP *sits up slowly and then quickly throws off clothes and runs behind cyclorama.*
Music up gradually.)

Taro.
Are you all right over there, Yukiko?
Yukiko.
Yeah, I've got a good spot over here.
Taro.
Now don't be scared.
Yukiko.
I'm not scared, Taro! (*Hesitantly.*) Are you?
Taro.
(*Bravado.*) No!
Yukiko.
Just a little?
Taro.
Well, maybe just a little.

(*Music becomes louder.*
Light on cyclorama reveals a shadow effect of KAP *dancing on rooftop. If no cyclorama,* KAP *can dance in special area.*)

Taro.
(*Loud whisper.*) There's something over there!
Yukiko.
I see it. A monster or something.

(*Strobe light flashes as they dash about in confusion.*)

Michio's Father.
(*Running in with lighted paper lantern.*) We've spotted something.
Michio's Mother.
(*With lantern.*) What is it?

(KAP *slips and falls from roof.*)

Everyone.

He's falling! He's falling!

(*Blackout as* KAP *slips under cyclorama onto stage. He lies on the ground unconscious. Everyone runs cautiously up as lights up slowly.* MOTHER *and* FATHER *carry* KAP *downstage.*)

Taro.

Yukiko, it's a kappa.

Yukiko.

A kappa!

Taro.

There's a shell on its back.

Yukiko.

And the water's spilled from its head.

Taro.

Stay back, everyone. It could still jump up and attack us.

Michio.

(*Running in.*) What's happened? Where's Kap?

Yukiko.

He's not here.

Michio.

Who's that?

Taro.

A kappa! We caught a kappa!

Michio.

Oh, no! Help him! We must get water quickly or he'll die.

(PROPERTY MAN *brings in water bucket.*)

Taro.

Why should we help a kappa?

Michio.

It's Kap.

Taro.

You're dreaming.

Yukiko.

It couldn't be Kap.

Michio's Father.

No, he's right. It's probably Kap.

Mother.

We thought we could disguise him as our child. But he is really a kappa at heart.

Yukiko.

Then let's help him.

Mother.

All of his water is gone. It may be too late.

Yukiko.

(*To children.*) It can't be too late. Please help us.

Michio.

(*To children.*) Kap cannot live without your help.

(*Music under.*)

Minstrel.

Everyone call out together:
> "Kappa prince who danced and fell
> May our water make you well."

Michio.

(*Chanting during ritual.*) Please, Kap, wake up.

Mother and Father.

Wake up, son, for us.

Taro and Yukiko.

Wake up, Kap.

(*Slowly* KAP *comes to consciousness. Sits up. Looks around at everyone. Then looks at himself, his hands, his shell, feels water in his head.*)

Kap.

(*To everyone.*) What are you looking at?

Michio.

At my brother.

Mother.

At my little boy.

Kap.

You're looking at a . . . a kappa.

Michio.

It doesn't matter, Kap. We love you.

Father.

That's right. We wouldn't have you any other way.

Taro.

You're great as a kappa.

Kap.

I thought I'd be like you . . . a real boy.

Mother.

You are *my* little boy.

Kap.

No, I remember everything now. I am Kap, prince of the kappas. I never could be a boy. I belong in my river kingdom, not here.

Yukiko.

Please stay with us, Kap.

Kap.

I can't live on land, I would only steal more cucumbers and play more tricks on you.

Taro.

If you stay, you can have all the cucumbers you want.

Yukiko.

We like your tricks, Kap. Please stay with us.

Michio.

Let's go home now, Kap.

Kap.

No, I must find the home from which I came . . . deep under the river. They must be waiting for me there even now.

Michio.

Don't leave us, Kap. (*To audience.*) Tell him not to leave.

Kap.

(*To children.*) You of all people should understand why I must return to the river. I can no more be a real boy than you could be a real kappa. When night falls, we must all return to our own homes. (*To* MICHIO's MOTHER *and* FATHER.) Good-bye, my human mother and father. Thank you for all you've done for me.

Father.

At first I didn't think you should stay with us, Kap. But now I want you to . . . I want you to be our son.

Mother.

No, husband, forgive me, but I must disagree with you
for the first time. Kap has to go back to his own home.
I was only thinking of myself when I wanted to keep
him as our own. His mother and father must miss him
just as we would miss Michio.

Kap.

Thank you, Mother. For you are my *human* mother,
and you always will be.

(PROPERTY MAN *hands him rolled-up paper streamers.* KAP *gives each person one end while he says
good-bye. He holds on to the other end.*)

Kap.

(*To* MICHIO.) Good-bye, my brother. Don't forget that
down in the river there will always be a kappa who
loves you.

Michio.

(*With a smile.*) I'll try to remember not to forget.

Kap.

(*To* YUKIKO *and* TARO.) Good-bye, Yukiko and Taro.
Thank you for letting me be your friend.

Yukiko.

Thank you for teaching us how to dance and have
fun, Kap.

Taro.

And, Kap, I wouldn't admit this to anyone else . . .
you are a better wrestler.

(KAP *breaks paper streamers one by one as he moves
back.*)

Michio.

(*Before his streamer breaks.*) Kap . . .

(KAP *stops.*)

Michio.

Kap . . . if you find your river home, will you leave
a cucumber on the shore for me tonight?

Kap.

I will, Michio. And I'll find my home, I know it.

(*Music under.*

He goes off. PROPERTY MAN *puts down a blue ribbon which he walks along . . . or blue lights.*)

Minstrel.

Come along, Kap, I'll lead you there.
I walk on water, I walk on air,
And I know the path a kappa should tread
When he returns to his riverbed.

Come along, Kap, they're waiting for you,
The water has turned a misty blue
From your mother's tears which are shed
From the royal water in her head.
And the King has canceled the Full Moon Ball
Until you return to the palace hall.

So come along, Kap, I'll show you the way
Along the river where you used to play,
To the trick-filled life that once you knew,
In the days when you were really you.

Kap.

I guess it doesn't matter where I dive in.

(*He jumps over blue cloth as if diving in. Cloth is then taken away.*

Media returns to underwater effects, if media is used.)

Kap.

How good the river feels . . . even better than the moon. Oh, I can hardly wait to see my parents again and the Pearl-White Palace.

Carpy.

(*Swims by, stops in amazement.*) Kap? Kap, is that you?

Kap.

(*Surprised.*) Yes, it's me. Kap.

Carpy.

Don't you remember your old friend, Carpy?

Kap.

(*Beginning to remember.*) Yes, I do remember! Yes . . . Carpy!

Carpy.

Where have you been, Kap? Everyone's been so worried about you. Your mother hasn't eaten a cucumber since you disappeared. Kappas have been searching all through the river. There is a big reward for anyone who finds you.

Kap.

Well, you found me, Carpy.

Carpy.

But the reward is a cucumber. And I hate cucumbers.

Kap.

Cucumbers! I'm hungry.

Carpy.

Jump on my back, and I'll take you to the Pearl-White Palace.

> (KAP *holds on to his back and they swim about.*
> KING *and* QUEEN *swim in sadly.*
> CARPY *swims nearby with* KAP.)

Carpy.

There's your mother and father. You go alone and surprise them.

> (CARPY *swims off.*
> KAP *swims up to parents.*)

Kap.

Quock!

Queen.

(*Surprised.*) Quock? Quock!

King.

Quock! Quock!

> (KING *and* QUEEN, *quocking, run to* KAP.
> *The three of them join hands and dance a kind of jig together. Music under.*)

King.

This calls for a celebration. Let us all dance on the roof of the Pearl-White Palace by the light of the pearl-white moon.

Kap.

Before we start, may I take a cucumber?

King.

Of course, son. Take all you want.

Kap.

I only need one.

(KAP *swims to audience and gives cucumber to a child there.*)

Kap.

If you see Michio, will you give this to him for me. (*Runs back to* FATHER.) And now, let the dance begin.

King.

Court Minstrel . . . court Minstrel . . . where is he?

Minstrel.

(*Running in through audience.*) Oh, let me through, please, let me through, I shall be late.

King.

There you are at last. Where were you when we needed you?

Minstrel.

I've been playing at a harvest festival on land but it's over now and I am back.

King.

Well, don't go wandering off again . . . Play, play, play . . . and let everyone dance.

Minstrel.

(*To audience.*) The King has decreed that everyone shall dance. Come, let us celebrate Kap's return to the river kingdom. Let us all dance at the Full Moon Ball.

(*Music comes on strongly.* MINSTREL *invites children in audience to dance with kappas until music ends. All actors join dance.*)

Minstrel.

(*Striking gong.*) The King has decreed the Ball is over. Good-bye, everyone, come and visit us again soon here in the kappa kingdom.

(*Actors exit through audience.*)

Names and Nicknames

by James Reaney

PREFACE

The idea for this play came from an old speller owned by my father. It is called *The Practical Speller* and was published in 1881 by W. J. Gage & Co., Toronto. The various lessons in a section called "Familiar Words" are based on such themes as "At Home" or "On the Way to School" or "Boys Sometimes Are"—

dull	noisy	steadfast
cross	merry	untidy
wise	stupid	uncivil
rude	patient	respectful
manly	sincere	impertinent
busy	faithful	boisterous
witty	playful	ingenious
jolly	mirthful	ingenuous

Try murmuring these words over to yourself, and you get a picture in sound of a great many boys—slow ones, fast ones, hopping about, standing very still.

In the early days of this script, readers would say to me: "But, it's nothing but lists of words. I just can't see how it is going to work, particularly with a young audience." Since this could still be a possible reaction, perhaps it's best if I explain as much as I can—right from where I myself come from to the première directed in Winnipeg by John Hirsch who did see a great deal more in my text than just lists of words. *Names and Nicknames* grew out of not just my father's speller, but also out of the fact that I grew up with a mother and father both at one time or another very interested in acting and plays. From the turn of the century on, this interest flourished in the context of a farming district near Stratford, Ontario. At the Irish school where my father went, he won first prize in a mime contest the teacher, Mr. Macgregor Easson, conducted; from an excellent imitation of milking a cow my father went on to star in the title role of a play called *Ebenezer Scruggins*; people from Stratford (the high school principal) came out to see this performance and told him he ought to go into vaudeville, but he didn't think he'd be able to get up the dancing. And so my father submerged into the farming world again, but with always a beautiful sense for a play and a great help to me even when he was quite old in helping me see my own work. Not only did there seem to be a lot of plays put on in our neighborhood right up to the mid-thirties (*Dotty, the Miners' Daughter* from Samuel French with my mother as the gypsy fortune-teller), but there were also Christmas and Halloween concerts, spelling and geography matches, shivarees, Normal School productions of Shakespeare in the City Hall (two different casts for two different evenings) as well as fall fairs, radio programs (Nila Mac's "Let's Pretend" every Saturday morning, the Singing Lady, Little Orphan Annie joining a troupe of players on a southern showboat whose play formed one episode in this radio serial), circuses, parades (Orange Lodge), Christmas Carol productions in the City Hall (the title-role player was thereafter known as "scrooge" Willoughby), and last of all—Sunday School concerts and visiting evangelists with theremins. I think, too, that it was before I started school that I had a basic dramatic thrill: Miss Helen Coveney, my first teacher, appeared before the kerosene footlights as Aunt Jemima with rolling pin. Was it her, or wasn't it?

During high school I started writing plays and eventually had some put on for adults; but one of my early ambitions had always been to teach in a one-room school so I could direct the Christmas Concert. *Names and Nicknames* would have been the long play two thirds of the way through, a play in which the entire school could take part and after which Santa Claus would arrive. The choruses in *Names and Nicknames* are where everyone gets a chance; they are connected with memories of choral reading which Miss Evelyn Freeborne introduced in the mid-thirties (part of a progressive wave that hit teaching practice then—I thought it was "coral" reading and could see how the voices and maybe the bodies were supposed to intertwine); memories of rhythm bands— at my school, Elmhurst, S.S. No. 9, South Easthope, we made our own instruments after looking at the catalog and tried the idea out for a while without too many re- sults. But these were pre-Carl Orff days. The nickname idea behind Grandpa Thorntree's power over people grew out of a story my mother told me about an old man at Brocksden who always ruined babies' names by suggesting the possible nicknames. Since I have myself rejoiced in such nicknames as Rainy River and Redhead- ed Woodpecker I well know the dread of someone getting at your name, but in my father's speller there seemed to lie an antidote. There is this formidable list of first names; could not the old villain and name-spoiler be stumped by so many names for a child that he couldn't possibly ruin them all?

Directors, as I mentioned were daunted by the word lists; but eventually in the summer of 1963 John Hirsch, who was then at the Manitoba Theatre Centre, asked me for something his young actors could use as an exercise for their imaginations. These actors included Martha Henry and Heath Lamberts; later on that fall (1963), I watched them transform my text into a flow of gesture, mime, sound, and play-feeling I had only hoped could be there. It was the mime possibilities in the word-list chor- uses which John Hirsch surprised me most with. Kenneth Winter's setting of the songs, the playing of the child actors (so exuberant in the pig-feeding sequence) also surprised me in that I hadn't realized it could all be so energetic and like a river. After watching two public per- formances in which a whole balconyful of kids nearly leapt out of it in joining the dogs who are sicked on Thorntree (audiences of children are like live volcanoes) I returned to London, Ontario, where I started my own drama group (Listeners' Workshop)* and created more plays using the choruses and other ideas in *Names and Nicknames*. Since it is a theater of play, like games, their production needs only a few words, a drum, a piano maybe, and something will evolve. One early dramatic experience I haven't talked about yet was that of running across the fields to a schoolyard where games, not just scrub baseball, but real games were being played: crack the whip, London Bridge, skipping, stilt-walking, finger games with pieces of wet paper, Prisoners' Base, dramatic games with two sides and heroes, games such as "Old Witch" that my mother found still being played in a schoolyard of the early sixties. This schoolyard situation which I've tried to reduplicate in my play is the best imitation of what the world is like I've yet seen; its games contain tragedy, comedy—all the modes, but they contain it in a floating way: the way gods see things.

One day I sent the boy who was playing the hired man in a production at the Simcoe Street public school here to visit my father who at seventy-seven had become a patient at Westminster Hospital, the local veterans' hospital. My father got out of bed and showed this young actor how to mime harnessing a horse to a seed drill and how to milk a cow.

JAMES REANEY
October, 1972

*See "Ten Years at Play," *Canadian Literature* #41, for some more material on this workshop and its aims.

CHARACTERS

Farmer Dell
Mrs. Annie Dell
Rob, the hired man
Grandpa Thorntree
Reverend Hackaberry
Cousin Etta
Chorus
Baby One
Baby Two

It begins.

Chorus and Chief Actors.
The farm in the morning. The Farm.
Farmer Dell's Farm.

(*For the next sequence, the six chief actors mime the words they are saying. For "copse" they bring up-lifted hands together and someone whistles a bird song. For "barn" they build a barn, and so on. Not every word gets a gesture and the whole thing must be kept flowing, but the actors do say these words with their bodies as well as their mouths.*)

Vale hill dell dale
Bush rock bank field
Pool wood pond creek
Ridge hedge copse yard
Swale lane fence wall
Path road ditch post
Barn shed tree house

Farmer Dell's Farm.

(*The actors lie down as a rooster crows, some of them on the benches. Now, the sleeping* DELLS *bestir themselves. There can be mime of dressing, alarm clocks, etc.* ROB, *the hired man, goes out to get the cows. The* CHORUS *utter moos and some of them pretend to be cows.*)

154

Rob.

I get up in the morning and go and fetch the cows.
Cobossy coboss Cobossy coboss (*Ad lib repetition.*)

Chorus.

Moo moo moo moo.

Rob.

Come on cushy cows and come to be milked.

Chorus.

Moo.

(*Select two female members of the* CHORUS *to be cows.*)

Rob.

(*He drives them with a stick.*) Here—here's the short-est way.

Chorus.

Moo. We have to follow our cowpath.

Rob.

And it winds up and down.

Chorus.

Our names are Blossom, Josephine, Moo, Rachel, Betty, Moo. Next year, let's make the path curve more here. Rachel, Betty, Blossom, and Josephine. Not too fast or we won't let down our milk.

Rob.

Coboss coboss coboss coboss.

Chorus.

Moo.

Farmer Dell.

Come cushy cows and we will milk you.

(*He and* ROB *mime this with pails and milking sounds.*)

(*The moos and milking sounds slowly change into the sound of a cream separator, which* ROB *turns while* DELL *pours in milk. An actor turns about pretending to be the revolving cream separator. Perhaps over to one side we also see the women preparing breakfast.*)

Rob.

Turn the separator, turn the separator.

Cream out one spout. Skim out the other.
Turn the separator, turn the separator.

Chorus.

The bell goes tink tink tink.

Farmer Dell.

If the bell goes, you're turning it too slow.

Chorus.

(*Faster and fade.*) Tink tink tink tink . . .

Rob.

Sorry Sam, I'm still half asleep.
Turn the separator, turn the separator.
Cream out one spout. Skim out the other.
Turn the separator . . . (*Slows down.*)

Chorus.

Tink tink

Rob.

(*Faster.*) Cream out one spout. Skim out the other.

(*The pig sequence is about to start. This will take some humility, but it's worth trying. Everyone crouches down at their troughs and makes a rich oinking sound as* FARMER DELL *and* ROB *feed them.*)

Farmer Dell.

We get up in the morning and fetch the cows
And then we milk them
And then I slop the pigs and the cows
And then I count them
ONE FIVE TEN FIFTEEN TWENTY
little pigs.

Chorus.

One Five Ten Fifteen Twenty little pigs.
Oink oink oink oink oink.

(*A rising frenzy of sound—pigs at the feeding trough.*)

Rob.

Ouch! You stepped on my foot, Charley.

(FARMER DELL *drives off while* ROB *hops about on one foot.*)

Farmer Dell.

>Giddup Bradley. Up there Charley
>This oats and barley we've got to be sowing
>Must get it in so it can start growing
>Giddup Bradley. Git up there Charley
>Gee! Bradley! Gee! Charley!
>Haw! Bradley! Haw! Charley!

>MR. THORNTREE *appears.*

>(*Now, a transition sequence. Don't be afraid to let the "knee deep" sound carry on. Gradually, it will change into the harsher sound of the* THORNTREE *sequence.*)

Chorus.

>So spring on Farmer Dell's Farm.
>The snow has melted, the snow has gone.
>Tra la la   Tra la la   Tra la la
>The bare trees have put their green leaves on.
>Tra la la   Tra la la   Tra la la
>Knee deep   knee deep   knee deep   knee deep
>The frogs in the pond sing
>Knee deep   knee deep   knee deep   knee deep
>The frogs in the pond sing.

>(*They hum, a sound interrupted by various farm noises—a cow mooing,* FARMER DELL *shouting at the horses, a bird whistling, frog song dying away. Slowly, a chorus of crows cawing is built up and reaches a peak as* GRANDPA THORNTREE *enters and dominates the stage.* FARMER DELL *and the* HIRED MAN *have faded away.*)

Chorus.

>Caw caw caw caw
>Caw caw caw caw
>Raw raw raw raw
>Raw raw raw raw
>Old Grandpa Thorntree. Old Grandpa Thorntree.
>Old Grandpa Thorntree. Old Grandpa Thorntree.

(*A ragged, gnarled old man enters with the remains of a top hat on his head. It is the top hat and the cane that make him into* THORNTREE. *When last we saw him, he was one of the horses, one of the men around the* DELL *farm.*)

Farmer Dell.

> Hey Rob! One of them's got away!
> Nineteen little pigs!

(*They pursue the runaway pig, who leads* ROB *into the pig wallow—from which he emerges a dripping pillar when the pig is caught and returned.*)

Rob and Dell.

One Five Ten Fifteen Twenty little pigs.

Chorus.

Oink oink oink oink oink

(ROB *takes out a harmonica and plays it to the pigs. At certain points in his piece, one pig will stop eating and look up in rapture.*

Now the horse sequence starts. Two of the CHORUS *can be the horses. Two of the* CHORUS *can sit on the bench and drum with noise sticks to imitate the sound of their hooves.*)

Farmer Dell.

Rob, go now and catch the horses.

Rob.

Which ones, Sam? Sandy and Charley or Bradley and Dobbin?

Farmer Dell.

Today, we're sowing oats and barley, so hitch up the sorrel horse and old Charley.

Rob.

(*With pail of oats and a rope.*) Here Bradley. (*Whistles in a neighing way.*) Here Charley. (*Whistles.*)

Chorus.

> (*Two gallop about and are very hard to catch.*)
> We won't come. We won't come.
> We want to eat grass and play in the sun.

Rob.

Here Bradley
Here Charley. (*Whistling.*)

Chorus.

We won't come. We won't come.
We want to eat grass and play in the sun.

(*With a drum, quite a race can be suggested, but eventually, after much neighing and hitching, the horses are caught and hitched to a seed drill—a bench.*)

Chorus and Farmer Dell and Rob.

(*Interspersed.*) Harnessing horses.
Harnessing horses.
Collar and hames collar and hames
Lift up the neck yoke
Tongue tongue tongue
Tache up the traces to
Whipple trees double trees whipple trees
Whipple trees double trees whipple trees

Thorntree.

You children always tease me.
You children always tease me—you kids!

(MEMBERS *of the* CHORUS *jump forward and mock him.*)

Chorus.

Haw haw haw. Old Mister Thorntree
Swallowed a peck of rusty nails
Spits them out and never fails
To make them twice as rusty
To make them twice as rusty.
Swallowed a peck of rusty nails
Spits them out and never fails
To make them twice as rusty
To make them twice as rusty.

Thorntree.

Brat! How can I carry on my profession with you kids putting me in such a bad temper all the time.

Chorus.
What is your profession?
Thorntree.
Being a fence viewer. I go around seeing that people's
fences are straight.

(*He uses his stick to line up the children, who now
pretend to be fenceposts in a fence.*)

Thorntree.
Aye—there's where it goes crooked. It's gone crooked
here, too. That post should be a little to the—a whole
sliverful of property should really be on this side of the
fence. Was that post that way before? I keep thinking
of the nasty little tricks the children played on me at
the crossroads coming home from school—and I can't
think straight. All the posts are out of order. They're
all dancing in a circle around me!

(*He turns on the* CHORUS *who make up a fence, then
dissolve, then make up a fence again.*)

Thorntree.
Brat!
Chorus Boy.
What?
Thorntree.
Little girl!
Chorus Boy.
I'm a boy!
Thorntree.
No, you're not. You're a girl. You certainly resemble
a girl. That's a girl's sweater you're wearing, anyhow.
The colors are just a shade too bright for a boy's
sweater.
Chorus Boy.
(*Dissolving and tearing off sweater.*) Oh—I told
Mother I wouldn't wear this sweater. Oh!
Chorus.
Albert's a girl. Albert's a girl. Albert's a girl.
Thorntree.
Now *you're* a boy!

Chorus Girl.

I am not. I'm a girl!

Thorntree.

(*Pause.*) Kind of plain for a girl, aren't you?

Girl.

Oh boohoo. Boohoo.

Chorus.

(*Turning on her.*) Mary's a boy. Mary's a boy!

Thorntree.

Now if any of you ever get feeling cross with one of
your playmates and want some assistance in making
them feel punk—come to me.

Chorus.

Caw caw caw caw
Caw caw caw caw
A crow stole Grandpa Thorntree's hat.
Raw raw raw raw
Raw raw raw raw

(*They snatch and play ball with the old man's bat-
tered hat.*)

Now, he's sorry he called me a brat
And me a girl. And me a boy.

Thorntree.

Oh I'll never be sorry about that.
Because I'm going to get back at all kids.

Chorus.

(*Recovering.*)

Caw caw caw caw
You'll never get back at us.
You never do and you never did
Caw caw caw caw.

Thorntree.

Do me no do's and did me no did's
I'll get my revenge on some of you kids.

Chorus.

Haw haw haw. Old Mister Thorntree
Swallowed a peck of rusty nails
And garter snakes with wriggly tails

Spits them out and never fails
To make them twice as rusty
Twice as wriggly he makes
The snakes
And twice as rusty—the nails.

Rev. Hackaberry.

(*Enters.*) Children, you should not tease Mr. Thorntree. (*When last seen, too,* HACKABERRY *was one of the
horses.*)

Chorus.

But he's so mean to us, Reverend Hackaberry.
When he is so mean we cannot be merry.

Rev. Hackaberry.

But weren't you mean to him first?
And he cannot help his meanness, you know.

Thorntree.

Oh, I can't, eh—(*Comes out from behind a tree—the
step ladder.*)
I'll get you, Reverend.
I'll some evil to you send.
For sticking up for me, for trying to help me.
I don't need your help. I don't need your charity.
I can view fences in the summer
And trap animals in the winter.
And you—you're not youngsters
You're all—moungsters and monsters!

(*He chases the children.*)

Rev. Hackaberry.

Thorntree, you'll go too far some day
And turn into a thorntree by the way.

Thorntree.

How do you know?

Rev. Hackaberry.

Look. There's a thorn sticking out of your arm already. I'll swear it grew there.

Thorntree.

(*Laughing it off.*) It did grow there, Hackaberry. It
did grow there. And I'll tell the shrikes to put their
victim birds on it when it's good and sharp.

Rev. Hackaberry.

(*Running after.*) Don't run away like that, Thorntree. Come back and listen to reason.

In MRS. DELL'*s kitchen.*

(*Last seen scattering in front of* THORNTREE'*s malice, the* CHORUS *now reenter bearing dishes and kettles, and other kitchen utensils. One of them bears a large flashlight tied up in orange cellophane to represent the setting sun. The* CHORUS *with their bodies build up a suggestion of the kitchen, mime windows, cupboards, doors, and so on. The* CHORUS'*s sunset song should go quite quickly—despite the slowness of real sunsets.*)

Chorus.

Sunset in Farmwife Dell's kitchen.
Cups and saucers. Spoons and forks.
Knives and plates. Tea in kettles.
Fire in the stove. Bread in the oven.
Plants in the windows. Wood in the woodbox.
Towel on the roller. Water in the pail.
Dipper in the water. Kitchen kitchen
Supper supper. Sunset sunset.
Sunset in Mrs. Dell's kitchen
Sunset in Mrs. Dell's kitchen.

(MRS. DELL *and* COUSIN ETTA *enter with saucepans and dishes. They mime various kitchen tasks, using* MEMBERS *of the* CHORUS *and their particular utensils.*)

Mrs. Dell.

Look, Etta. What a beautiful sunset. Sam and Rob should soon be in for supper.

Cousin Etta.

Doesn't the sun gleam pretty on the pots and pans?

Mrs. Dell.

Etta, could you take this knife and go down into the orchard and cut some asparagus? It'll just be ready.

Cousin Etta.

Why, a feed of asparagus would be wonderful for supper.

Farmer Dell.

(*Entering with* ROB.) What you got for supper, Mrs. Dell?

Mrs. Dell.

All sorts of things, Samuel, including some asparagus fresh out of the orchard. Etta is just bringing it up.

(FARMER DELL *and* ROB *mime washing and drying themselves.*)

(*Everyone at the* DELL *farm is now bedded down for a good night's sleep—a baby's crying particularly rocks the hired man. At length, morning comes. The* CHORUS *pretend to be chickens in the henhouse. A rooster crows and they all awaken.*)

Dawn.

Chorus.

Occioccieroccioccer. Occioccericciocceroo.

Time to get up. Time to get up.

Hear about the baby? Heard about the baby?

Cousin Etta.

(*Enters and sprinkles feed for the chickens. Whenever she scatters it, they run and pick it up making hen cackles and any other chicken noises that come to hand.*)

Chorus.

Chook chook chook chook chuokk!

Chook chook chook chook chuokk!

Cousin Etta.

Oh, Sam and Annie. What are you going to name her?

Mrs. Dell.

We thought Amelia.

Cousin Etta.

And you're going off to get the Reverend Hackaberry to christen her Amelia? A beautiful name. A beautiful,

beautiful name. But, oh, my dear, be careful. I saw old Grandpa Thorntree coming down the road and he looked so mean. He might say something mean about the baby or—

Farmer Dell.

I'm not afraid of anything old Grandpa Thorntree can do.

Thorntree.

(*Suddenly entering.*) Out of my way, you dratted hens. (*They all run off.*) Trying to trip me up as usual, you stupid clucks. So you aren't afraid of me, eh, Farmer Dell? Why aren't you afraid of me?

Farmer Dell.

I don't know. I'm just not, that's all.

Cousin Etta.

You clear out of here, Grandpa Thorntree. The very look on your face would sour fresh milk in a pitcher. And you've just kicked two of my best Black Minorcas.

Thorntree.

Oh, a good fat hen likes a playful kick now and then. Well, Farmer Dell and Annie Dell, what are you naming the new little baby?

Cousin Etta.

Don't tell him. I heard that yesterday he vowed revenge on all the children of the neighborhood, even the ones that couldn't possibly harm or tease him.

Thorntree.

Why that's not true, Etta dear. I've got a little present for the baby, as a matter of fact. What's its name?

Mrs. Dell.

She isn't named yet. We're just taking her to be christened.

Farmer Dell.

Her name's going to be Amelia.

Thorntree.

Oh. It's going to be Amelia, is it? Well it isn't! I have sworn revenge on every child in the neighborhood and my special revenge against babies is that I spoil their christening by thinking up a terrible nickname for

them that will stick and stick and stick, it's so sticky.
No, they won't call this baby Amelia though you may
christen her that. They'll call her—what does the name
Amelia—Mealy! All the children will call her that at
school—Oat Mealy!

(*He goes off laughing and repeating the nickname.
The* DELLS *are thunderstruck.*)

Cousin Etta.

Oh, pay no attention to him. Go ahead and have her
christened anyhow. Christen her some other name.

Mrs. Dell.

No, Etta. Her name has to be Amelia. But we can't
christen her that until Mr. Thorntree's not around
anymore. And when will that be? I couldn't bear to
send her off to school and have him meet her and say
Mealy to her. And the other children might repeat it,
too. Oh!

Farmer Dell.

What are we going to do, Annie?

Mrs. Dell.

What can we do but take her back home. No christening today, poor dear.

Farmer Dell.

What else can we call her but Baby One. We'll call her
that until we can christen her properly.

(*They go out.*)

THORNTREE *at the schoolyard.*

Chorus.

(*They come marching on. As in the first scene, they
imitate these words with bodily action. They jump
across the ditch, for example.*)

A schoolyard a schoolyard a schoolyard
Where is the schoolyard
Where the ground is stamped hard
With the children's stamping feet

We're on the way to find it
Find it find it
On the way to school
Dew dust mud hail
Snow ice frost smoke
Road lane ditch track
> Truant officer
>> Tree
>> Pebble
>> Water
>> Splash!

    (*The* CHORUS *divide up into a line of boys and a line of girls and file into school where the teacher and immediate class will be the other five chief actors seated on benches.*)

Chorus.

In the school room.

Mrs. Dell.

(*As schoolmarm. The kids repeat words after her and mime, or the kids could name the invisible things she points to.*)
> Desk   bell map chart
> Clock   book   slate   globe
> Chalk   paper   ferrule   ouch!
> Blackboard   children   teacher   printer
> Student   satchel   pencil   crayon
> Register   ink bottle   dictionary

Rob.

I'd like to go to school again. I never did get my Entrance. Etta, the hired girl is so cruel to me. She says I'm such an ignoramus she'd never dream of marrying me. But if I could just get my Entrance, she might consider it. I wonder if the children would let me come back.

Chorus and Mrs. Dell.

    (*Use as much mime as possible.*)

What pupils do
> Read   write   parse   solve

> Think   reckon   think   learn
> Think   listen   think   attend
> Study   recite   declaim—
> Recollect   and reckon   compose   compute
> Recollect   recollect   recollect—
> Remembrance   remember   remembrance
> Calculate   analyze

There's the Dell's hired man looking in the window!

Chorus.

There's that old Thorntree leaning in the other window.

Thorntree.

Listen, kids. He's too old to go back to school. And he's too dumb. Just look at him. All he knows is how to play the harmonica.

Chorus.

Go away, Rob. You're too old.

Rob.

Then how am I to get enough education so Etta will marry me? She says I can get my Entrance if I really care to. And care for her.

Chorus.

That's just too bad. That's your look out.

Thorntree.

Etta's got her Entrance, Rob. Why don't you try some other girl that's not so highly educated. There's Leota Throughopper down the road. She never got out of primer class. She'd have you. She's about your speed.

Rob.

Well—I guess that's it. I've just set my sights too high. And my eyes are turned on too low. (*Exit.*)

(*The* CHORUS *take over the stage now. We are in the schoolyard.* THORNTREE *is watching.*)

Chorus.

Recess   recess   Games!   games!
A schoolyard   a schoolyard   a schoolyard
Where the ground is hard
With the stamping children's feet.

(*They stamp their feet, then break into a games sequence.*)
Crack the Whip!
Send them flying!
Prisoner's Base
    (*Have kids on stilts, playing tug of war, etc.*)
Come pull away, pull away
    Bull in the ring
    My bar's made of gold
    My bar's made of iron
    My bar's made of steel
    My bar's made of stone
    (*Have actual skipping, but watch the knots in those ropes!*)
Skipping skipping. The girls are skipping
    Rosy apple lemon pear
    These are the colors she should wear
The boys are walking on stilts
    I am a girl guide dressed in blue
Skipping skipping. The girls are skipping.
    (*For the individual games and skipping rhymes, break the* CHORUS *up into groups.*)
    These are the actions I did do
    Salute the king. Turn to the queen
The boys are walking on stilts
    Turn your back on the baseball green
I'm the king of the castle
Get down you dirty rascal
    Blue bells cockleshells
    Evie ivie over
My mother said that I was born in January,
February, March, April, May, June, July, August,
      September
    A house to let apply within
    A woman put out for drinking gin
    I call in—(*Name the child.*)
    All in together girls
    Very fine weather girls
    One two three four five
    Salt vinegar mustard pepper

Cedar cider red hot pepper
Hide and go seek   Hide and go seek
Eeenie meenie minie moe
Catch a fat one by his toe
If he hollers let him go
Eenie meenie minie moe
O-U-T spells out and
OUT you must go
(*Child who is "It" counts up to ten and then yells—*)
Anybody hiding round my gool*
Whether he be hidden or not
He shall be caught
One two three on Walter!

(*A sulky* CHILD *goes over to* THORNTREE.)

Child.
Mr. Thorntree. You said if ever we wanted to get back at somebody, we might just come to you. Well, those kids haven't let me up to bat yet—what names can I call them?

Thorntree.
Well—you can call 'em (*Whispers.*) and you can— (*Whispers.*)

Child.
(*Goes over to the* CHORUS *and starts a name-calling sequence.*)

Hi—scummy!
Hi—sissy!

Chorus.
Monkey Ape Foxy Toothy
Fatty Warty Greasy Smelly
Stinkpot (*Repeat ad nauseam.*)

(*The games fade away, and the* CHILDREN *stand about moping listlessly.*)

I won't hold the skipping rope for her
Not after the nicknames she's called me.
Hey! Let's make a snow man and then smash him to bits!

*Goal is pronounced "gool" in Southwestern Ontario.

Winter isn't finished yet.
The frogs have stopped singing!

(*They have cotton-batten snowballs. But, as the snowballs fly, we still hear the first song.*)

A schoolyard   a schoolyard   a schoolyard
Where is the schoolyard
Where the ground is stamped hard
With the children's stamping feet
We're on the way to find it (*Stamping.*)
Find it find it
On the way to school
Dew dust mud hail
Snow ice frost smoke
Road lane ditch track
   Truant officer
      Tree
      Pebble
      Water
      Splash!

Another baby at the DELLS.

(*If one of the girls is really good at skipping, you might have a skipping cadenza here using one of the skipping rhymes to finish the schoolyard scene with. Perhaps a fade-out to suggest that the skipping girl goes on forever. Perhaps the "January, February" skipping song should melt here into the time bridge.*)

Chorus.
      Two years later in the summer
      Two years later in the summer
      Summer summer summer summer
      Another little baby was born.
      While the birds were singing
         (*Bird whistles of various sorts here.*)
      And Queen Anne's Lace was blossoming
      And ox-eyed daisy fading

And raspberries ripening
And honey bees humming
(*Humming of bees here continues for some time.*)
Beneath the golden sun
Beneath the golden sun
Two years later in the summer
Two years later in the summer
Summer summer summer summer
Another babe was born—while
(*Bird whistles and then bee hums.*)
While while while while

(ROB *and* FARMER DELL *enter, miming the making of haycocks.*)

Rob.
I never thought I'd see us making this hay, it's been raining so. But the rain sloped off at last.
Farmer Dell.
Another forkful for that coil, Rob.
Rob.
What are you naming the new boy, Sam?
Farmer Dell.
Well—we thought and we thought. It has to be a name that Grandpa Thorntree can't make a horrible nickname of.
Rob.
Yessiree. There's twenty babies without names in this neighborhood and all because of him and his terrible tongue.
Farmer Dell.
We couldn't name him Abel.
Rob.
No. You couldn't name him Abel.
Farmer Dell.
Because then Thorntree would sneer—Unable.
Rob.
Why so he would. So he would.
Farmer Dell.
We couldn't call him John. Because then old Grandpa

Thorntree might call him Jack in the Pulpit or even
worse—Jackass.

Rob.

It would be just like him to do that.

Farmer Dell.

So what we're going to do is have Reverend Hackaberry come over to the house at dinner time so we
won't have to take the baby out onto the road to the
church where we might meet old Thorntree, and we're
giving the baby five names, five names so if even he
hears the names, he can't possibly spoil five names all
at once and we'll call the baby by the name he doesn't
have time to get out.

Rev. Hackaberry.

(*Entering.*) Well, Sam, what have you decided to call
this baby boy of yours?

Farmer Dell.

We're going to call him Paul John Peter James Martin.

Rev. Hackaberry.

Yes. That's very wise in view of the difficulty with
Thorntree. Let us repair to your house then: and Rob,
you might pump a pail of fresh cold water to christen
this child with. Good day, Annie. Good day, Etta, and
good day, Baby One.

(BABY ONE *should be played by a member of the*
CHORUS. *Enter these with a doll as the new one.* BABY
ONE *is now a little girl.* ROB *mimes pumping and*
THORNTREE *begins to climb up the stepladder or, if
you like, onto the roof of the house, where he listens
down the chimney. A member of the* CHORUS *can be a
pump.*)

Chorus.

   Down underground it's cold as winter
   Down at the bottom of the well
   Pump pump pump pump
   Pump pump pump pump
   Up above it's fire hot summer
   The sun like a golden butter nut
   Pump pump pump pump
   Pump pump pump pump

Pump up winter into summer
From the secret underground stream
That flows beneath us like a dream
Pump! Splash! Gurgle gurgle.
Pump pump pump pump
Gurgle gurgle gurgle gurgle

(*The family arrange themselves, and* ROB *brings in the pail of water.* THORNTREE *is now at the top of the stepladder.*)

Rev. Hackaberry.
And now, Farmer Dell, what names do you give this child. This little man.

Thorntree.
Names? I wish they'd clear their chimney better so I could hear properly. Names?

Mrs. Dell.
Did you hear something on the roof? (*To audience, inviting their participation.*) Does anyone hear anything on the roof?

(*The children in the audience may tell her about* THORNTREE *but just as she looks, he ducks down his head.*)

No. I guess there isn't anybody up there.

(*With careful control, the audience can again be brought in here. Every time they point out* THORN-TREE, *by the time she turns round he has ducked down. Ad lib to temperature of the occasion.*)

Farmer Dell.
It's the fir tree scraping against the shingles in the summer breeze. I name this child Paul.

Chorus.
Paul. (*They repeat the other names after* FARMER DELL.)

Farmer Dell.
John Peter James Martin

Rev. Hackaberry.
(*Taking the baby.*) And now little baby I name thee—

Thorntree.

Five names! Too many names. Fat name. Too many names. Fat name. Yah! Fat name, fat name! (*He opens his umbrella and leaps off the roof.*)

Mrs. Dell.

Oh, Sam. He was up on the roof listening to us down through the chimney. He heard the baby's names!

Thorntree.

That makes the twenty-first child whose name I've ruined. (*Laughs.*)

Farmer Dell.

Sic the dogs on him. Sic him, Rover. Sic him, Bluebell. Sic him, Daisy. Sic him, Rollo. Get him Gnasher. (MEMBERS *of the* CHORUS *leap forward.*)

Chorus.

> Bow wow wow! Bow wow wow!
> Grr grrr grr! Grr grr grr!
> Bow wow wow! Bow wow wow!
> Bite him, fellow. Bite him!

(*They chase* THORNTREE *around the stage and finally off. If he goes through the audience, you're going to get audience participation.*)

Farmer Dell.

You'd better whistle the dogs back, Rob, before he does something to them.

Rob.

(*Whistles.*) Here, Rover. Come on back. Here Bluebell. Back you silly dogs. You're no match for Thorntree. It's no use. They won't come back for my whistle, and he's hitting them with his cane.

Farmer Dell.

We need more whistlers. Anybody here good at whistling dogs back for us? (*The audience whistles.*) Louder and higher than that. (*Renewed efforts. The dogs reluctantly return. Perhaps they run off, in which case the audience has to whistle them in again.*) Thatta boy, Rover. Thatta boy, Rollo.

Mrs. Dell.

What will we call this baby, Sam?

Farmer Dell.

I guess we'll have to call him Baby Two.

Mrs. Dell.

Baby Two. I couldn't bear to have a child called—Fat Name.

Cousin Etta.

I think we should get the village constable.

Mrs. Dell.

Reverend Hackaberry, what are we going to do if we have another baby and cannot name it either? Nor apply for a birth certificate for them?

Rev. Hackaberry.

Let us all go up to the church and pray about it. Come with me. God will surely suggest something. We'd better speak in sign language just in case there might be listeners—behind that thicket—in the ditch, underneath us in the culvert. So—speak in sign language. Now at first, Sam and Annie, you tried this —(*He holds his hands a small space apart as in a fish story.*) Then this last time (*A wider distance.*), but the next time the methods we use against Grandpa Thorntree must be this—(*Stretches his hands way apart, then whispers in their ears.*)

Mrs. Dell and Farmer Dell.

First we tried this—(*Gesture.*) Then we tried this— (*Larger gesture.*) next time try this—(*Biggest gesture. Have the gesturing and whispering repeated among the whole cast.*)

Farmer Dell.

It will take some study. Why, there must be hundreds of them.

Mrs. Dell.

It will not only take some study but also the production of a third child. Where shall we find that?

Rev. Hackaberry.

Both can be found. Meanwhile, as I see it, the problem is not to be solved this way—(*The first gesture.*) but only in this way—(*The final gesture.*) But let us go up to the church and pray.

In the fall.

(*They leave. Across the stage, the children blow like falling leaves. The main characters return to mime—*)

All.
Fall and harvest on the farm.

Rye oats	mangel-worzels
Wheat barley	turnips corn
Apples pears	geese and hogs
Chaff straw	sheaf stook
Pumpkins buckwheat	potatoes grain
Ducks drakes	chicks parsnips

(*Scything, turnip pulling, and stooking can be mimed here.*)

Crops and roots	crops and roots
Granary full	root-cellar full
Silo full	cellar full
Harvest, harvest	harvest, harvest
Fall, fall, fall, fall	
Autumn, autumn,	
autumn, autumn	

(*They hum and whistle like the wind. The children whirl by again. Part of the group chant "The leaves are leaving the groves" underneath the following lines. Later on select another repeat line and chant it under.*)

Oak leaves falling, fir needles stay
Ash leaves falling, birch birch
The elms are golden and soon are bare
Beech leaves are brown and beechnuts are ripe
The leaves are leaving the groves
Under the gray sky, the bare woods and
The squirrel's asleep and the ground
Smoke from the chimney and frost on the ground.
The stream is still with
   still still
Ice Ice Ice Ice

(*The idea of things that are flowing suddenly—still —They make the wind song again and sprinkle snow from their hands. Enter* THORNTREE *in snowshoes. This is his moment of triumph, and the* MEMBERS *of the* CHORUS *can be the various animals in his traps. Their being caught in the traps can be mimed.*)

Thorntree.

> While the other people sink in the snowy ooze
> I float about it on my snowshoes
> And everybody's afraid of me
> And everybody respects me
> While other people sink in the snowy ooze
> I float about it on my snowshoes
> Fifty unchristened babies, ha ha!
> Nameless but nicknameful
> Even the children with their names
> Dread my tongue's destroying flames
> And now I'll see what my traps are doing.

(*He bats each animal into a heap in the center of the stage as he speaks.*)

Thorntree.

> Ah! Here's a rabbit the steel is chewing
> Rabbit foot not so lucky, eh?
> Well stay there!
> Well, what have we here ready for a box
> But a full grown red-coated black-tailed fox
> Get over there!
> What have you caught old rusty spring?
> Why, I do believe, two priceless ermine!
> Get over there!
> And what's in you my favorite trap?
> Why, guess—a ferocious old bobcat
> Get over there!
> Hurray!
> I'll have to go off to get my sleigh
> To haul my trapped animals away
> And then I'll skin them ha ha ha
> And then I'll sell them—ha ha ha

While other people sink in the snowy ooze
I float above it on my snowshoes (*Exit.*)

(*Optionally, the animals put him into a frenzy by
escaping from his traps. The stage darkens, the* CHORUS
*rise from the heap with lighted flashlights, which they
move about with like the winter stars.*)

> Stars on a frosty night
> In the depth of winter.
> Stars on a frosty night
> In the depth of winter

(*If each child has two flashlights, quite a few con-
stellations can drift over the stage: the Big Dipper, Cas-
siopeia's Chair, and, last of all—Orion.*)

> Shine on the sleeping fields
> Sleep beneath the snow
> On the trees turned upsidedown
> Their sap sunk below
> Orion, Orion, Orion, Orion,
> The cruel sworded giant
> Made of stars he marches on
> Over the snowy world.
> Stars on a frosty night
> In the depth of winter
> Stars on a frosty night
> In the depth of winter

(*A rooster crows, and it becomes light again. Bird
whistles.*)

Spring on Farmer Dell's farm
The snow has melted, the snow has gone
Tra la la Tra la la Tra la la
The bare trees have put their green leaves on.
Tra la la Tra la la Tra la la
Knee deep knee deep knee deep knee deep
The frogs in the pond sing
Knee deep knee deep knee deep knee deep
The frogs in the pond sing.

(*They hum and occasionally say "knee deep" under the following dialogue. The* CHORUS *fade into less distinct "knee-deeps" and change into trees and fence posts along the road.*)

The third baby.

Rob.

(*As if walking into town.*) Oh, dear me. I've got the time off to go in and write the examination. I shall never be able to enter the building. As to entering the room, they'll all be young kids twelve or fourteen, and here I am eighteen. I'll tower over them like a bean pole. They'll be people younger'n me writing their university entrance, let alone the high school entrance. I've got to quiet my mind with something—I'll see if I can kick this stone all the way into town—I never knew I had nerves till now—if I can kick it all the way into town, that means I'll pass the exam, but if I— let's see, I'll go over the arithmetic rules in my head and then I'll do my memory work.

A number that divides two or more numbers exactly is called—(*He kicks the stone about in a circle.*)

Thorntree.

(*Picking up the stone.*) Talking to himself. The first sign of advanced madness.

Rob.

You give me that stone!

Thorntree.

Ah. A special stone, eh? You intend kicking it all the way into town and if you don't lose it, you'll pass, eh? Well—you're going to lose it. Unless—

Rob.

Unless what?

Thorntree.

Unless you tell me what's been going on at the Dell farmhouse lately.

Rob.

I won't tell you anything.

Thorntree.

I'll follow you all the way into town telling people how old you are and what exam you're trying.

Rob.

I don't care.

Thorntree.

I'll look in the window at you—I'll keep saying to myself, but you'll hear it—"Wrong, Rob, wrong, Rob."

Rob.

Oh—

Thorntree.

I only want to know one thing, Rob. Is there a new baby at the Dell's?

Rob.

No. Not that I've heard of.

Thorntree.

(*Laughing.*) And is it going to be christened today?

Rob.

No. It is not!

Thorntree.

(*Throwing back the stone.*) That's all I want to know. That's all I want to know.

Rob.

Oh, you old devil. (*Picks up the stone and rushes off.*) Now he'll ruin that baby's name too.

(*The* DELL *family march out of their house,* FARMER DELL *holding the third and latest baby.* BABY ONE *and* BABY TWO *are walking now.*)

Thorntree.

Well, Farmer Dell. So this is the latest little Dell. And all the family with you. Baby One and Baby Two I see. Hello, Baby One.

Baby One.

You are a bad man, Grandpa Thorntree.

Baby Two.

Mooly moo dirly irly a doidle.

Thorntree.

Yes, and where might you all be going? Off to church, • perhaps?

Farmer Dell.

We're going off to church to get our children christened.

Thorntree.

And what are you going to name them? These two's names I know—Oat Mealy, wasn't it? And Fat Name or too many names of Fatty for short. You might as well tell me what you're going to name this infant right now. So I can tell you what nickname I'll brand it with if you dare christen it.

Rev. Hackaberry.

(*Entering with a basin of water.*) What names do you give these children, Samuel and Anne Dell?

(*With him enter the children, who later block off* THORNTREE's *escape.*)

Farmer Dell.

This one's to be Amelia. This one's Paul John Peter James Martin, and I want to name this one—

Thorntree.

Yes, yes. Let's hear the ridiculous name so you can stop the christening party before it's too late.

Farmer Dell.

We're going to call our third boy baby

(*A drum underlines the growing river of names.*)

> Aaron Abel Abijah Abner
> Abraham Adam Adolphus Albert
> Alexander Alfred Algernon Alonzo
> Alvin Ambrose Amos Andrew
> Anthony Archibald Arnold Arthur
> Asa Augustus

Mrs. Dell.

> Baldwin Basil
> Benedict Benjamin Bernard Bertram
> Caleb Calvin Cecil Cephas
> Charles Christopher Clarence Clement
> Cornelius Cuthbert Cyril Cyrus

Baby One.

> Daniel David Donald

Baby Two.
>Dionysius

Rob.
>Duncan Ebeneezer Edgar Edmund
>Edward Edwin Egbert Eli
>Elias Elijah Enoch Ephraim
>Erastus Ernest Eugene Eustace
>Ezekiel Ezra Felix Ferdinand
>Francis Franklin Frederic

Etta.
>George
>Gideon Gilbert Godfrey Gregory

Thorntree.
>Stop stop stop stop.

Etta.
>Gustavus Guy Harold Henry
>Herbert Herman Hezekiah Hiram
>Horace Horatio Hubert Hugh
>Humphrey Hugo Ira Isaac

Farmer Dell.
>And also Jabez Jacob James

Chorus.
>Jasper Jerome Jesse Job
>Jobin Jonas Jonathan Joseph

Thorntree.
>Stop stop stop stop
>I cannot stand all these names
>Names names names names

(*He sinks to the ground, then shoots up and begins to dance a thorntree dance to the names.*)

Mrs. Dell.
>Joshua Josiah Julius Justin

Chorus.
>Lambert Lawrence Lemuel Leonard
>Levi Lewis Lionel Lorenzo
>Lucius Luke Luther

Rob.
>Mark

    Marmaduke Matthew Maurice Martin
    Michael Miles Morgan Moses

Baby One.

    Nathan Nathaniel Nicholas

Baby Two.

    Norman

Etta.

    Octavius Oliver Orlando Oscar

Chorus.

    Patrick Paul Peleg Peter
    Philip Phineas oh—oh

(*They hum as everyone gathers up speed.*)

Farmer Dell.

    Ralph Raphael Raymond Reginald Reuben

Chorus.

    Richard Robert Roderic Roger Roland

Mrs. Dell.

    Rufus Rupert Samson Samuel Saul

Chorus.

    Seth Silas Silvanus Silvester Simeon

Farmer Dell.

    Simon Solomon Stephen Sydney Thaddeus

Chorus.

    Theodore!

Farmer Dell.

    Theophilus Thomas Timothy Urban

Chorus.

    Vincent!

Farmer Dell.

    Walter Zachariah!

(*By this time,* THORNTREE *has danced himself off the stage.*)

Rev. Hackaberry.

Quick Rob. Go and see what's happened to the old trapper. I thought I saw him fall down there.

Farmer Dell.

It worked. We named Old Grandpa Thorntree so many

names he couldn't think of a nickname. Couldn't think
of anything toward the last there but just to get away.

Rob.

(*Bringing in a dead thorntree.*) Well, look what's happened to him. He's changed into a thorntree, at least
I think he has.

Etta.

That's his hat, and there's his cane.

Mrs. Dell.

How did he do that?

Rev. Hackaberry.

He was so balked, his envy and spite were so frustrated
that they turned in upon themselves and produced this
awful miracle.

Baby One.

Poor old Grandpa Thorntree.

Mrs. Dell.

Don't you dare touch that dead tree, Amelia. It might
still hurt you! Amelia—I can call her by her rightful
name. And Paul. Little Paul. I can call you by your
name now. And which of his hundred names will we
call this little dear?

Farmer Dell.

Whichever the first name I said was.

Mrs. Dell.

Aaron. Little Aaron who struck the rock and forth
came water.

Rev. Hackaberry.

Think of all the other babies who can now be properly
christened.

Etta.

But now we must go home and have enough christening dinner for three little christened ones. But where
were you this afternoon, Rob? We missed you.

Rob.

I was to town. Etta, do you see this stone?

Etta.

I certainly do. Is there anything extra-special about
it?

Rob.

When I was walking into town today to write my examination, I said to myself, "If I can kick this stone all the way into town and back, I'll probably pass." And I did. And you know how hard that is.

Etta.

Yes, Rob.

Rob.

If it turns out I did pass the Entrance examination, will you marry me?

Etta.

Rob, I've been thinking. I'll marry you whether you pass it or not. Now that Grandpa Thorntree is gone, it's safe to get married and have babies with proper names again. That's really what was troubling me.

Mrs. Dell.

So we must make this a betrothal party as well as a christening party. What will we eat at this party? (*The words are arranged in a "Turkey in the Straw" pattern which the six main actors dance while the* CHORUS *chant. A dance of girls with dolls is a possibility here, since all the young children in the district can now be properly christened.*)

Chorus.

Oh—buns and rolls, soups and teas
Sauces and pies, sauces and pies
Stews and muffins, biscuits waffles
Butter and pastries, porridge and milk
Pancakes and crackers, doughnuts, dumplings
Pancakes and crackers, doughnuts, dumplings
Blanc mange puddings sandwiches cocoa
And other good things to eat, to eat.

(*Everyone laughs. Then—switch the mood to—*)

Vale hill dell dale
Path road ditch post
Barn shed tree house
Long ago   long ago   on
Farmer Dell's Farm.

The Comical Tragedy or Tragical Comedy of Punch and Judy

A Play with Music
in Six Scenes and
Several Interludes

by Aurand Harris

An adaptation suggested by various traditional Punch and Judy puppet plays.

PREFACE

I am often asked, "But why do you write plays for *children?*" It is true there is little prestige or literary acclaim, and the royalties are small. But I like children, and I like what children like in the theater—a good story, interesting characters, excitement, suspense, fantasy, beauty, and fun.

There are other reasons, too. Unlike Broadway, which is provincial, children's theater in America is national, offering the playwright a varied audience. And unlike Broadway, children's theater is growing both in quantity and in quality. There is an open and eager market. There is a need for variety in the kinds of plays. A writer enjoys unlimited creative freedom. There are a growing number of good producing groups. Your plays can have a first-rate production.

For too long, plays for children's theater were mostly dramatizations of fairy-tale classics, and were usually produced by amateurs whose lack of theater training was compensated for by genuine enthusiasm. We thank them for the beginning they made. But now plays and performances have changed. There are still many productions of well-known titles, as there should be. Each new generation has a right to enjoy the best of the old. Also, the parents, who buy the tickets, feel secure with a known story. But since the popular stories have already been successfully dramatized, the contemporary playwright must dig deeper, explore less well-known but equally good stories, new stories, and original plots. This makes it necessary for the playwright to expand his horizon and makes for a growing library of children's plays.

Every playwright wants and deserves the best possible production of his scripts. Now in children's theater an increasing number of productions are first-rate. The première of *Punch and Judy* presented by the Atlanta Children's Theater is an example. Staged by Charles and Carol Doughty, the play was rehearsed with an Equity cast under the Doughtys' professional direction. The script was tightened and polished. The resulting performance was brilliant.

There is also an opportunity to utilize a variety of styles in writing children's plays. I have enjoyed the creative freedom of writing a popular lyrical play, historical epic, commedia dell'arte caper, realistic slice-of-life drama, audience-participation romp, musical melodrama, and, in a still different style, *Punch and Judy,* a dark comedy.

When I started to write the play, and I do feel the Punch and Judy puppet show is part of our children's heritage (one which many of them have never had the opportunity to enjoy), I wanted to keep the essence of childlike slapstick fun that has always been inherent in Mr. Punch in whatever country or whatever century he performed. After researching many puppet scripts performed in America and England, I found that although each puppeteer created his own individual play, certain basic scenes and characters were usually included. It is upon these that I built my play. I also found that musical, comical interludes were often used, and I have included these between scenes. I purposely set the play in no particular period. But to me Punch and Judy reflect England during Queen Victoria's reign. I did not, however, use the last scene which was often added in the Victorian scripts, showing Mr. Punch being eaten by a crocodile that "punished" him and ultimately allowed Victorian morality to triumph.

Mr. Punch is the only character throughout the history of dramatic literature who dares to be free and is *not* punished at the end. As Mr. Punch says, "It is the wickedest play that ever was—and the one that's run the longest." One psychologist has explained that Punch's play has been a success because it draws its strength from the darkness within us all. Another thinks the play has survived throughout the centuries because Mr. Punch is a fearless hero who conquers all the restraints man has imposed upon himself—and has the urge at some time during his life to break: family (Judy and the Baby), society (Professor, Doctor, Policeman), superstition (Ghosts), death (Hangman), and sin itself (Devil), which that writer feels makes it a great morality play.

Punch and Judy is an action play, one to be seen and heard, rather than read. The movement, the color, the music heighten the mood and the meaning and the fun. The original score written for the production by Glenn Mack is a delightful blending of rhythms and sounds which adds to each scene. So I ask you, as you read the Tragical Comedy or the Comical Tragedy of Mr. Punch, try to hear, try to see his "Rottle-dee-tottle-dee-toot", the drifting of the Ghosts, the wild police chase through the audience, and the clapping and cheering of the children when Mr. Punch gives the Devil the final slap of his stick.

Aurand Harris

CAST

Punch
Judy
Toby
Professor
Hector
Doctor
Policeman
Guards
Hangman
Ghosts
Devil

SCENE

A deserted Punch and Judy Puppet Theater.
Scenes of the Puppet Play:
  1. *Home Sweet Home*
  2. *Dog Bites Nose*
     Professor Loses Head
  3. *Dancing Horse*
     Dr. Cure-All
  4. *Fly Away Baby*
     Off to Jail
  5. *Hung by a Rope*
  6. *Out Pops the Devil*
There is one intermission.

(*NOTE: Except for Punch, Judy and Toby, all the other parts
may be played by three or four actors, making it possible for the
play to be performed by a cast of six or seven. It is suggested all
the actors wear black tights, which will give a unity, and which
will make costume changes simple, requiring only a jacket, a cape,
a robe, a hat, to complete a costume.*)

ACT ONE

*There is soft music. Cue 2, THERE WILL ALWAYS
BE A PUNCH AND JUDY, and the curtains open.
On a bare stage, in subdued light, stands an old Punch
and Judy puppet theater. The words "Punch and Judy"
are faded, the little curtain is drawn, and a large sign
reads, "Closed." After a pause, the little curtain shakes.*
TOBY, *a hand-puppet dog, peeks out. He looks to R
and barks sadly, then to L and gives another mournful
bark. He shakes his head and gives a loud sighing
growl. He leans out, points to the sign, shakes his head,
lifts his head and howls sadly, then collapses with a
big sigh. He lifts his head inquiringly, looks quickly to
each side, then toward audience, sees the children,
barks excitedly, holds out his paws eagerly, then claps
happily. He barks loudly, meaning, "Stay there," and
waves. He disappears behind the little curtain but immediately reappears and barks again, "Stay there,"
waves and disappears. The barking continues and*
TOBY, *an actor dressed like the dog puppet, enters
from behind the puppet theater and hurries downstage.
Cue 3 optional. Lights come up gradually. Over the
footlights he greets the children again with happy
barks, waves, and a wagging of his tail. He runs to
puppet theater, lifts his head and barks loudly.*

Punch.
(*Off, inside the puppet theater.*) What's going on?
What's going on? What's up?

(TOBY *twists and barks and points, trying to tell*
PUNCH *there are children out front. The little curtain
moves violently and* PUNCH, *a hand puppet, appears.*)

193

What's the calling? What's the brawling? What's up?

(TOBY *barks and motions for* PUNCH *to look at the audience.*)

Quiet! Go back to sleep.

(TOBY *shakes his head and barks.* PUNCH *leans over the stage shelf and talks consolingly.*)

I know. You want to give a puppet show. So do I. But no one comes to see Punch and Judy anymore. Mr. Puppet Man has gone and left us. We are faded and old and forgotten. Go—go to sleep. Our little show is over.

(TOBY *turns to audience, shakes his head angrily and barks with determination.* PUNCH, *surprised looks at* TOBY *again.* TOBY *runs to footlights, barks and motions toward audience.*)

What is it? Who is it? Is someone there?

(*He peers.* TOBY *barks and motions for children to answer, too.*)

Who? Children! An audience! Have you come to see the puppet show?

(*Sings and dances.*)

Well, rootle-tee-tootle—tee-toot! We've been saved, Toby!

(TOBY *barks.*)

Punch and Judy have been saved by the children. Don't go away. I'll be with you—I'll be with you before you can say—

(*Puppet disappears behind little curtain.* PUNCH, *an actor dressed exactly like the puppet, immediately hops from behind the puppet theater.*)

—Punch and Judy!

(*Dances down to footlights.*)

Oh, allaca-zoop, allaca-zand! It's Mr. Punch. Give him a hand.

(*He applauds himself.* TOBY *claps and encourages children to applaud.* PUNCH *bows.*)

How do you do? How *do* you do? How do *you* do?

(*Dances.*)

Rootle-dee-tootle-dee-toot! How many are here. I'll count.

(*Points and counts audience.*)

One, two, three, four—five-five!

(*Stretches out the word.*)

He is a big one! Six, seven, seven-and-a-half. She is a small one. Eight, nine and nine. Twins! And there's Tom. Hello, Dick. Hello, Mary. And Mrs. Bigger and her baby! Which is bigger, Mrs. Bigger *or* her baby?

(TOBY *barks and shakes his head.*)

Why, the *baby*, because he is a *little* bigger!

(*Dances.*)

Rootle-dee-tootle-dee-toot! We'll give you a show. We'll always give you a show! For your enjoyment we proudly present—the Comical Tragedy—or the Tragical Comedy—of Punch and Judy.

(*Aside.*)

It is the wickedest play that ever was—and the one that's run the longest.

(*Dances.*)

Rootle-dee-tootle-dee-toot! I'll call Judy. Oh, Judy's a beauty. Wait until you see her.

(*Calls.*)

Oh, Judy, my dear. Judy, my love. Judy, my little dove.

(*Shouts.*)

Judy, stick your head through that curtain!

Judy.

(JUDY, *a hand puppet appears in front of the little curtain of the puppet stage.*) Yes, Mr. Punch?

Punch.

Knock, knock; knock.

Judy.

Who is there?

Punch.

Children! Children!

Judy.

(*Peers.*) Children?

Punch.

Punch and Judy have been saved by the children.

Judy.

Saved by the children! Oh, I'm so happy I am going to cry.

Punch.

No, Judy. Smile! Everyone laughs at Punch and Judy. Oh, rootle-dee-tootle-dee-toot! Tell me what is black and white and red all over?

Judy.

You tell me.

Punch.

A blushing zebra! Oh, rootle-dee-tootle-dee-toot! We'll begin the show. Call the others! The Doctor, the Policeman, the Horse, the Devil.

Judy.

Yes, Mr. Punch. Oh, oh! We're going to have a show!

(*Puppet disappears behind curtain.*)

Punch.

(*To* TOBY.) Start the music! Beat the drum. Ring the bell. Oh, rootle-dee-tootle-dee-toot!

(TOBY *runs quickly behind puppet theater. Punch points to audience.*)

One to get ready. Two for the show. Hold on to your
seats. Here—we—go!

(*Music begins. Cue 4.* PUNCH *runs to L back of
puppet theater. Immediately* TOBY *comes around R of
theater, ringing a bell.* JUDY, *an actor dressed exactly
like the puppet, marches after him, hitting a tambou-
rine.* PUNCH *follows last, beating a drum. They circle,
then line up at front and sing.*)

> Punch and Judy are coming today,
> Punch and Judy are coming this way.
> Punch and Judy are near—

(TOBY *rings bell and barks a long—OOOOOOOO-
OO.*)

Punch and Judy are here.
 (TOBY *repeats bell and howl—OOOOOOOOOO.*)

> Punch and Judy are coming this way.
> Punch and Judy are coming today.

With your kind permission—
Judy.
And your polite attention—
Punch.
We will begin our Punch—

> (*She bows to him.*)

And Judy—

> (*He bows to her.*)

Show!

(TOBY *barks a long "OOOOOOOOOO," rings bell
and runs off L.* PUNCH *and* JUDY *"cakewalk" off as
march music swells. She exits.* PUNCH *embraces audience and shouts.*)

> I love you. I love you.
> I love you divine.
> Save me your chewing gum,
> You're sitting on mine!

> (*He exits R.*)

Scene One

Same music continues softly. TOBY *enters L and puts up sign on an easel which reads, "Scene 1," and exits. The sign may also have printed on it, "Home Sweet Home."* PUNCH, *off R, waves the main curtain. He puts his arm out and waves, then waves his hat, then waves a shoe, then peeks out and grins, pulls back, then lifts a leg out and kicks, peeks out again, pulls back, shakes curtain violently, then marches out to C. He carries a slapstick hooked to his belt. Note: it is advisable to have two extra slapsticks on each side, off stage, in event that his breaks. Music stops.*

Punch.

Ladies and gentlemen, how do you do?
If you are all happy, I'm happy too.
Stay and hear my merry little play—
If I make you laugh, I need not make you pay.
(*Sings. Cue 5.*)
Mr. Punch is a jolly good fellow,
His coat is always scarlet and yellow,
With a bump on his nose and a hump on his back
And a big stick to give you a whack!
(*Slaps stick in air. Speaks.*)
My fame is known from sea to sea!
My name is known, but pronounced differently.
In Italy—I am called PULCINELLA!

(*Italian music. Cue 6. He dances Italian steps and shouts in Italian.*)

In Russia—they cheer and I appear—PETRUSHKA!

(*Russian music. Cue 7. He dances Russian steps and shouts in Russian.*)

In France—they shout and I come out—POLICHI-NELLE!

(*French music. Cue 8. He dances French steps, shouts in French. Sings.*)

But—

(*Speaks quickly.*)

Pulcinella, Petrushka, Polichinelle—

(*Sings. Cue 9.*)

Anywhere and everywhere,
Whatever the name,
I am always the same,
A bump on my nose and a hump on my back
And a big stick to give you a whack!
Oh, it's so glorious to be so notorious!

(*Calls.*)

Judy! Judy, my beauty.

(*Aside.*)

Oh, her eyes twinkle and shine—like mine. Her nose is like a rose—like mine. Her mouth runs from north to south—

(*Points to audience.*)

like yours! JUDY!

Judy.
(*Enters R, sweeping with broom. All the scenes can be played downstage, almost leaning over the footlights, as if leaning out from the puppet stage. The close contact with the audience is part of the effectiveness of a puppet show.*) Mr. Punch, I am sweeping and keeping the house clean . . .

(*Sweeps in short strokes, backing* PUNCH *across the stage.*)

Working all day while you are away . . . Rubbing and scrubbing . . . knitting and sitting . . . like a good wife . . .

(*Aside.*)

My house . . . my family . . . are the joys of my life.

Punch.
(*Romantically.*) Oh, Judy, my love.

Judy.

Mr. Punch.

Punch.

Judy, my dove.

Judy.

Mr. Punch.

Punch.

(*Aside.*) Oh, Judy is my beauty.

(*Offers his hand. She takes it. Music. Cue 10. They dance in circle, then face audience. He sings.*)

> Judy is my wife,
> Down the aisle I led her,
> She promised to obey me
> That's why I wed her.

(*She holds dance pose. He turns to audience and speaks fast.*)

> Now that I've got her
> She'd rule the house and me,
> All she ever thinks of—
> Is the family.
> Now that I've got her
> She tries to order me,
> But I can tell you who
> Will win that victory.

Me!

(*They dance, then bow sweetly to each other.* PUNCH *aside.*)

Watch and see!

(*They dance again. The music ends as the dance ends with a bow.*)

Judy, my beauty, give us a kiss.

Judy.

I have other things to do—all of them for you.

Punch.

Come, Judy. A little smack—right on the kisser.

(*Puckers mouth.*)

Judy.

I have to polish the brass and shine the looking glass.

Punch.

(*With romantic abandonment.*)

> Oh, love is a wiggle thing.
> It wiggles like a lizard.
> It wraps its tail around your heart
> And crawls into your gizzard.
> > (*Dances.*)
> Rootle-dee-tootle-dee-toot!

Judy.

A husband should think of money, mortgages, and security.

Punch.

Oh, Judy, don't be an old shoe.

Judy.

An old shoe!

Punch.

> Oh, Judy is an old shoe,
> And I'm a fine piece of leather.
> Hammered and nailed—
> And here we are together!

Judy.

(*Aside.*) He called me an old shoe! I work and work and all you do is Rootle-dee-tootle-dee-too!

Punch.

(*Dances.*) Pickles are green,
> Violets are blue,
> I am the boss.
> I'll show you.

Judy.

(*Angrily.*) I'll show you what a wife can do!

Punch.

Give us a kiss.

Judy.

A kiss?

Punch.

Give us a smack.

(*Puckers lips.*)

Judy.

A smack?

Punch.

Right on the smacker.

(*Shuts his eyes, ready.*)

Judy.

I'll give you a smack.

(*Raises broom.*)

Punch.

A big one.

Judy.

A big one! A smack for the money you don't bring home!

(*Hits* PUNCH *with broom.*)

A smack for the husband you should be!

(*Hits again.*)

Punch.

Oh, Judy! You kiss too hard!

Judy.

And a smack for the family!

(*Hits him again.*)

Punch.

Stop! Stop kissing me! No more kisses! No more kisses please!

Judy.

Remember you are a husband, a father, a breadwinner!

Punch.

I am Mr. Punch. I am——me!

Judy.

(*Sweetly.*) Now I will cook and bake and make your favorite dish.

(*Sweeping to R.*)

Mend and patch each hole, and feed the goldfish in the bowl.

(Aside.)

Oh life is sweet. Life is complete in my home sweet home.

(Exits R.)

Punch.

(Sings, comically. Cue 11.)

Oh Mr. Punch is a sad sad fellow,
His coat is always scarlet and yellow,
With a lump on his nose and a bump on his back,
And on his head he got a whack!

Some men fight dragons. Some men fight windmills. Mr. Punch hereby announces—he will fight for his right—to be free!

(Sings. Cue 12.)

Nobody is going to make and shape, roll and
    mold me in a form,
Nobody is going to make and take and break
    me 'til I conform.
Each rope, each chain, each fetter that would
    hold and mold all men fast,
I'll fight, I'll fight, I'll fight, I'll fight,
    I'll fight them all to the last.
I will be—the man *every* man wants to be.

I'll be—me!

(Holds stick high. Sings fast and joyfully. Cue 12A).

I'll give a smack, smack, smack on the chin.
I'll give a whack, whack, whack on the shin.
A whack-whack, a smack-smack, and I'll win!

Let's begin!

(Dances off R.)

Rootle-dee-tootle-dee-toot!

Scene Two

Music. Cue 13. TOBY *appears at L, puts up second sign which reads, "Scene 2." It may also have printed on it, "Dog Bites Nose. Professor Loses Head."* TOBY *wears a large cap and a large bow around his neck. Also around his neck hangs a hand mirror. He admires himself in the looking glass. At C he sings.*

Toby.
(*To audience.*)

> I've got my cap set for you,
> I've got my tie tied for you,
> I've trimmed my beard for you.
> I've got my eye on you.
>
> Be my friend, be my pal,
> Be my buddy, be my gal,
> Cross your heart and swear it's true,
> And I'll be a pal to you . . .

(*Holds up mirror and reflects light from it onto faces in the audience.*)

> To you . . . to you . . . to you . . . to you.
>
> I've got my cap set for you,
> I've got my tie tied for you,
> I've trimmed my beard for you,
> I've got my eye on you.
>
> Without a friend, without a pal,
> Without a buddy, without a gal,
> It's a life I don't recommend,
> It's a dog's life without a friend.

(*Reflects light from mirror again onto faces in audience.*)

Come on—

> Be my friend, be my pal,
> Be my buddy, be my gal,
> Cross your heart and swear it's true,
> And I'll be a pal to you . . .
> To you . . . to you . . . to you . . . to you.
>
> I've got my cap set for you,
> I've got my tie tied for you,
> I've trimmed my beard for you,

I've got my eye—eye—eye—
I've got my eye on you.

(TOBY *exits L and immediately returns and bows and exits.*)

Punch.
(*Enters R.*) Toby. Toby.

(TOBY *enters and bows again, throwing kisses.*)

Toby. Toby! Go away. Get off the stage.

(TOBY *keeps bowing.*)

Toby! It is scene two. Go! Get! Skdoo!

(TOBY *gives him an aloof look, shakes his tail at him and continues to bow to audience.*)

Tob—y!
(*Raises his stick.* TOBY *turns on him, growls and raises fists.*)
I think he woke up on the wrong side of the bed.

(TOBY *growls louder.*)

I think he fell out of the bed!

(TOBY *growls.*)

Nice Toby. Sweet Toby. Look at him smile.

(TOBY *bares his teeth and advances.*)

He wants to shake hands. Here old friend, take my hand.

(TOBY *bites* PUNCH's *hand.*)

Oh! He thinks it is a piece of baloney. I said, "Shake." Not bite.

(TOBY *growls and put up fists.*)

Oh, you want to fight. All right! Round one!

(*They circle, facing each other. Music optional. Cue 14.* TOBY *hits at* PUNCH.)

Around two!

> (*Punch gives him a hit with the stick.*)

Around three!

> (TOBY *bites and holds* PUNCH's *nose.*)

Oh, my nose! Let go! Let go! O-o-oh! You bit my
nose. My beautiful nose!

> (PUNCH *sits wailing.*)

Toby.
> (*Dances to side, sings. Cue 15.*)
> > I've got my eye—eye—eye—
> > I've got my eye on you.

> (*He takes a final bow and exits.*)

Punch.
> (*Rises.*) Judy! Help! Judy, come. Judy, run! Mr.
Punch has been eaten—for lunch!

Judy.
> (*Enters R, sweeping.*) Shout! Shout! Shout! What is
it about?

Punch.
My nose! My beautiful nose. Oh, Judy, how will I
smell without a nose?

Judy.
> (*Pointedly.*) Terrible.

> (*Exits R, sweeping.*)

Punch.
> (*Wails loudly.*) O-o-oh! When you smile the world
smiles with you, but when you cry—you use your
own handkerchief.

> (*Takes handkerchief from pocket, dabs eye, holds
handkerchief away, squeezes concealed sponge and
water drips.*)

O-o-o-oh!

> (*Wipes other eye, holds handkerchief away, squeez-
es tightly and much water pours.*)

O-o-o-o-oh!

Professor.

(*Enters L.*) Mr. Punch. Good morning. Good afternoon. Good evening. How do you do.

Punch.

(*Awed.*) Who are you?

Professor.

I am the Professor, Ph.D., A.B.C., M.A., U.S.A.

Punch.

A professor!

Professor.

A teacher. My head is full, crowded, crawling with information, observations, and generalizations.

Punch.

He's got a big head!

Professor.

I make and shape the mass media. I am a walking talking encyclopedia.

Punch.

That's the trouble with teachers. All they do is talk.

Professor.

Problem one. What is one thing a bird can do which you cannot do?

Punch.

Take a bath in a saucer! Rootle-dee-tootle-dee-toot.

Professor.

We will now verify, clarify, and qualify your knowledge of dogs.

Punch.

Oh, I have a dog.

(*Calls.*)

Toby. Toby.

Professor.

Is he a *bird* dog?

Punch.

No. He can't sing a note. Rootle-dee-tootle-dee-toot!

Professor.

Is he a *watch* dog?

Punch.

No. When I hear a noise I bark myself. Wolf-wolf-wolf!

Professor.

Mr. Punch, I must teach you your responsibilities.

Punch.

Responsibilities?

Professor.

To your wife, your home, your country. You must—reform.

Punch.

Reform?

Professor.

And conform! Throw away your stick. The days of whacking are over. Instead—use your head. Fill your head with dates and weights, historical situations and geographical locations.

Punch.

Stop! Your head will pop!

Professor.

Good or poor or mean or rich, each man must fit into a niche. Learn the rule and pass the test.

Punch.

(*Aside.*) And be a fool like all the rest? No, I will be —Mr. Punch.

Professor.

Lesson one.

Punch.

School has begun!

Professor.

I will give you something for your head.

Punch.

No. I will give *you* something instead!

(*Raises stick.*)

Professor.

Ready?

Punch.

Ready!

(*Swings stick.*)

Professor.
Fact one.
Punch.
Whack one!

(*Slaps at* PROFESSOR.)

Don't try to chain, rein, or bridle me!
Professor.
Help. My head is whirling.
Punch.
Or tie, twine, or shackle me!

(*Slaps.*)

Professor.
Help. My head is swirling.
Punch.
Don't try to curb or bind or muzzle me!

(*Slaps.*)

Professor.
No more facts! My head is full.
Punch.
Don't tell me what to do! I'll paddle my own canoe!

(*Slaps.*)

Professor.
Help! Help! I am *losing* my head!

(*Runs behind puppet theater at L.*)

Punch.
(*Aside.*) Big heads always do!

(*Runs behind puppet theater at L. There is a big crash.*)

Professor.
(*Off, shouts.*) HELP! I HAVE LOST MY HEAD!

Immediately the PROFESSOR's *body runs out from the R side of puppet theater, but without a head.* PROFESSOR *ducks inside his robe which covers his head. Headless, he darts this way and that, exiting at R.*

PUNCH *follows his zigzag path, holding the* PRO-FESSOR's *head [papier-mâché with hat on it] on a stick, which he picked up as he ran behind the puppet theater.*)

Punch.

(*Happily waves at audience.*) Rootle-dee-tootle-dee-toot!

(*He exits R, dancing.*)

Scene Three

TOBY *enters L and changes sign, which reads "Scene 3." It may also have printed on it, "Dancing Horse. Dr. Cure-All." He waves and exits. Off R, the head of a horse peeks around the curtain. Then* HECTOR, *a comical dancing horse—two actors under horse costume—canters to C. He pats his foot—one—two—three and the music starts. Cue 16.* HECTOR, *with great abandonment, dances. His fast dance is suddenly stopped by* PUNCH *calling off R.* HECTOR *stops. Music stops.* HECTOR *looks off R, then runs UC to puppet theater, hides at the L side of it, head concealed behind it, but his back legs still in view.*

Punch.

(*Off R.*) Hector! Hector! Where are you? Hec—tor-or-or.

(*Enters and crosses.*)

Hector! Hector! My horse has run away. Hector! Hector! This is Scene Three. Now where the heck can Hector be!

(*He exits L.* HECTOR *immediately canters downstage and taps his foot—one—two—three. Music starts.* HECTOR *dances wildly. The dance is stopped again by* PUNCH *calling off L.* HECTOR *hides at R of puppet theater.* PUNCH *calls off.*)

Hector! Hector! Hec—tor—or—or!

(*Enters L.*)

Hector! Where can my horse be? Hector! Hector! Oh, where in the heck is Hec-Hec-Hector!

(*He exits R.* HECTOR *comes DC and taps his foot—one—two—three. Music starts and* HECTOR *dances.* PUNCH *reenters.*)

Hector!

(*Dancing and music stop.*)

Hector, you are dancing again.

(HECTOR *nods his head.*)

And you are dancing in public!

(HECTOR *lowers his head.*)

How many times must I tell you—a horse does not dance. A horse is a noble beast.

(HECTOR *nods.*)

He runs.

(HECTOR *runs in one spot.*)

He trots.

(HECTOR *trots.*)

He jumps.

(HECTOR *jumps.*)

He gallops.

(HECTOR *gallops.*)

But he never dances.

(HECTOR *bows his head low, then slowly collapses to the floor.*)

Come! We must do the next scene. The famous scene when Punch rides the horse!

(*Dances.*)

Rootle-dee-tootle-dee-toot. This is the part I like! You will see how gracefully I ride without a saddle, stirrup, spur, or dangles! Watch Punch ride in circles, squares, and rectangles!

(*Straddles the collapsed horse.*)

Hector! Up! Leap, lope, gallop away.

(*Slaps stick in the air.* HECTOR *shakes his head.* PUNCH *turns around, straddling and facing the back end of the horse*).

Hector! Getty-up, getty-up, getty-up—GO!

(*Hits slapstick at* HECTOR's *rump.* HECTOR *suddenly stands up, shaking and bucking.* PUNCH *yells and falls off.* HECTOR *gallops in a circle around him, kicks a back foot at* PUNCH *on the ground and exits* R.)

Help! Help! Help! I've been kicked. Oh, my head! Oh, my feet! Oh, my seat! Judy! Come! Judy! Help!

Judy.
(*Enters R, stirring with spoon in a bowl.*) Shout, shout, shout. What is the noise about? I am making and baking and spicing and icing a cake.

Punch.
Get the Doctor. Run! Run! Run! Oh, Doctor, come, come, come—before—I die.

(*Falls back stiffly.*)

Judy.
(*Alarmed.*) He is hurt! He is in pain. He has been slain! What will become of me? of my home? of my family? Oh, Mr. Punch, remain. Oh, Doctor, come. Oh, St. Pa-nat-o-my! Mr. Punch has had a punch in his a-nat-omy!

(JUDY *exits L. Music starts for a series of fast crosses. Cue 17. First* TOBY *skips across jumping a rope. He exits R.*)

Punch.
(*Sits up.*) Oh, Doctor. No!

(*He falls backward. As* TOBY *exits,* PROFESSOR's *body, long robe without a head, but carrying a head on a stick, runs across from R to L and exits.* PUNCH *sits up.*)

Oh, Doctor. No!

(*He falls backward.* HECTOR *gallops across from R to C, does a dance step, kicks his back leg toward* PUNCH, *and runs off.* PUNCH *sits up.*)

Oh, Doctor. No!

(PUNCH *falls back again.*)

Doctor.
(*Enters R. He is wild and comical.*) The Doctor is here. The Doctor is here!

(*Music stops.*)

Punch.
(*Sits up.*) Oh, Doctor.
Doctor.
(*Points at* PUNCH.) Someone is ill! Someone wants a pill!
(*Sings with fervor. Cue 18.*)
Oh, I examine every part
Lungs, and your liver and your heart.
Oh, oh, oh,
I can't wait. (*Shivers.*) Until I start!
Oh, stethoscope and microscope—
With a knife and doctor there is hope.
Oh, oh, oh,
I can't wait, (*Shivers.*) Until I start.
If you have a break, a bruise, an itch,
I will cut and sew a fancy stitch.
Oh, palpitation, vaccination,
Circulation, hallucination—
Oh, oh, oh,
I can't wait (*Shivers.*) I have to start!
Punch.
Oh, Doctor!

Doctor.

(*Jumps with joy.*) A patient! (*Runs to* PUNCH.)

Punch.

I am dying—dying—

> (*Falls back stiffly.*)

—dead.

Doctor.

Tell me, Mr. Punch, how long have you been dead?

Punch.

(*Rises.*) Three years.

> (*Falls back.*)

Doctor.

When did you die?

Punch.

(*Sits up.*) Yesterday.

Doctor.

Oh, blood and bones and kidney stones! I must examine you. Let me see your pulse.

> (*Holds* PUNCH's *wrist. Nods head and taps foot in rhythm.*)

A-one, a-two, a-three. A waltz! Let me hear your tongue.

> (PUNCH *puts out tongue and says a prolonged* "Ah.")

Doctor.

Say "Three" four times.

Punch.

Twelve.

Doctor.

Twelve?

Punch.

I am in a hurry!

> (*Puts tongue out and shouts,* "Ah, ha-ha-ha-ha.")

Doctor.

(*Happy and excited.*) Smelling salts and turpentine, rubbing alcohol and iodine—stand up.

Punch.

(*Getting up.*) Oh, Doctor. I will never be able to stand up—see. (*Stands.*)

Doctor.

What is the time? (*Takes out a 12-inch watch.*) Ah, it is time—to time the beat of your heart. I will time. You will beat.

Punch.

Beat?

Doctor.

Beat.

Punch.

(*Nods, smiles, and raises stick.*) Beat!

Doctor.

Ready?

Punch.

Ready!

Doctor.

(*Puts one hand on* PUNCH's *chest, holds watch with other.*) Time!

(DOCTOR *nods.*)

Beat!

(PUNCH *nods.*)

One . . . two . . . three . . .

Punch.

Out goes he!

(*Slaps at* DOCTOR.)

Doctor.

Stop! Stop! Your heart is beating too fast!

(*Shakes watch.*)

Oh, time is runing out. It is half past time—to take your medicine.

(*Hands watch to* PUNCH.)

Punch.

Ah, see—time flies.

(*Tosses watch off R.*)

Doctor.

(*Gleefully.*) Oh, medicine, lotions, herbs, and potions
—I love you all!

(*Hands* DOCTOR's *bag to* PUNCH *who holds it. Sings.
Cue 19.*)

> A pinch of sulphur, whiff of slate,
> Mix and grind and add some fishing bait.

(*Pulls wiggling worm from bag.*)

> Oh, oh, oh,
> I can't—I can't—I can't wait.
> Cherry root, an onion shoot,
> Apple cider, and a spider,

(*Pulls wiggly spider from bag.*)

> Oh, oh, oh,
> I can't wait—(*Pause.*)—Until I start.
> With a dew dew berry duplicate,
> With a lizard's gizzard medicate!
> Oh, vaccinate, fumigate,
> Oh, lubricate, intoxicate.
> Oh, oh, oh,
> I can't—I can't—I can't wait!

Get ready. Open your eyes. Shut your mouth and
take your medicine.

(*Grabs* PUNCH *and shakes him.*)

Punch.

What are you doing?

Doctor.

(*Aside.*) Shake well before taking!

(*Takes slapstick from* PUNCH.)

First a dose for fever—

(*Slaps at* PUNCH.)

For chills up your back—

(*Slaps at* PUNCH.)

For whooping cough and sacroiliac!

(*Slaps.*)

Punch.
I don't like your medicine.
Doctor.
For influenza, extra doses—for sniffles and tuberculosis—

(*Slaps.*)

For lumps and bumps—
Punch.
Stop! No more medicine!
Doctor.
For humps and mumps and halitosis!

(*Slaps.*)

Punch.
Stop! No more medicine! I am well!
Doctor.
Well?

(*Sings, elated. Cue 20.*)

Wonder—wonder—wonder—wonder wonderful is
    medicine.
I'm certain you'll agree.
Oh, wonder—wonder—wonder—wonder wonderful
    is medicine.
I'm certain you'll agree.
Punch.
(*Sings, aside.*)

> Not the medicine he gives to me.
> Not the medicine he gives to me.

Doctor.
Oh, take a dose—

(*Holds up stick.*)

Punch.
Oh, no no no.

Doctor.
Oh, take another—
Punch.
No no no no no!
Doctor.
Oh, one more. Oh—
Punch.
No no.
Doctor.

Oh, wonderful is medicine!
And you are out of bed!

Punch.
Or dead!
Doctor.
Now you must pay me. Pay the doctor's fee. (*Holds out hand.*)
Punch.
Pay you?
Doctor.
I cured you. You pay me.
Punch.
Oh.

(*Smiles with an idea, takes stick.*)

Certainly.

(*Aside.*)

I'll pay him back. I'll give him back every whack he gave me! Are you ready? Shut your eyes. Open your mouth and take *your* medicine.

(*Slaps.*)

Doctor.
Stop! A doctor never takes his own medicine.
Punch.

(*Sings without music.*)

Wonder—wonder—wonderful is medicine—
for shivers and shakes and twisters—measles, warts
and blisters!

(*Slaps.*)

Doctor.
Help! Help!

(*Runs. Aside.*)

Is there a doctor in the house?
Punch.
For heat and fever parches; feet and fallen arches!

(*Slaps.*)

Doctor.
Help! Help! A nurse! A bed! Before the Doctor—is dead!

(*Exits L.*)

Punch.
(*Sings loudly and joyfully. Cue 21.*)

Wonder—wonder—wonder—wonder wonderful is
 medicine.
I'm certain I agree.
Oh, wonder—wonder—wonder—wonder wonderful
 is medicine
When it's not given to me!

(*He exits dancing at R.*)

Scene Four

TOBY *enters from L and starts to change the sign.*
HECTOR *peeks in at R, and enters.* TOBY *quickly looks
to R and to L, then nods his head and motions for
horse to C. Cue 22.*

Toby.
Presenting Hector the Dancing Horse—in—a Dance
of the Nations.

(HECTOR *bows.*)

From Ireland—the Irish jig.

(HECTOR *does a fast jig. Music. Cue 23.*)

From Austria—the Vienna waltz.

(HECTOR *waltzes to waltz music. Cue 24.*)

From Scotland—the Highland Fling.

(HECTOR *does a funny Highland Fling. Cue 25.*)

From Hawaii—the hula hula.

(HECTOR *circles, twisting his hips. Cue 26.*)

And last a march from the U.S.A.!

(*March music. Cue 27.* HECTOR *marches with high steps.* TOBY *puts small American flag in horse's mouth, which* HECTOR *waves as he exits.* TOBY *applauds.* HECTOR *runs back in, bows and starts dancing again and dances off R.* TOBY *goes to sign, puts up new one, which reads, "Scene 4." It may also have printed on it, "Fly Away Baby. Off to Jail."* TOBY *exits.*

JUDY *enters R with a* BABY RAG DOLL *in her arms. She hums and comes to C and sings. Cue 28.*)

Judy.
Sleep, sleep, sleep little baby,
You've had a busy day.
Sleep, sleep, sleep little baby,
Dream the night away.
Rock-a-by, rock-a-by, rock-a-by, rock-a-rock-a-a-by.
Punch.
(*Calls, off R.*) Oh, Judy! Judy, my beauty!
Judy.
Sh, Mr. Punch. You will wake the baby.
Punch.
(*Off.*) Judy, I am hun-gry.
Judy.
I cooked you an egg omelet.
Punch.
(*Enters R.*) I ate it, but next time—break the eggs.

(*Dances.*)

Rootle-dee-tootle-dee-toot.

Judy.

Sh! The baby is asleep.

Punch.

(*Tiptoes to* JUDY, *baby-talk punches* BABY *harder and harder in the stomach.*) Oh, little Punchie-Punchie joy. You are Mr. Punch's Punchie-boy. (*Aside.*) Isn't that a picture! Oh, Judy is my beauty. Did you know we were married in a bathtub? It was a double ring ceremony. Rootle-dee-tootle-dee-toot.

Judy.

Sh!

Punch.

Sh!

Judy.

Take the baby, Mr. Punch. I am going around the corner.

Punch.

Me rock the baby? That's a mother's duty.

Judy.

I forgot the bread, the cabbage head, and the jelly spread.

Punch.

(*Aside.*) She is so forgetful she powders her shoes and shines her nose.

Judy.

Take the baby.

Punch.

(*Screws up his face.*) I can't. I have a cold in my head.

Judy.

Oh, how can you say so many stupid things in one day?

Punch.

I get up early! Oh, rootle-dee-tootle-dee-toot.

Judy.

It is a father's duty to help care for the baby.

Punch.

Duties, duties, duties.

Judy.

Are you big enough, brave enough to look after a baby? Are you a man or a mouse? Well, squeak up!

Punch.

(*Grabs* BABY.) Give him to me. I'll rock him. I'll knock him. I'll sock him!

Judy.

Be careful!

Punch.

(*Sings, comically. Cue 29.*)

> Sleep, sleep, sleep little baby,
> You've had a busy day.
> Sleep, sleep, sleep little baby
> Dream the night away . . .

Judy.

I will be right back. You can wave from the window as I pass.

(*She points to* L. TOBY *enters L, carrying a window which is a self-standing unit. He places it at L and exits.*)

Judy.

Good-bye, little Punch.

(PUNCH *starts to sing loudly.*)

Sh!

(*Going off R.*)

Let me think. Bread . . . cabbage head . . . jelly spread. No, no, instead . . . salt . . . malt . . . custard and mustard!

(*Exits R.*)

Punch.

Confused . . . confused. Judy is so confused she is knitting a sweater with spaghetti! Rootle-dee-tootle-dee-toot.

(*Tosses* BABY *around. To audience.*)

Sh! you will wake the baby. That's a good idea. It's no fun sleeping the day away.

(*Shakes* BABY *violently.*)

Oh, little Punch! What would your nose be if it were twelve inches long? A foot!

(*Tosses* BABY *high in air.*)

Rootle-dee-tootle-dee-toot. Wake up! We'll have fun! We'll put bugs in jars and smoke cigars!

(*Whirls* BABY *around by feet.*)

Wake up! Wake up!

(BABY *cries loudly.*)

Quiet! Quiet!

(*To audience.*)

Now see what you did! You made him cry! Quiet! Quiet!

(*Shouts.*)

Stop! Shut up! Stop. Don't cry. Stop or you'll get a black eye!

(BABY *cries louder.*)

Oh, stop the waterworks. Turn off the waterfall!

(*Runs to R.*)

Judy! Judy! What will I do? Judy, he's calling for you!

(*Shakes and tosses* BABY *high.*)

Stop the yelling. Stop the bellowing!

(*Holds* BABY *out to audience.*)

Here, you take him. Take him . . . take him . . . shake him . . . shame him. Oh, flood! Get a boat. Get a float. Swim for your life!

(*By window, calls.*)

Judy, are you there? I'm drowning. Give me air! Judy, please pass by.

(*Swings* BABY *as if going to throw it through the window as he sings. Cue 30.* TOBY *enters, and moves about to catch the* BABY.)

> Fly, fly, fly little baby,
> Fly, fly, away.
> Fly, fly, fly little baby,
> I've had enough today.

One . . . two . . . three . . . goodby!

(*Throws* BABY *through the window.* TOBY *catches it and exits.*)

Judy.

(*Enters R.*) I heard a cry like a baby. Then it stopped —like it was dropped. Mr. Punch, where is the baby?

Punch.

The baby?

Judy.

The baby.

Punch.

The little angel?

Judy.

The little angel!

Punch.

The little angel—flew away.

(*Motions to window.*)

Judy.

(*Runs to window.*) Flew away!

Punch.

Out the window.

Judy.

Mr. Punch, you threw the baby out the window!

Punch.

I gave him a little help.

Judy.

You big nose, red nose, lobster nose, know-nothing! I'll make you cry for help!

(*Takes his stick.*)

Punch.

(*Aside, innocently.*) Every father wants to throw a crying baby out the window. I did it!

Judy.

You selfish-selfish tootle-dee-toot.

(*Slaps at him.*)

You mean-minded, hardhearted galoot!

(*Slaps at him.*)

Punch.

Help! No, Judy. No more kisses.

(*Runs.*)

Judy.

You double-dyed, cross-eyed, tongue-tied goof!

(*Slaps.*)

You half-wit, dimwit, nitwit nincompoop!

(*Slaps.*)

Punch.

I know you love me, Judy, but no more kisses. No more kisses.

Judy.

(*He runs. She chases, hitting when she can.*) Muddle-head, addlehead, dopehead, empty head, bonehead, pinhead, blockhead, wooden head!

Punch.

Stop!

(*Grabs stick.*)

I am Mr. Punch! No one punches me! I'll show you how and what a husband should be. Here are a few kisses from me! A smack and a whack!

(*Slaps at her.*)

Judy.

(*Running.*) Help! Help!

Punch.

A kiss and a hug and a squeeze!

(*Slaps.*)

Judy.

Help! Help! Save me!

Punch.

A little cuddling and wooing! A little billing and cooing!

(*Slaps.*)

Judy.

Save me! Doctor, lawyer, merchant—POLICE! POLICE!

(*Exits R.*)

Punch.

(*Gives a triumphal slap and sings. Cue 31.*)

> Oh Mr. Punch is a jolly good fellow,
> His coat is always scarlet and yellow.
> His wife and his baby he gave a toss,
> And now he is—his very own boss!

Rootle-dee-tootle-dee-toot. I've done it! No family ties for me. Mr. Punch is free!

(*There are three loud slow knocks off R.*)

Knock—knock—knock.

(*Three knocks are repeated.*)

Someone is coming after me! Oh, what have I done? What have I done? *Whatever* I've done was done in fun!

Policeman.

(*Off.*) Open the door! Open the door in the name of the law!

Punch.

The police!

Policeman.

(*Enters R.*) Mr. Punch.

Punch.

He knows my name!

Policeman.

I am a Policeman.

Punch.

But I don't want the police.

Policeman.

But the police wants you!

Punch.

Oh.

Policeman.

I have a notation in my pocket to lock you up.

(*Turns and reaches into pocket.*)

Punch.

I have a notion to knock you down.

(*Raises stick.* POLICEMAN *turns.* PUNCH *smiles and puts stick down.*)

Policeman.

Here is a list of your offences. Do you know your rights?

Punch.

Yes, this is my rights and this is my lefts. (*Holds out right and left hands.*)

Policeman.

(*Holds up narrow scroll.*) You hit a dog.

Punch.

He bit me first.

Policeman.

You smacked your wife.

Punch.

It was a kiss.

Policeman.

You cracked a professor.

Punch.

His head was too full.

Policeman.

You whacked a doctor.

Punch.

I gave him back his own medicine.

Policeman.

You threw a baby out the window.

Punch.

What else can you do with a crying baby?

Policeman.

You will be in jail a *long* time.

Punch.

But it was a *short* baby.

Policeman.

When you break a law, there are other laws to punish you. You are under suspicion.

Punch.

(*Looks up.*) I am?

Policeman.

You are under arrest.

Punch.

Oh, no—no! Mr. Punch is free. I won't go! You will have to catch me!

(*Runs.*)

Policeman.

You cannot escape the arm of the law.

(*Extends his arm and runs after him.*)

Punch.

Help! Judy! Judy, my beauty! Help! Save me!

(*Runs into audience.*)

Policeman.

The law will catch you!

(*Blows whistle and runs after him into audience.*)

Punch.

Oh, Tom! Dick! And Mary! Save me. It was all in fun.

(*Looks over shoulder.*)

O-o-oh, Mr. Punch, run, run, run!

Policeman.

Desperate criminal loose in town! Dangerous man turning law upside down!

Punch.

Call the police! Oh, police, save me from the police!

Policeman.

Search and find every clue and trick. Find the man with the stick.

(*Blows whistle.*)

Punch.

Someone guide me! Some hide me!

(*Grabs scarf and lady's purse from first row.*)

Thank you.

(*Puts scarf over his head and runs back onstage.*)

Policeman.

Stop!

(*Blows whistle and points.*)

Mr. Punch, the law has caught you and brought you to justice.

Punch.

(*Speaks in a woman's voice.*) I am an old lady, sir. Are you talking to me?

Policeman.

Oh, I am sorry, madam. I beg your pardon, lady.

Punch.

I should think so! Stand aside, young man, and let a lady pass.

(*Swings pocketbook at* POLICEMAN *and walks away.*)

Policeman.

Mr. Punch! Mr. Punch has escaped!

(*Blows whistle.*)

Punch.

(*Throws scarf and pocketbook away.*) Rootle-dee-tootle-dee-dee. No one gets the best of me.

Policeman.

There he is! Surround, attack, throw a net. We'll catch him yet!

> (*Blows whistle and starts chase.*)

Punch.

I must leave you—fly! Rootle-dee-tootle and good-by!

> (*Runs to R.*)

Doctor.

(*Enters R, stopping* PUNCH.) Mr. Punch.

Punch.

The Doctor.

Judy.

(*Enters R with* BABY.) Mr. Punch!

Punch.

Judy—and the baby!

Policeman.

(*At his L.*) Mr. Punch.

Punch.

(TOBY *enters L, barks angrily.*) What—you, too Toby!

> (PUNCH *is in center. Others close in on him and sing.* Cue 32.)

Others.

We're looking at you, you, you, you, you, you, Mr. Punch.

Punch.

Me?

Others.

Yes, at you.
Nobody else would do, do, do,
Such awful, terrible things as you.
Nobody else would do, do, do,
Such awful, terrible things as you.
Oh, we've added your crimes, one by one,
All the wicked wicked things you have done!
But there comes an accounting day, day, day,
When for all your crimes you must pay, pay, pay.

Judy.
He's a menace to the family . . .
Policeman.
Security . . .
Doctor.
Community . . .

(TOBY *gives a loud "Rauff!" on beat.*)

Others.
Behind prison bars he shall be!

(POLICEMAN *ties rope around* PUNCH.)

Punch.
I'm being bound by propriety—
Others.
He's a menace to the family.
Punch.
Tied by rules of society—
Others.
He's a menace to security.
Punch.
This must not happen, not to me—
Others.
He's a menace to community.
Punch.
I'm Mr. Punch. I'm always free!
Others.
   Oh, Mr. Punch, you are in a fix,
   No more smacks or whacks or selfish tricks.
Punch.
      I'll fight for my right to be me.
      I'll fight for my right of liberty!
Others.
   Oh, Mr. Punch, you are in sad shape,
   And this time—there is no escape!
   We must keep, keep, keep the social order,
   The state and family group;
   To keep the status quo, he must go—
Punch.
   No, no.

Others.

> (*March off R with* PUNCH.)
>
> So—throw him in the—
> Throw him in the—
> Throw him in the coop!

(*All exit R.* PUNCH *immediately returns, end of rope being held behind him offstage.*)

Punch.

Don't give up hope. What's a twist of rope? I'll be back and you'll see who gives who a whack! Rootle-dee-too-

(*He is pulled backward by rope, offstage.*)

oo-oo-oo-oo-oo-oot!

(*Music swells to climax. Cue 33.* TOBY *enters and puts up new sign which reads "Short Intermission."* TOBY *waves and exits. If no intermission, then he will put up the sign which reads "Scene 5", and the play continues with entrance of two guards.*)

INTERMISSION

ACT TWO

Overture. Cue 33. Scene is the same march music. Cue 34. Two brightly dressed guards march in from R. They do a short comic military dance. They change the sign, which reads, "Scene 5." It may also have printed on it, "Hung by a Rope."

Scene Five

The GUARDS *carry in from L a barred prison-cell front which is a self-standing unit and put it DL. This can*

*be the same frame as the window, which was removed
during intermission, but now has bars on the front.*
POLICEMAN *pushes* PUNCH *in from L and leaves him
behind the bars.* POLICEMAN *and* GUARDS *exit.*)

Punch.
(*Puts head out between bars. Sings. Cue 35.*)

> Oh oh oh oh oh,
> Hear my cry, hear my sigh, here stand I
> Behind prison bars, locked with a key,
> Help! Help! Help! Someone rescue me!
>
> Oh oh oh oh oh,
> If I were a butterfly, I'd fly, I'd flee.
> But I'm not a butterfly, as you can see.
> Help. Help. Help. Someone rescue me!

(*Shouts.*)

Let me out! Let me out! Let me ou-ou-out!

> (*Two* GUARDS *march in from R. They carry a gal-
> lows and stand it DR.*)

Punch.
What is that? It has one branch on the top. It's a tree!
If I could reach—I'd eat a peach.

(*Calls.*)

Yoo-hoo, you and you. Who is the tree for?

(*They point at him.*)

Me!

(GUARDS *fix rope.*)

What are they doing? They are stealing my fruit! Help!
Thieves. They are fixing a rope—with a loop. Yoo-
hoo. The rope—with the loop—who is it for?

(GUARDS *point at him.*)

ME!

(*Guards march off R. Punch sings. Cue 36.*)

Oh oh oh oh oh,
A rope swings high with a noose that's crooked.
If I swing high, my goose is cooked.
Help. Help. Help. Someone let me loose!

Oh oh oh oh oh,
There is no doubt, I must get out.
Quick as quick as quick as quick can be.
Help. Help. Help. They're going to hang me!

(*Yells and shakes bars.*)

Let me out! Let me out! Let me ou-ou-ou-out!

(*Off L, heavy drumbeat footsteps are heard.*)

Someone is coming.

(HANGMAN *strides in and takes a stance. He wears a masking hood, but he should not be all in black. There should be some colorful accents. He is a comical* HANGMAN. PUNCH *shakes and speaks in a frightened voice.*)

Who is there?
Hangman.
I am the Hangman.
Punch.
Oh!
Hangman.
I have come to hang you.
Punch.
No!
Hangman.
(*Takes out little book.*) The book says: I will fling the rope over your head. You will swing until you are dead, dead, dead.
Punch.
I am going to die *three* times.
Hangman.
You have broken the laws of the land.
Punch.
No! I didn't touch them!

Hangman.

The book says it is the hour to hang you. Come out.

Punch.

I like it here.

Hangman.

Come out! Before my temper goes. I am in a hurry.

Punch.

I am in no hurry at all.

Hangman.

Come out! Or I'll hang you by the nose!

Punch.

(*Comes around cell front to C.*) Oh, no. No. Not my beautiful beautiful nose.

Hangman.

Have you made your will?

Punch.

My will?

Hangman.

Your last will and testimony. You have to make a will before I can hang you.

Punch.

Then I never will—make a will. Rootle-dee-tootle-dee-toot!

Hangman.

The book says—hang you! And hang you I will, will or no will! Stand there.

(*Points to noose.*)

Punch.

Why?

Hangman.

The book doesn't say why. It says stand there!

Punch.

Where?

Hangman.

There!

(PUNCH *stands behind noose.*)

And stay! Now listen well while I tell you the words to say: good-by, good-by—farewell.

Punch.

I'd rather say, good-by, good-by—

(*Waves.*)

and go away.

(*Starts.*)

Hangman.

Stop! You are doing it all wrong! You must do it right!

Punch.

(*Nods.*) Right—

(*Marches.*)

Right, left, right, left, right, left—

Hangman.

Halt! Stand there.

(PUNCH *does.*)

And stay.

Punch.

And pray.

(*Clasps hands together.*)

Hangman.

Attend! The hanging will begin. First the rope I
bend—

Punch.

It is the end of Mr. Punch.

Hangman.

What are you doing?

Punch.

Saying my prayers.

Hangman.

What prayers! (*In a tantrum.*) Oh, nothing, nothing
is going right!

Punch.

(*Marches.*) Right, right, left, right, left, right, left—

Hangman.

Halt! Come back!

(PUNCH *does.*)

Say your prayers. And be quick!
Punch.
> (*Kneeling, opens mouth, then starts to stammer.*) I-I-
> I-I-I-I-I can't remember.

Hangman.
> Say something. So I can hang you!

Punch.
> Humpty Dumpty sat on a wall.
> Humpty Dumpty had a great fall.
> All the king's horses and all the king's men
> Had scrambled eggs for breakfast again.

Hangman.
> Amen. We will begin.

Punch.
> I had a little dog, his name was Tim.
> I put him in a bathtub to see if he could swim;
> He drank all the water and ate all the soap,
> And almost died with a bubble in his throat.

Hangman.
> Amen. We will begin.

Punch.
> Fuzzy-wuzzy was a bear.
> Fuzzy-wuzzy cut his hair.
> Then Fuzzy-wuzzy wasn't fuzzy, was he?

Hangman.
> Amen! We will begin—NOW! (*Picks* PUNCH *up by
> the collar.*) Put your head through there.

Punch.
> Where?

Hangman.
> There.

Punch.
> How?

Hangman.
> Now!

> (PUNCH *puts head below noose.*)

No, not below!

> (PUNCH *puts head above noose.*)

No, not above!

(PUNCH *puts head at side.*)

No, not to the side! Oh, idiot numbskull! Dumbskull!

(PUNCH *puts arm in noose.*)

No! Not your hand, not your arm! Put in your head!
Punch.
Where?
Hangman.
There! in the noose, you silly goose!
Punch.
How should I know. I've never been hung before.
Hangman.
I will hang you according to the book.
Punch.
The book?
Hangman.
I will quote what it says: Page one. Give your head—
Punch.
(*Points to* HANGMAN.) Your head?
Hangman.
No, your head.
Punch.
My head?
Hangman.
Yes, *your* head.
Punch.
Oh, *your* head.
Hangman.
No, no, not my head. Your head.
Punch.
Your head.
Hangman.
No, no, you blockhead. *Your* head!
Punch.
That's what I said you said, your head.
Hangman.
No, no, no! Listen to what I say!

Punch.
You say?
Hangman.
I say.
Punch.
I say.
Hangman.
No, no, not you—me!

(PUNCH *opens his mouth to speak.*)

Don't say anything! Watch me!
Punch.
You?
Hangman.
Me!
Punch.
Me?
Hangman.
No. Me!
Punch.
Me!
Hangman.
No, Me! Me! Me!
Punch.
(*Sings up the scale.*) Do-ra-ME-fa-so—
Hangman.
Quiet! I will *show* you what to do.
Punch.
Show me?
Hangman.
You are so stupid, you don't know your head from my
head. So I will use *my* head to show you where *your*
head should be. Now watch. I am going to put my head
in the loop.
Punch.
You are going to put your head into the noose?
Hangman.
Yes!
Punch.
(*Aside.*) I know what to do with *his* head, don't you?

Hangman.

(*Puts head through noose.*) Page one: you give your head a thrust—Clearing the rope is a must—Page two: as it tightens tightly around, You speak your last words and sound. Three! Good-by, good-by, farewell.

Punch.

It is as easy as A.B.C. One: pull the rope!

(*Pulls rope.*)

Hangman.

No!

Punch.

Two: do it fast—

Hangman.

NO!

Punch.

And it is the last—

Hangman.

OH!

(*Drops his head forward and turns around, back to audience.*)

Punch.

Good-by, good-by, farewell. There is no more to tell!

(*Tosses book over his shoulder. Sings. Cue 37.*)

> Mr. Punch is a jolly good fellow,
> His coat is always scarlet and yellow.
> They could not hang him from a shelf
> Because the hangman hung himself!

Rootle-dee-tootle-dee-toot! I'm free! I have escaped death! There is nothing now that can get me!

(*Ghost music is heard. Cue 38. Two* GHOSTS *"float" in from L.*)

Brr-r-r-r. I feel a cold—wind—blowing. I feel—an icy hand—on each shoulder. Whoo-oo-oo can it be?

First Ghost.

Whoo-oo-oo.

Punch.

It sounds like a ghost.　•

Second Ghost.

Whoo-oo-oo.

Punch.

Like two ghosts!

First Ghost.

We have come for Mr. Punch.

Punch.

Mr. Punch!

Second Ghost.

Do you know him?

Punch.

Yes. Oh, yes. Do you know him?

Ghosts.

No.

Punch.

Oh! So—you don't know him, do you? Then I'll show him—to you.

(*Points to gallows.*)

There he hangs!

(*Aside.*)

He was wet so I hung him up to dry. Rootle-dee-tootle-toot.

Ghosts.

(*Float to noose.*) We have come to take him away.

Punch.

Such fast service. Take him. Take him. He's yours.

Ghosts.

Thank you . . . thank you.

Punch.

You're welcome . . . you're welcome.

(GHOSTS *remove noose and put a ghost cover over* HANGMAN. PUNCH *speaks to audience.*)

Rootle-dee-tootle-dee-toot. Spooks and ghosts dance

in a ring and sing. Tell me, what sings better than *two* ghosts?

(*Points to three* GHOSTS.)

Three!
Ghosts.
(*Ghost music. The two* GHOSTS *with the* HANGMAN *now a* GHOST, *float to footlights.*) As we fade away from your view . . . this is what we say . . .

(*Each points to a child as he speaks.*)

to you . . . and you . . . and you . . .

(*They shout.*)

Boo!

(*They float quickly off L.*)

Punch.
(*Sings. Cue 39.*)
Mr. Punch is a jolly good fellow,
His coat is always scarlet and yellow.
There are no laws that can mold him,
There are no bars that can hold him.

(*Two* GUARDS *enter R and carry off cell front. Return and carry off gallows.*)

Take away! I've fought them all. Mr. Punch and his individual—ity are free! Rootle-dee-tootle-dee-toot!

(*Remembers.*)

There is one more. The last fight of every man. He must fight—win or lose—with—the Devil. Oh, Rootle-dee-tootle-dee-toot! I'll fight—I'll fight the Devil him-self, if he comes after me!

(*Aside.*)

And he will be in the next scene. What a fight you'll see! And there will be one winner.

(*Aside.*)

Guess who that will be? ME! Rootle-dee-tootle-dee-toot!

(Dances off R.)

(TOBY *enters and changes sign which reads, "Scene 6." It may also have printed on it "Up Pops the Devil." The sign is on a red background.* TOBY *waves his paw as if the sign is hot, blows on his paws, looks back at the sign, jumps, barks, and exits quickly.)*

Scene Six

The stage begins to glow with red light. Smoke effects may be used. Cue 40. The DEVIL *with horns and tail and dressed in bright red, dances in from R. He is gleeful in his wickedness. Sings.*

Devil.

> Fiery furnace, horns and hoops,
> He skips and steps and steps and hops,
> Anywhere, everywhere,
> He'll be there. Out pops—the Devil.
>
> He's an imp, a scoundrel, a rascal, a rogue,
> A fallen angel with a tail,
> A robber, a thief, a pirate, a cheat,
> A crook who ought to be in jail.
> But oh, the fun, the fun, fun, fun when one
>   is a little devilish.

(He looks and points at audience.)

Hello . . . hello. So many people I know. So many friends of mine. Ah, I see you. You are one of my little devils!

(Points to second child.)

And you! Ah, you're a devilish little devil!

(Points to third.)

Ah ha! You over there! You are going to be one of my best big devils!

(*Opens his arms to all.*)

Oh, come—everyone! We'll have fun—fun—fun!

(*Sings. Cue 41.*)

Get in line, the fire is fine,
We'll skip and step with steps and hops,
Anywhere, everywhere,
I'll be there. Out pops—the Devil.

He's a traitor, a squealer, a heel, a rat,
He's a villain with mischief to sell:
He lures, he tempts, he slanders, and hates,
He's a sneak, a stinker, a *skunk* with a smell.
And oh the fun, the fun, fun, fun, when one
   is a little devilish.

Suit of red, flame, and smoke,
We'll skip and step with steps and hops,
Call my name. Play my game.
I'll be there. Out pops—the Devil.

Someone is coming. Ah, it is Mr. Punch. I have my tail—pointed at him! And today I will get him. Today Mr. Punch is going to go to hel—to where I dwell. First, I must disguise myself because—*you* know the Devil never *looks* like the Devil when he is with you.

(DEVIL *exits L.* PUNCH *enters R.*)

Punch.
(*Walks to C, talking to audience.*) Walking along the street today . . . walking in my leisurely way . . . think- ing of a joke to say . . . Why does a humming bird al- ways hum? He hums because he doesn't know the words. Oh, rootle-dee-tootle-dee-toot.

Devil.
(*Enters L, disguised as Blind Man.*) Mr. Punch.

Punch.
I smell smoke.

Devil.

Mr. Punch. I am old and wise. I will give you a great future.

Punch.

I feel hot air.

Devil.

I can make you famous. I can write your name in the history book, if—

Punch.

If?

Devil.

If you shake my hand.

(Offers red-gloved hand.)

Punch.

It's red! It's red hot!

(Aside.)

There's something devilish here! It is—it is the Devil in disguise! This is the way I shake hands with the Devil! Shake.

Devil.

(Laughs cunningly.) Shake.

Punch.

(Slaps stick at DEVIL, *who runs off, calling,* "Help . . . help.") And may the Devil take you.

(Walking to C.)

Walking along the street today . . . walking in a leisurely way . . . thinking of a joke to say . . . If a cow married a zebra, what would she give? Striped milk! Oh, rootle-dee-tootle-toot.

Devil.

(Enters, disguised as a Rich Woman.) Mr. Punch.

Punch.

I smell smoke again.

Devil.

I am rich, rich, rich. I can give you wealth—money, jewels, lands, checkbooks.

Punch.

I feel hot air again.

Devil.

All the riches in the world can be yours.

Punch.

Mine?

Devil.

If—

Punch.

If?

Devil.

If you will sign on the dotted line.

(*Opens book.*)

Punch.

Red ink! There is something devilish here! You are no lady. You are a shady Devil. This is the way I sign up with the Devil!

(*Slaps stick at* DEVIL, *who runs off R, crying,* "Help . . . help.")

And the Devil keep you!

(*Walking to C.*)

Walking along the street today . . . thinking of a joke to say. One morning a mother hen laid an orange. What did her little chick say? "Oh, see the orange mar-ma-lade!" Rootle-dee-tootle-dee-toot.

Devil.

(*Enters, disguised as an Old Man.*) Mr. Punch.

Punch.

(*Aside.*) Can't you smell it? Fire and brimstone!

Devil.

Mr. Punch. I have great power. I can give you power, too.

Punch.

And I can give you a whack!

Devil.

You can rule the world if—

Punch.

If?

Devil.

If you give your soul to me.

Punch.

Never! Mr. Punch is free!

Devil.

No man is free from me.

(*Tosses off disguise.*)

I am the Devil.

Punch.

The Devil you are?

Devil.

The Devil I am and I have come to take you.

Punch.

(*Aside.*) Fires in Hades! It is Old Nick himself!

Devil.

You have escaped from the others, but you will not escape from me. The Devil is the last fear of man.

Punch.

Escape? Oh, yes I can! I've fought the fetters of the family, the shames of society. I've cheated death himself. Now I'll fight for my life hereafter. Prepare!

(*Holds up stick.*)

Devil.

(*Holds up bright red slapstick or red pitchfork.*) Beware! This is the end of your story, Mr. Punch. There will be no more to tell. I will win. And you will go to—

(*Suddenly there are loud claps of thunder. The stage glows with red light. Smoke and lightning effects may be used. Fight music begins. Cue 42.* PUNCH *and the* DEVIL *start their famous fight, which is fast, frantic, and comic. The* DEVIL *laughs when he is winning.* PUNCH *"Rootle-dee-tootle-dee-toots" when he is winning. They may run through the audience. Finally* PUNCH *slaps the* DEVIL *down and stand heroically, the winner. All effects and music stop. Lights become bright.*)

Punch.

Hooray! The Devil is dead! Take him away!

(*Two* GHOSTS *float in L, pick up* DEVIL *under the arms and pull him, feet dragging, off L, as* PUNCH *speaks.*)

Mr. Punch has won the fights, the strife, that every man meets in his life! (*Sings. Cue 43.*)

> Mr. Punch is a jolly good fellow,
> His coat is always scarlet and yellow.
> Mr. Punch is the man, certainly,
> That every man wants to be.

(TOBY *runs in and barks.*)

This is the end of our merry little play. We'll see you again when we come this way.

(*Music. Cue 44. He holds out his hand for* JUDY *who enters R. They sing.*)

Punch and Judy.

> There will always be a Punch and Judy,
> Always be . . . It's true.

Punch.

> 'Cause there's a little bit of Punch,
> A little of me, in everyone of you.

Punch and Judy.

> There will always be a Punch and Judy,
> Always be . . . it's true,

Judy.

> 'Cause there's a little Judy,
> A little of me, in everyone of you.

Punch and Judy.

> Oh, fight for what you really do believe in,
> If it's true . . . always do,

Punch.

> 'Cause there's a little bit of Punch—

Judy.

> And Judy—

(TOBY *barks, "And me!" Music and singing sudden-ly stop. Pause. Then music starts again. The three back up to puppet theater, singing softly.*)

> There will always be a Punch and Judy,
> Always be . . . it's true.
> 'Cause there's a little bit of us
> A little of us, in everyone of you.

(PUNCH *exits behind puppet theater, then* JUDY. TOBY *barks and waves to audience, then exits behind puppet theater. Lights dim slowly. Immediately the hand puppet of* PUNCH *pops up in front of the little curtain of the puppet stage.*)

Punch.
(*Sings.*)
> Oh, there will always be a Punch and Judy,
> Always be . . . I hope . . . I hope . . .

Judy says—

Judy.
(*Hand puppet of* JUDY *pops up.*) Good-by.

(*Throws kisses and disappears.*)

Punch.
Toby says—
(*Hand puppet of* TOBY *pops up and waves while* TOBY *barks loudly. Puppet disappears.*)

And Mr. Punch says—good-by, good-by, good-by.

(*He waves. Music continues. He disappears, but immediately reappears.*)

Rootle-dee-tootle-dee-toot!

(*Puppet waves and disappears. The puppet theater stands as it was at the beginning of the play, deserted in a pool of soft light and the music lingers, as the main* CURTAIN *closes.*)

The Marvelous Adventures of Tyl

A Commedia for Children

by Jonathan Levy

PREFACE

I began writing children's plays several years ago as a lark, for friends who had a cast of children and no script. I found, much to my surprise, that I enjoyed it. I enjoyed the purity of the actors and the freshness of the audience. So, when that first production was over, I continued writing plays for children. And I have found myself apologizing ever since.

Most children's theater in this country needs apologizing for. It is a closed shop that produces a shoddy article, to wit: pedestrian scripts, mounted in productions that (like the sisters in *Decline and Fall*) are either Flossie or Dingy—either show-biz musicals on the boyhood of James Knox Polk, or *The Shoestring Players* doing Goldilocks in sheets; directed with the heaviest of stock hands; and acted in a nineteenth-century "indicating" style that no longer gets by even in opera.

It is no mystery why the shop is closed: no one with an alternative wants in. For who would voluntarily enter a profession in which there is no money, prestige, or security?

Actors go into children's theater as a stopgap or a stepping-stone, not as a career. Directors—with a few saintly exceptions—do the same. And ultimately even the saints run down, wear out, or give up. No one can —or should be asked to—run forever on his own steam.

Worst of all, perhaps, is the scarcity of playwrights. Professional writers either write *adult* plays, with which there is a chance of recognition or money; or children's *books*, which is a steady and honorable profession.

The dilemma is depressingly circular: no one wants to

write for a marginal, lackluster theater; and a theater without an influx of good new plays is bound to stay marginal, and lose whatever luster it has.

The situation is bad and can only get worse if we unthinkingly continue doing what we are doing: patching instead of rebuilding. The time has come, I think, to pause and collectively rethink our premises. As a first step, this means coldly and critically sifting through the mass of received clichés that clutter the art.

For, although no branch of our theater is in worse shape than our children's theater, no branch is more enamored of—and shackled by—its clichés: clichés of subject matter, of length, of acting style, of everything that matters. It is as if we hoped the accumulation of deadwood we have inherited would somehow magically transform itself into a Living Tradition.

For we have not inherited a strong, native tradition of children's theater in America. Yet we hesitate to innovate or borrow inventively. And so we neither grow nor change.

We must reconsider what children's theater is and is not; what best nourishes it; and what it optimally could be.

Children's theater is not adult theater simplified and coarsened. It has its own ends, effects, and conditions. It is a difficult and specialized art, whose practitioners must be specially trained for it. It cannot live on cast-offs from the adult theater, as it is generally forced to do in America.

Nor can it live by endless self-imitation; and could not even if the original models were of Shakespearean excellence.

Moreover, it cannot flourish if it is expected to be self-supporting. Children should no more be expected to pay for their theater than they should be expected to pay for their education. As it stands now, it is usually the actors—unpaid or poorly paid—who subsidize children's theater. This is not only grossly unfair, it is also the best way to make sure that children's theater remains the province of beginners and amateurs. Not that there is anything wrong with either beginners or amateurs. They are necessary but not sufficient.

If our children's parks were as bad as our children's theaters, parents and teachers would be shouting in the streets, and congressmen would be falling over one another introducing recreation bills. But no one is shouting—or even grumbling audibly—about the state of our children's theaters; and I suppose that is because few adults know enough of the possibility of the art to feel deprived, or sense what their children are missing. When most Americans think of children's theater, they remember the tatty Cinderellas they were brought up on—though they often forget the deep impression even these tawdry shadows made on them—and see no need for perpetuating more of the same. And they are right.

But children's theater does not have to be like that. The clichés we have inherited are not laws of nature. They can be changed. Children's theater can be—and at its best is—as quirky, subtle, funny, serious, various, and playful as children are themselves.

JONATHAN LEVY

Style:

The style of *Tyl* is essentially that of the commedia dell'arte. However, it is in the early, rough tradition of the commedia—wolf skins and cloven hooves, not dominos and small feet. Particular care should be taken with the movement in the production—the mime, dance, and transformations. It should be muscular and acrobatic, not pretty. This is a very physical play.

Sets:

The set for *Tyl* should be colorful, sturdy, and portable. The play was designed to tour. Consequently, the fewer elements the set contains the better. One possibility: a single-colored, light backdrop with movable geometrical forms—perhaps in Mondrian colors—in front of it. These forms, alone and combined, should be used over and over during the course of the play. For example, one form might serve as a school desk, a butcher's table, and an executioner's block. Another might serve as a doorway, a mirror frame, or—turned on its side—a shopwindow. Each side of the forms might be painted a different color, like children's blocks. One side might be painted black, one side blue, one side white, etc.; so that the mood and decor of a scene could be established merely by turning the forms either 45 or 90 degrees.

Costumes:

Everyone in the cast changes his costume. Everyone except Tyl (and perhaps the actress who plays Suzanne, Sarah, and Serafina) changes his character several times. Tyl changes his age, without props. All character changes should be accomplished with as little external help as possible—a hat, a stick, a stoop, a different voice should be enough.

The strong costumes (the Rich Man's, the Doctors', etc.) should be simple and vivid, like the king in a pack of cards. Perhaps the simplest way to effect the costume changes is for the cast to wear tights or leotards over which they can slip serapelike garments.

Note: All the unenlightened characters in the play—the

256

Grandmother, the Teacher, the Doctors, etc.—wear half-masks on the top half of their faces. These masks are fitted with large eyeglasses.

Music:

The music for the play should be original and taped, unless the cast can make all the music itself. Where indicated, the cast *must* make its own music. If any member of the cast can play an instrument—especially guitar—he should be encouraged to do so.

Text:

As in any commedia script, the director should tailor the text judiciously to match the particular talents of his company. This is especially true of the role of Tyl.

Cast:

The cast is composed of seven actors, four men and three women. They divide all the roles in the play among themselves.

For the director's convenience, the scenes have been numbered. However, the action of the play should be fluid and continuous.

CHARACTERS

Tyl
Father
Mother
Grandmother
Cousin Suzanne
Teacher
Sarah
Butcher
Rich Man
Serafina
Old Margaret
Executioner
Doctors, Soldiers, a Juggler, an Acrobat,
a Calf, a Lamb, Students, Two Old Women
Dietrich, a cut-out figure

OVERTURE

The overture begins with the house lights on. About halfway through it, they fade.

1

The birth of TYL.

FATHER, MOTHER, DOCTOR, GRANDMOTHER. *Then* TYL. *Then* COUSIN SUZANNE *and a* DOG.

The MOTHER *is in bed, profile to the audience. She is covered with a sheet that masks the bed's legs. There is an exaggerated semicircular bulge over her belly. The* FATHER, GRANDMOTHER, *and* DOCTOR *stand around the bed.*

The music dwindles into a single drum.

Mother.
(*In time to the drum.*)
        Oh. Oh. Oh my. Oh.
        Oh goodness, Martin, I . . . OH.
        I do think he . . .
Father.
. . . he's just . . .
Grandmother.
. . . just about to . . .
Father and Grandmother.
. . . to be . . .
Mother.
. . . OH!

Doctor.
BORN!
(*Big drum beat.*

The sound of a baby crying. All stand back. TYL, *crying, emerges from under the sheet. A baby's dress is attached to his neck so that all the audience sees of the actor playing* TYL *is his head and his hands. As* TYL *emerges, the bulge subsides.*

TYL *continues to cry. He looks around the room from one face to another. His crying turns to laughter. A puzzled reaction from all.*)

Grandmother.
(*Peering closely.*) They're not supposed to laugh. They're supposed to cry.

(TYL *points at her and laughs more.*)

Grandmother.
Well, really.

Doctor.
Stand back.

(*They do. He grabs* TYL *and examines him like a specimen.*)

Doctor.
What a curious child.
Very fat and very fair.
With a full set of teeth
And a full head of hair.
Broad of back and long of limb.

(TYL *being held too tightly, makes gasping noises.*)

Doctor.
I'll just pound a little life into him.

(*The* DOCTOR *holds* TYL *up and pounds him as if on the backside.* TYL *howls in surprise, then pain. He turns and bites the* DOCTOR's *hand.*)

Doctor.
OW. He bit me!

(TYL *laughs.*)

Father.

> Louder . . . and louder . . . and louder.
> How could any father be prouder?
> What shall we name him? Walter? Will?

(TYL *shakes his head "no" after each name.*)

Mother.

Timothy? Thomas?

(TYL *shakes his head "no."*)

Grandmother.

Terence?

(TYL *shakes his head vigorously "no."*)

Father.

Tyl.

(TYL *shakes his head "yes" and points at himself.*)

All.

Tyl.

Tyl.

(*Aside.*) Tyl.

Mother.

Come to your mother, Tyl. (*She takes him. He gurgles in her arms.*) Such a sweet face.

Grandmother.

(*Hovering.*) Look at me, Tyl. I'm your grandma.

(TYL *growls.*)

Father.

Such intelligent eyes.

(TYL *gurgles happily.*)

Grandmother.

Here, Tyl. Come kiss grandma.

(TYL *growls.*)

Mother.

Such a nice mouth.

(TYL *sighs and smiles.*)

Grandmother.
I'm your *grandma. Kiss* grandma.

(*She leans between* FATHER *and* MOTHER, *holds* TYL's *head, and kisses him loudly.* TYL *howls, turns, and bites her hand. She yelps.*)

OW. He bit his grandma.
Doctor.
He bites everybody.
Tyl.
(*Aside.*) What can I do? I'm too young to explain.
Grandmother.
(*To* MOTHER.) Marjory, I have to tell you something. I'll be a hundred and ten years old in March and I've seen a lot of children in my time. But I have *never* seen a child like this one.
Doctor.
And neither have I.

(*Music.* TYL *comes downstage and eats jam out of a pot with his hands. The* GRANDMOTHER *and* DOCTOR *are shocked.*)

Doctor.
Look at your cousin Dietrich.

(DIETRICH, *a cut-out figure on wheels, is rolled to the middle of the stage. He is hinged at the waist and bows politely.*)

Grandmother.
And look at your cousin Sue.

(SUZANNE, *very ladylike, comes downstage as if on wheels. Music out.*)

Suzanne.
> Little boys make horrid noise
> And get in scrapes and messes.
> Little girls wear cultured pearls
> And long expensive dresses.

(TYL *smears jam on her outstretched hand. She pauses, turns, then smears the jam on his face. He puts both hands in the jam pot and is about to smear her dress when the* GRANDMOTHER *takes her hand and drags her away.*)

Grandmother.
Suzanne! (*The* GRANDMOTHER *slaps her hand. Beat. She turns and slaps* TYL.) Don't lower yourself.

(*Music in.*)

Doctor.
Even the *dog* has manners.

(*A smarmy dog crosses as if on wheels.*)

Grandmother.
And good Lord look at you!

(TYL, *squealing and squalling, collapses into babyhood.*)

Mother.
He's just a baby.

(*The* FATHER *and the* MOTHER *come downstage.* TYL *crawls and acts babyish.*

Note: TYL *telescopes six or seven years of growth into the next scene. Vocally, he goes from baby sounds to syllables to words to sentences. Physically, he goes from babyhood to boyhood.*)

2

TYL *learns to talk.*

TYL, *the* MOTHER, *and the* FATHER.

Tyl.
(*Making baby sounds.*) Ah . . . ah . . . mm . . . aa . . . mm. Mama. Papa. (*He points out.*) People! (*He points up.*) San.

Mother.

Sun, Tyl. That's the *sun.*

Tyl.

San. (*Aside.*) I know it's the *sun.* I just can't say it, yet. (*He puts his hands on the ground.*) Err. Erse.

Father.

Ear*th,* Tyl. The good earth.

Tyl.

Ears-th. (*He begins to eat the earth.*)

Mother.

(*Stopping him.*) Don't eat it, Tyl.

Tyl.

(*Aside.*) If it's good, why can't I eat it?

Mother.

Look, Tyl. Look at the moon.

Tyl.

Moom.

Mother.

Moon, Tyl. Say *moon.*

Tyl.

(*Getting to his knees.*) Moon. The sun and the moon shine on the earth. (*Aside.*) It's getting easier. (*Aloud.*) And on all the earth's people.

(*The* FATHER *and the* MOTHER *exchange a proud look.*)

Father.

That's marvelous, Tyl.

Tyl.

Oh yes. It is. It's . . . marvelous.

(*The sound of bells.*)

Mother.

Tyl, hurry. You'll be late for school.

(*More bells, becoming musical. The* MOTHER *and the* FATHER *prepare* TYL *for school.*)

3

School.

STUDENTS. *Then the* TEACHER. *Then* TYL.

While TYL *is being prepared for school downstage, the scene upstage becomes a schoolroom. Actors straggle in, perhaps muttering sums. Two actors carry in a ladder to which a color wheel is attached.* DIETRICH, *the cut-out figure, is rolled in and seated. All take their places.*

Mother.
Good-bye, Tyl.

(*The* FATHER *and* MOTHER *wave to* TYL, *who waves back, then exits.*

The bells stop. The STUDENTS *turn forward. Enter the* TEACHER—*one actor on another's shoulders. The* TEACHER *wears a long gown and a mortarboard hat. The top actor wears a half-mask. He carries a pointer.*)

Teacher.
Good morning, class.
Class.
Good morning, sir.
Teacher.
Quiet down, now, quiet down. You. Stop that idiotic grinning. This is school and school is serious. Yesterday, you remember, we studied the numbers. To review: how many fingers am I holding up? (*He holds up five.*)
Class.
Three.
Teacher.
Good. And now? (*He holds up eight.*)
Class.
One.
Teacher.
Excellent. You're making progress. Today, class, we will study the colors. You may think that telling one

color from another is a simple matter. Believe me, it
is not.

(*He has turned his back on the class. Enter* TYL
stealthily. He tries to sneak to his seat. The TEACHER
continues without turning around.)

Tyl, you're late.

(*The* TEACHER *turns.*)

How do you expect to learn anything if you don't get
to school on time? Or do you think you know it all
already? Hm?

(*He turns back to the color wheel.*)

We will begin at the begining with the color

(*He turns the wheel to a bright blue.*)

RED. Now red is one of the seven primary colors. You
can always recognize red by . . .

Tyl.
That's *blue*.

Teacher.
Nonsense, Tyl. This is a particularly clear shade of
red. Our second color . . .

Tyl.
It's *blue*.

Teacher.
(*Turning, exasperated.*) I've already told you twice
this color is red. Tyl, why must you be such a trouble-
maker?

Tyl.
But it's *blue*.

Teacher.
Dietrich, is this red?

(DIETRICH *bows "yes."*)

Teacher.
You see? Class, what color is it?

Class.
Blue.

Teacher.

(*Raising stick.*) I'll ask the question again. What color is that, class? RED . . . or blue?

Half-Class.   **Half-Class.**

Blue.   Red.

Teacher.

That's better but not perfect. (*He raises his stick and shakes it.*) Once more. RED . . . or blue?

Class.

(*Except* TYL, *who is silent.*) RED.

(TYL *turns to the audience and pronounces "blue" silently.*)

Girl.

(*Whispering to* TYL.) Stop it. He'll keep us in after school.

Tyl.

(*Looking in the* GIRL's *eyes.*) What lovely red eyes you've got, Sarah. (TYL *makes faces at her until she laughs.*)

Teacher.

Sarah, stop laughing. I'm surprised at you. Tyl, get back to your seat. (*The* TEACHER *turns and faces the* CLASS.) If it's blue you want, class, I'll show you blue. (*He turns the wheel to orange.*) Now that is blue.

Tyl.

(*Aside.*) It's orange.

Teacher.

(*Pointing to purple.*) And that is yellow.

Class.

(*Dully.*) Yellow.

Teacher.

(*Pointing to white.*) And that is green.

Class.

Green.

(TYL *has snuck out of his seat and climbed the ladder so that he is just above the* TEACHER's *head. He lifts the mortarboard as if it is on a hinge. Each time the* TEACHER *names a color,* TYL *lifts out another ob-*

ject, as if from the TEACHER'*s head. The* CLASS'*s
responses turn to laughter and the order of the classroom breaks down—some* STUDENTS *come forward to
pick up the objects* TYL *throws, some cavort, etc.*)

Teacher.
(*Pointing to red.*) And that is black.
Class.
Black.

    (TYL *pulls out a dog-eared book.*)

Teacher.
(*Pointing to black.*) And that is white.
Class.
White.

    (TYL *pulls out an old shoe.*)

Teacher.
I hope I'm not going too fast for you. (*He points to
brown.*) And that is gold.

  (TYL *pulls out a coil of rope with bows tied to it
and a cowbell on the end of it.*)

Teacher.
Say gold, class.

    (*The* CLASS *is now in semi-chaos.*)

Teacher.
And that is . . . that is . . . clearly . . .

  (TYL *roots around in the* TEACHER'*s head as if
scraping an empty pot. Finding nothing, he takes off
the* TEACHER'*s glasses.*)

Teacher.
My glasses! Where are my glasses?
Class.
(*Ad lib.*) Glasses. Where are his glasses. Etc.

  (*The* TEACHER *stumbles around.* TYL *holds the
glasses out. The* TEACHER *makes several grabs for*

*them, then gets them and puts them back on. He is
staring directly at* TYL.)

Teacher.
Tyl! I might have known.

(TYL *jumps down from the ladder. The* TEACHER
chases him, swinging his pointer. TYL *avoids him,
jumping over and under the pointer, then hiding.*)

Teacher.
Where is Tyl?
Class.
(*Ad lib.*) Tyl. Where's Tyl. Etc.
Tyl.
Here I am.

(*The* TEACHER *roars. Music. The chase turns into a
kind of bullfight, the* TEACHER *charging,* TYL *gracefully avoiding him. The* CLASS *becomes spectators and
they react to the action. They get rowdy.*)

Tyl.
No, here. No. Over here.

(*He leaps out the window. The* TEACHER *makes a
last swipe.*)

Teacher.
CLASS. Class, come to order.

(*The* CLASS *quiets down quickly.*)

Teacher.
Get back to your desks.

(*They do, and sit mute and cowed.*)

Teacher.
That's better. Why can't you all be more like Dietrich?

(*Light on* DIETRICH'S *face. Freeze. The light fades
slowly. Reenter* TYL *downstage.*)

4

TYL *gets glasses.*

TYL. *Then the* DOCTOR.

Tyl.

(*To the audience.*) Maybe there's something wrong with me. All I know is, I see what I see.

(*The freeze breaks. All but* TYL *exit.*)

Tyl.

I can't help it. Can I? Well, can I?

(*Enter* DOCTOR.)

Doctor.

Of course you can help it. You're just not trying. (*He looks closely at* TYL.) Just as I thought. You need glasses.

Tyl.

I do?

Doctor.

Everybody needs glasses. Here. Try these. (*He gives a pair of glasses to* TYL, *who puts them on.*) That's better now, isn't it?

(*Awkward music.* TYL *stumbles around the stage.*)

Tyl.

Oh, yes. Much better. I can see perfectly now.

(*The* DOCTOR *saves him from falling off the stage. Music out.*)

Doctor.

What kind of day is it today, Tyl?

Tyl.

It's warm and sunny.

Doctor.

It isn't warm, Tyl. It's freezing cold.

Tyl.

(*Shivering.*) Of course, you're right. It's freezing cold.

Doctor.
And it's raining.

Tyl.
(*Protecting himself from the rain.*) It's raining very hard.

Doctor.
What are you talking about, Tyl? It's not raining. The sun is shining. And it's very hot out.

Tyl.
Of course, of course. That's what I meant.

Doctor.
I think, Tyl, you are ready for the army.

5

The Army

TYL. *The* DOCTOR. *Then a* SERGEANT *and two* SOLDIERS.

Martial music. The SERGEANT *is heard counting cadence off-stage.*

Doctor.
Sergeant. Here's a new recruit for you.

(*Exit the* DOCTOR *with* TYL's *outer cloak.* TYL *is now dressed as a soldier. Enter a* SERGEANT *and two* SOLDIERS, *marching. The* SERGEANT *is counting cadence.*)

Sergeant.
. . .hup two three four, hup two three four—you, there. New man. Fall in line. Hup two three four etc.

(TYL *falls into step. The* SERGEANT *marches the men around the stage and stops down center.*)

Sergeant.
Company, halt.

(*They halt. From here until* TYL *loses his glasses, the* SOLDIERS *execute the* SERGEANT's *orders perfectly.*

The result is a cross between a dance of marionettes and a game of "Simon Says.")

Sergeant.
Company, right face. Left face. About face. Company, eyes right. Eyes left. Eyes front. Eyes up. Eyes down. Company, lean left. Lean right. All fall down.

(TYL's *glasses fall off and slither downstage.* TYL, *on his stomach, grabs for them.*)

Sergeant.
Company, on your feet.

(TYL, *no longer an automaton, is bewildered and looks around. From here on,* TYL *begins to elaborate on each movement to keep himself interested. For example, he does a little hop on "right face," a drag step on "present arms," etc.*)

Sergeant.
Attention. Company, parade rest. Company, attention. Company, present arms. Company, left face. Right face. About face. STOP! You. New man. When I give a command I want it obeyed exactly. No making things up. When I say "right face" I *mean* right face, without a dumb little hop in it . . . like this.

(*He does what* TYL *did.* TYL *then does it again.*)

Sergeant.
And when I say "present arms" I mean present arms, not some skipping nonsense . . . like this.

(*The* SERGEANT *does what* TYL *did.* TYL *does it again.*)

Sergeant.
Right. That's exactly what I don't want you to do.
Tyl.
What about this?

(TYL *does a more elaborate move. The* SERGEANT *does it after him.*)

Sergeant.
That's right. None of that either.

(TYL *does several more moves, more and more elaborate. The* SERGEANT *does each after him.*)

Sergeant.
Or that. Or that. And especially not that.

(*The movement becomes more of a dance step than a military maneuver.* TYL *leads, the* SERGEANT *follows.*
Music. TYL *and the* SERGEANT *do a short circular dance based on the movement. The other two* SOLDIERS *watch, then they dance too, mirroring the* SERGEANT *and* TYL.)

Sergeant.
(*Coming back to himself.*) Stop it! Stop DANCING! You're spoiling my soldiers. Back in line now, all of you.

(*Music out.*)

On the double.

(*They do.*)

Company, attention. Right face.

(*All turn right except* TYL, *who turns left.*)

Forward, march. Hup two three four etc.

(*Exit the* SERGEANT *and* SOLDIERS *to the music they entered to. Reenter the* DOCTOR.)

Doctor.
Here, Tyl. You dropped your glasses.
Tyl.
I don't think I want to wear glasses. They make me feel strange.
Doctor.
You probably just had the wrong kind. Try a new pair. (*He gives him other glasses.*)
Tyl.
(*To audience.*) Should I put them on?

Doctor.

Of course you should. Here. I'll help you.

(*He does. Awkward music.* TYL *focuses, swaying back and forth.*

Enter two OLD WOMEN *with shopping baskets. They walk around* TYL *and talk about him without talking to him. Music out.*)

First Woman.

I call it a disgrace.

Second Woman.

That's just what it is. It's disgraceful.

First Woman.

A boy his age without a job.

Second Woman.

I've worked all my life. I don't see why *he* shouldn't work.

Doctor.

(*As third* OLD WOMAN.) Look at him. My dears, just look at him. Who would hire him?

(*Enter* BUTCHER.)

Butcher.

I'll hire him. I need an apprentice. I'll make a butcher out of him in no time at all.

6

TYL *becomes a butcher.*

TYL. *Then a* BUTCHER. *Then a* CALF *and a* LAMB.

The scene becomes a BUTCHER's *shop. A* BUTCHER's *block with equipment hanging from it—two large knives, a sharpener, a funnel, etc. The* BUTCHER *takes one knife and gives the other one to* TYL.

Butcher.

Here, Tyl. Do what I do and repeat after me.

(*The* BUTCHER *illustrates with large motions of his knife. The result is like air painting.* TYL *imitates him.*)

Butcher.
One slice up and one slice down . . .
Tyl.
One slice up and one slice down . . .
Butcher.
A slit in the gizzard and a slit in the crown . . .
Tyl.
. . . in the gizzard and a slit in the crown . . .
Butcher.
Lop off the head and the tail and the feet . . .
Tyl.
. . . and the tail and the feet . . .
Butcher.
And there is your carcass remarkably neat.
Tyl.
. . . markably neat.
Butcher.
Very good, Tyl.
Tyl.
Very good, Tyl.
Butcher.
I have to leave the shop for a while, Tyl. You're in charge while I'm gone. Here. Tie on the apron.

(*He takes off his apron and gives it to* TYL. TYL *puts it on. The* BUTCHER *puts on a hat.*)

Butcher.
There's nothing much for you to do while I'm away.

(*He leads out a* LAMB *and a* CALF, *bleating and mooing.*)

Butcher.
Just slaughter these two and cut them up the way I showed you. The mayor eats steak

(*The* CALF *moos.*)

and his wife eats lamb chops.

(*The* LAMB *baas.*)

Remember, now. Just the way I showed you.

(*Exit* BUTCHER.
TYL, *whistling, sharpens his knife and tests its sharpness. The* CALF *and the* LAMB *moo and baa with increasing apprehension. Their noises become—*)

Calf.

Moo. Mooo-cy.

Lamb.

Baaa. Baaa-ee . . .

Calf.

. . . mooo-ciful.

Tyl.

(*Repeating his lesson with gestures.*) One slice up and one slice down . . .

(*The* LAMB *and the* CALF *baa and moo, scurrying around.* TYL *chases them shouting angrily.*)

Come on, now, you. Hold still.

(*He catches the* LAMB.)

Got you.

(*He drags the* LAMB, *baaing pitifully, to the block. He raises his knife.*)

One . . . two . . . thr . . .

(*The* CALF *leaps at him and knocks off his glasses.*)

MY GLASSES. Where are my glasses?

(*He looks around. The* LAMB *tries to escape.* TYL *stops her.*)

No you don't. I've still got my knife.

(*He raises it.*)

One . . . two . . . three.

(*Now looking the* LAMB *in the eye, lowers the knife slowly.*)

But you . . . you're . . .

Calf.

(*Extending his hoof.*) I'm Moo-rice.

Lamb.

And I'm Baaa-bara.

(*The* CALF *cries.*)

Tyl.

Moorice, you're crying.

Calf.

I was sooo frightened.

Lamb.

He's very sensitive. He's artistic. He paints.

Calf.

I paint moo-rals and make moo-saics.

Lamb.

He sings, too. He's a baa-ritone.

Tyl.

Sing us something, Moorice.

Lamb.

Yes, do. It will cheer us up.

Calf.

(*Shyly.*) What shall I sing.

Lamb.

Sing "Moorish Moon."

Calf.

"Mooo-rish Mooon?" That's a very hard song. You'll have to help me. (*He vocalizes. Music.*)

(*Note: This song should be slow, and sound like a cow mooing. The words are not important. The song should be slow in tempo. The* BUTCHER'*s song, which interrupts it antiphonally should be quite fast.*)

Calf.

(*Sings.*)

> That mooney June we used to croon
> This moody tune on the lagoon,
> To a bassoon.
>> Oh Moorish Moon, Oh Moorish Moon,
>> You look like a maroon balloon.

I wish I had a big harpoon
To move you with, Oh Moorish Moon.

(*In the middle of the chorus, the* BUTCHER *is heard singing offstage.*)

Butcher.
(*Offstage.*)
Ham chops, lamb chops, ribs and roast,
Smidgens of pigeons served up on toast.

Tyl.
Shh. (*He listens. The voice gets closer.*) He's back. Run.

(*The animals scurry around.*)

Tyl.
Hide. *Hurry.*

(*After some confusion, the animals hide. The* BUTCHER'*s singing has gotten louder. Just as the animals are out of sight, the* BUTCHER *enters.*)

Butcher.
(*Singing.*)
Saddle a veal and a nice jellied eel,
Make a magnif, a magnificent meal.
Where are those carcasses? I can't wait to get to work. Where's my knife?

(TYL *gives it to him.*)

Butcher.
Ah. (*He waves it in the air.*) Help me on with my apron. And then . . .

(*The* BUTCHER *performs an operation on the air.* TYL, *avoiding the swipes of the knife, helps him on with the apron, succeeding in tying his hands behind his back in the process.*)

Butcher.
One slice up and one slice down . . .

Tyl.
Just slip this over your head. There.

Butcher.
A slit in the gizzard and a slit in the crown . . .

Tyl.
Put your arm through here. That's right. And the other one through here. I'll hold the knife.

Butcher.
Lop off the head and the tail and the feet . . . (*He is tied up now. He struggles.*) I can't move! What have you done to me?

Tyl.
(*Cutting near the* BUTCHER.) One slice up and one slice down . . .

Butcher.
Don't do that. It's dangerous.

(*The* LAMB *and the* CALF *emerge.*)

Calf.
You're telling us it's dangerous.

Butcher.
THEY'RE STILL ALIVE! Get out of my shop.

(*The* LAMB *and the* CALF *play near the* BUTCHER, *mocking him.*)

Butcher.
Not you. *Him.*

(*Exit the* LAMB *and the* CALF *joyfully.*)

Butcher.
(*Struggling, to* TYL.) Out. Get out.

(TYL *takes the funnel off the block and blows it at the* BUTCHER. *It makes a noise like a noisemaker.*)

Butcher.
Right this minute.

(TYL *blows the funnel again.*)

Butcher.
And don't you ever dare come back.

(TYL *blows again.*)

Butcher.

You have no head for business!

(*The* BUTCHER *struggles, then freezes.* TYL *comes downstage making tentative sounds on the funnel. Enter the* DOCTOR.)

Doctor.

Tyl, you're very careless. You've lost your glasses again. Luckily I've got another pair in my pocket. (*He reaches into his pocket.*)

Tyl.

No thank you.

Doctor.

But you have to wear glasses.

Tyl.

Why?

Doctor.

Because everybody wears glasses. *I* wear glasses.

(DIETRICH, *the cut-out figure, is pushed on.*)

Doctor.

Your cousin Dietrich wears glasses. Don't you want to be like Dietrich?

Tyl.

No. (*He shoves* DIETRICH *who folds in half.*)

Doctor.

Don't you want to be like *me*?

Tyl.

NO.

Doctor.

NO!?

Tyl.

NO! I want to be like *me*. Now why don't you just go away and let me play my trumpet.

Doctor.

(*Angry.*) What trumpet?

Tyl.

This trumpet.

(*He elongates the funnel which becomes a heraldic trumpet. He blows on it. It makes a lovely sound. The*

DOCTOR *freezes in a pose of consternation.* TYL *plays a little more. Exit the* BUTCHER *and the* DOCTOR.)

7

The Orchestra.

TYL. *Then most of the company.*

TYL *plays, walking around the stage. He plays behind pieces of scenery, into the wings, etc. calling a band of* MUSICIANS *up one by one. The entire company joins him, except for the actor who will play the* RICH MAN *and the actress who will play* SERAFINA. *Each actor plays a different instrument. They walk around as a band, if possible through the audience.*

8

The RICH MAN.

TYL. MUSICIANS. *A* RICH MAN.

Enter a RICH MAN *crying. He is dressed entirely in gold. The* ORCHESTRA *stops playing, raggedly. The* RICH MAN *cries louder. The* ORCHESTRA *feels sorry for him and tries to make him laugh—they make faces, play funny music, etc.—but the* RICH MAN *only cries louder. At last he raises his hand and stops the* ORCHESTRA.

Rich Man.
My friends, thank you for your kindness. I am touched by it and feel I owe you the courtesy of explaining to you why all your well-meant antics have failed to bring even the faintest smile to these old lips.

(*Music, not from the* ORCHESTRA.)

In there, in that sad room

(Two of the company raise a sheet between them, thereby creating a room.)

lies my only daughter, Serafina, sick unto death and worsening. Hour by hour she grows weaker, despite the constant attention of the two famous doctors I have brought here from the ends of the earth. But, alas, all their remedies have failed. As you may have guessed, I am not a poor man.

(He takes a bag of gold from his belt and jangles it. All react, especially TYL.*)*

If some new doctor were to appear with fresh ideas—not some adventurer, not some charlatan, but a real physician—and if by some miracle he were able to cure my dear Serafina, no reward

(He jangles the bag again. A second, larger reaction. Exit TYL.*)*

no reward at all would be too great for him. But if such a physician is to come in time, he must come soon.

(Enter TYL *as a doctor.)*

Tyl.
(Muttering.) Tibula fibula. Gluteus maximus. Etc.

*(*TYL *does some doctor business.)*

Rich Man.
Oh, what a marvel. My prayers are answered.
Tyl.
(Muttering.) Gobble gobble.
Rich Man.
A new physician. *(He examines* TYL *closely.)* Obviously a very deep thinker. But he's so young.
Tyl.
(Aside.) Young?

*(*TYL, *not pausing in his gibberish, becomes old—old voice, old posture, old mannerisms, etc.)*

Rich Man.

(*Staring, puzzled.*) Not as young as I thought.

(TYL *exaggerates.*)

In fact, he's ancient. Still, I'm sorry to see he's so thin.
I only employ fat doctors, because I believe only those
who are sleek and stout themselves can restore others
to a state of sleekness and stoutness.

Tyl.

(*Aside.*) Too thin? (TYL, *not pausing in his gibberish,
becomes fat—fat face, puffed-out robes, etc.*)

Rich Man.

(*More puzzled.*) Not thin either.

(TYL *exaggerates.*)

In fact, he's *huge*. Still and all, I could never think
of employing a doctor—even a fat, elderly doctor—
who had no apprentice. I can't believe a doctor without an apprentice can be truly first-rate.

(TYL *continues his gibberish, miming puzzlement:
how to get out of this? He mouths the word "apprentice." Then inspiration.* TYL, *still speaking, becomes
two people—the fat doctor behind his cloak [bass
voice, etc.] and a thin, small apprentice by his side
[high voice, etc.]*)

Rich Man.

He has an apprentice! I am satisfied. (TYL, *with a sigh
of relief, stops being the apprentice.* RICH MAN *to the*
SERVANTS.) You, there. Let this physician into my
daughter's room. At once. There's no time to lose.

(*The* SERVANTS *remove the sheet, discovering* SERA-
FINA *lying on a cot and two* FAT DOCTORS *pacing
around her. They stop, then pace in the opposite direction.* TYL *and the* RICH MAN *stand apart and watch.*)

9

The Sick Room.

Two DOCTORS *and* SERAFINA. *Then* TYL *and the* RICH MAN.

Doctor One.
More air.

(*He goes to the window and opens it wide.* DOCTOR TWO *runs to the window.*)

Doctor Two.
No air! She'll freeze to death.
Doctor One.
She'll suffocate if she doesn't get air, fool.

(*The two* DOCTORS *struggle with the window.*)

Doctor Two.
Who are you calling fool, fool?
Doctor One.
I'm calling *you* fool, fool.

(*They struggle noisily with the window, then realize they are being watched and stop abruptly.*)

Doctor Two.
Time to flip her.

(*He goes to the cot and takes the* GIRL's *arms.*)

Doctor One.
No flipping!

(DOCTOR TWO *turns the* GIRL *roughly half over. The* GIRL *groans. He then goes to her feet and grasps them.* DOCTOR ONE *goes to the head of the cot and grasps her arms. He turns her back the way she was as* DOCTOR TWO *turns her legs in the opposite direction. The* GIRL *groans louder.*)

Rich Man.
How is she, Doctors?

(*The* DOCTORS *shake their heads.*)

Doctor Two.
She's a very sick girl.

(*He pulls one of her arms. She groans.*)

See? We've tried everything. Hot baths . . .
Doctor One.
. . . cold compresses . . .
Doctor Two.
. . . stuffing her . . .
Doctor One.
. . . starving her . . .
Doctor Two.
. . . and pounding her with rubber hammers.
Doctor One.
Nothing works.
Doctor Two.
She's doomed.
Tyl.
(*Aside.*) No wonder she's sick.

(*He goes to the* GIRL, *looks at her, then kisses her on the forehead. The* GIRL *looks up at him.*)

Tyl.
No fever.

(*He and the* GIRL *look at each other. He smiles. Music. She smiles back.* TYL *convinces her in pantomime to play along with him. She understands, agrees, and lies back down. Music out. He then speaks to the* RICH MAN, *but loud enough for all to hear.*)

Tyl.
Who are these quacks?
Doctors One and Two.
(*Ducklike.*) Quacks? Quacks?
Tyl.
Yes, *quacks.* (*To the* RICH MAN.) I have magic eyes.
I can spot *quacks* in a minute.

(*The* DOCTORS *splutter.*)

Rich Man.

(*To* TYL.) Really, Doctor. That's very strong.

Tyl.

Strong? It's not strong enough. Watch. I'll test them. (*To* DOCTOR ONE.) You. How many hairs are there on a normal adult human head?

Doctor One.

Don't be preposterous. Nobody knows that.

Tyl.

Wrong. Everybody knows that.

Doctor One.

All right then, you, whoever you are. Tell me. How many hairs *are* there on a normal adult human head?

Tyl.

Five hundred fifty-five thousand five hundred and five.

Doctor One.

That's ridiculous. Prove you're right.

Tyl.

Prove I'm wrong. (*He turns quickly to* DOCTOR TWO.) And you. If you're such a marvelous doctor, let's see you do this. (*He does a somersault.*)

Doctor Two.

I don't see what that's got to do with anything.

Tyl.

You don't, do you? (*To the* RICH MAN.) All we real doctors learn to do that in our first week of school.

Doctor Two.

That's not true.

Tyl.

Of course it's true. (*He does a double somersault.*)

Doctor Two.

Get out of my way.

(*After many preparations and false starts, he tries to do a somersault and ends up flat on his back, stuck like a turtle.*)

Doctor Two.

Help me. Help me up.

Tyl.

(*To* DOCTOR ONE.) Well? You heard him. Help him up.

(DOCTOR ONE *goes to* DOCTOR TWO, *takes his hands, and tries to lift him up. They rock for a while, then both go over. They flap their arms and grunt.*)

Tyl.

Now it's my turn. Doctor Tyl. (*To the grunting* DOCTORS.) I need absolute quiet.

Rich Man.

(*To* DOCTORS.) Shh.

(*Silence.* TYL *dances backward and forward, making occult motions over the* GIRL.)

Doctor One.

What kind of a cure do you call that?

Tyl.

(*Dancing.*) That is called the dance cure, quack.

(*Music.*)

Rich Man.

Look. It's working.

(*The* GIRL *rises, slowly at first, then more quickly.* TYL *takes her hands and they dance together. Then she sings in a light voice.*)

Serafina.

(*Singing.*)

> The stag in the meadow,
> The doe and the deer,
> The birds in the forest
> Enrapture my ear.
> La la la la la, etc.

(*She dances around the room, delicately, like a figure on a music box. While she dances, the* RICH MAN *embraces* TYL.)

Rich Man.

Oh, my dear sir. Oh, my dear Doctor. She's well! Look how happy she is. How can I ever thank you?

Tyl.
Well, there's the money you promised . . .

(TYL *points at the moneybag. The* RICH MAN *moves it out of his grasp.*)

Rich Man.
No amount of silver, no amount of gold can ever repay you for the miracle you have worked.

Tyl.
Just give me my money.

(*He grabs at the bag again. Again the* RICH MAN *moves it out of his grasp.*)

Rich Man.
A miracle is what I called it and a miracle is what it is. Picture this. Serafina at death's door. No one can save her. Enter Doctor Tyl. Arise, says Tyl, and arise she does. Truly a miracle.

(TYL *has punctuated this speech by grabbing at the moneybag. Each time the* RICH MAN *has moved it just out of his grasp. The two* DOCTORS *on their hands and knees have been following this exchange like a tennis match.*)

Tyl.
Oh well. God helps those who help themselves. (*With a series of handclaps and fingersnaps he dazzles the* RICH MAN *and takes the money. To* SERAFINA.) Come on.

Rich Man.
He took my money. Stop him.

Doctors One and Two.
(*Still seated.*) STOP.

10

First Chase.

TYL, SERAFINA *and the* RICH MAN. *Then the company.*

Music. The RICH MAN *pursues* TYL *and* SERAFINA *all over the stage and, if possible, out through the audience. When he is just about to catch them, they turn into things—people, animals, features in the landscape. The fun of this scene is in the ingenious and incongruous things they become. For example, they could become a workman and his wheelbarrow, an organ-grinder and his monkey, a mother and her baby, part of a flock of sheep, or figures on a large clock. The transformations should be made quickly and fluidly, as if at the inspiration of the moment. During the chase, the* RICH MAN *might ask members of the audience if they'd seen his daughter,* SERAFINA *might ask if they'd seen her father.* TYL *and* SERAFINA *might even briefly become members of the audience. Each time the* RICH MAN *is foiled, he becomes more enraged. The music comes in and out.*

11

The Fair.

A JUGGLER, *an* ACROBAT, *and a* GIRL. *Then* SERAFINA, *the* RICH MAN, *and* TYL. *Then* DOCTORS ONE *and* TWO. *Then old* MARGARET.

Fair Music. A JUGGLER *crosses, juggling. Then an* ACROBAT *crosses doing flips. Enter a* YOUNG GIRL.

Girl.
A fair! Look. It's a fair.

(*The scene becomes a fair.* TYL *and* SERAFINA *set up as a sideshow. Their prop is a large mirror. The sides of the mirror must be wide enough to cover* SERAFINA's *changes. The props for her changes are preset behind the mirror's sides. Enter the* RICH MAN *at a run. He is bewildered at first, then becomes interested in the show. The* ACROBAT *and* JUGGLER *are off by now.*)

Serafina.

> (*As a barker.*) Hurry hurry hurry. Come one, come all, come great, come small, come rich and mighty, come poor and humble. Gather round, good people, and see nature's most marvelous prodigy, her most wonderful and strange creation, the magical, prophetic, all-seeing and all-knowing PROFESSOR TYL and his marvelous mirrors.
>
> (*Enter* TYL. *He is dressed fantastically, with mirrors on his hands, clothes, and eyes. He flashes patterns.*)
>
> Here he is. Need I say more? Step up, step up. See into your deepest character, learn the real truth about yourselves in Professor Tyl's miraculous mirror.
>
> (*If possible, the mirror glows or lights up.*)

Tyl.

> (*As if possessed, working his mirrors.*) Oooh. Ahh. Saturn in the House of the Moon. Taurus in Aries. Ascending. Ascending. Descending. I see many mansions.

Serafina.

> Who will be first? The fee is just one penny. And if the learned Professor fails to see into the deepest part of your heart, he will give you this bag of gold. (*She shakes the bag of gold.*)
>
> (*Music out.*)
>
> Who will be first? You, madam?

Margaret.

> Me? No, not me. No, really. (*She is encouraged by the others.*) All right.
>
> (SERAFINA *goes behind one of the sides of the mirror and emerges as* MARGARET's *mirror image. Enter the* DOCTORS.)

Rich Man.

> This is most amusing.

Doctors One and Two.

> It is. *Most* amusing.

Tyl.

(*Working his mirrors.*) Speak, Mirror, speak. And show this woman her true self.

(TYL *turns away, then speaks as* MARGARET. SERAFINA *mimes as he speaks.*)

Tyl.

I am old Margaret, the maid.
Oh, that's the part I've always played.
For thirty years I've scrubbed your floors
And opened other people's doors,
Made their beds and cut their wood,
Washed their clothes and cooked their food.
And yet you know inside of me . . .

Margaret.

(*Joining* TYL.)

Is a song bird longing to be free.
Free to sleep and take its ease

(TYL *drops out.* MARGARET *is now speaking alone.*)

And do precisely as I please.
If one day you ring and I do not come,
You'll know that Margaret has flown home.

(MARGARET *is abashed and confused to find she is speaking alone. She reaches into her pocketbook.*)

Serafina.

(*Reappearing.*) The Professor refuses his fee in this case.

(MARGARET *goes back to the others.* SERAFINA *shakes the moneybag.*)

All right, then, who's next?

Doctor One and Doctor Two.

(*Eagerly.*) We're next.

(*They jump in front of the mirror.*)

Tyl.

Speak once again, please, Mirror. Speak the truth to these two gentlemen.

Doctor One and Doctor Two.
> We're not gentlemen. We're DOCTORS.

> (TYL *and* SERAFINA *appear dressed outlandishly as doctors. They speak and move like puppets.*)

Tyl.
> Say "Ahh."

Serafina.
> Ahh. Say "Ahh."

Tyl.
> Ahh.

> (*They hold each other's mouths open and say* "Ahh.")

Serafina.
> I'm sorry to say you're a very sick man. Look at your tongue. It's got blue spots all over it.

Tyl.
> That's not my tongue. That's my *tie.*

> (*He hits her à la Punch.*)

Serafina.
> OW.

Tyl.
> Here. Let me take your pulse. (*He puts his hand on her wrist.*) Tick tick tick tick tick. *You're* the sick one. Your pulse is racing. Tick tick tick tick . . .

Serafina.
> That's not my pulse, stupid. That's my *watch.*

> (*She hits him à la Judy.*)

Tyl.
> OW.

> (*He hits her back. They fight, à la Punch and Judy. The others laugh and applaud.*)

Doctor One.
> Very amusing.

Doctor Two.
> Very inventive.

Doctor One.
Who are they supposed to be?
All.
You!
Doctor One.
Me?
Doctor One and Doctor Two.
US?

(*They roar and start for* TYL. *The* RICH MAN *restrains them.*)

Tyl.
Yes, *you.* Now pay your fee.
Rich Man.
Go ahead. Pay him. I haven't laughed so much in years.

(*The* DOCTORS *pay, grumbling.*)

Serafina.
(*To the* RICH MAN.) Now, sir, what about you?
Rich Man.
ME? No. I don't want to. (*She jangles the bag of money.*) Where do I stand?
Tyl.
Oh, Mirror, speak one last time. And, dear Mirror, be exact.

(SERAFINA *appears in gold clothes.* TYL *imitates the* RICH MAN's *voice.*)

Tyl.
I am rich and marvelous to behold.
You see that I am covered head to foot in gold.
I love my golden shoes, I love my golden dress.
I love my daughter just a little less.
Gold is my darling, gold is my delight.
I count it all day long and sleep on it at night.
I love to hear it clink, and see it shine,
And roll in it, like all the other swine.

(SERAFINA *rolls.* TYL *makes pig noises.*)

Rich Man.
It's not true. You all know me. I'm not like that at all.

(*The others are silent. They turn away. The* RICH MAN *stares at* SERAFINA. *Furious.*)

Why . . . that's my daughter. And that's my *money.*

(*He steps through the mirror frame, grabs his bag of money, and pulls off her disguise. He roars.*)

Doctor One and Doctor Two.
(*Of* TYL.) And he's the "doctor."

12

The Second Chase.

TYL, SERAFINA, *the* RICH MAN, *and the company.*

Rich Man.
Stop thief. Help. Somebody. Anybody.

(*The* RICH MAN *chases* TYL. *During the chase he is joined by the company, one by one. This chase is in dead earnest. It must be differentiated from the first chase, which was light and antic.* TYL *is as agile as ever, but he is feverish. The pursuers chase him with outstretched arms, closing him in. Silence. The only sounds are of hard breathing—mostly* TYL'*s—and feet on the floor.* TYL *avoids his pursuers several times, then is caught.*)

Rich Man.
Ahh.

(*Two of the company hold* TYL'*s arms behind his back. Slow, muffled drums. Enter a hooded* EXECU-TIONER, *carrying an axe.*)

13

The Execution.

TYL, SERAFINA, *the* RICH MAN, *the* EXECUTIONER, *and the company.*

A mournful procession develops, TYL, *under guard, followed by the others. The drum roll gets faster.* TYL, *his hands behind him, is forced to lay his head on a block. The crowd closes around him. The axe is raised and poised.* SERAFINA's *anguish. A long beat.* TYL *crawls through the legs of one of the crowd and crawls downstage. He has taken off his outer garment. He indicates that the audience should be quiet and then exits. The axe falls. The drum stops. Weeping and sobbing.*

14

Keening Scene.

The RICH MAN, SERAFINA, *and the company. Then* TYL.

The crowd breaks. TYL's *outer garment is suspended on a stick, like a headless scarecrow, in the center of the stage.*

First Woman.
He was wild but he wasn't bad. I liked him.
First Man.
At least he was honest. He said what he thought.
Second Man.
Can't be too honest in this world and live to be old.
Second Woman.
That's God's truth.
Serafina.
What will I do without him?

Rich Man.

(*Sobbing.*) He was right about me. I can't deny it
anymore. I'm a terrible man.

(*Louder general weeping. Enter* TYL, *disguised as
an old woman, crying louder than anybody.*)

Tyl.

(*Sobbing.*) He was so gentle, so good. And so young.
He never harmed a soul in his life.

All.

No. That's right. He never harmed a soul. Etc.

Tyl.

(*Sobbing more heavily.*) All he ever asked was a little
kindness. And what did he get? (*He imitates the sound
of the axe.*)

Rich Man.

It's true.

All.

(*Sobbing more heavily.*) How terrible. How awful.
Etc.

Tyl.

Oh, if only he were alive. There's nothing I wouldn't
do for him. Nothing I wouldn't gladly give him.

Rich Man.

Anything. Anything at all.

(*All weep more loudly.*)

Tyl.

(*With an eye on the* RICH MAN.) If only it would bring
him back, I would give him . . . my daughter's hand
in marriage and half my wealth.

(*All sigh and sob.*)

Rich Man.

Yes, I would. I would give him my daughter's hand
in marriage and . . . a quarter of my wealth.

Tyl.

Half my wealth.

Rich Man.

Half my wealth.

Tyl.

And the mayor's big house on top of the hill.

Man.

Yes.

Tyl.

And all the good pasture land around it.

Woman.

Oh yes.

Tyl.

And I swear on my honor, I'd never say another angry word to him as long as he lived.

All.

YES.

Tyl.

(*Unwinding his belt, which is a rope.*) Hold on to this rope and do just what I tell you. I know an ancient spell that might—just might—bring him back.

All.

Yes. Anything. Anything you say. Etc.

(TYL *walks around them and gives them each a piece of the rope to hold. He encircles all but* SERA-FINA.)

Tyl.

Now close your eyes . . .

(*They do.*)

and count to five. Slowly. After me. One.

All.

One.

(*Drumbeat.* TYL *makes a knot in the rope.*)

Tyl.

Two.

All.

Two.

(*Drumbeat.* TYL *pulls the rope tight. All gasp.*)

Tyl.

Eyes closed. Three.

All.

(*Constricted.*) Three.

> (*Drumbeat.* TYL *takes off his disguise and puts his outer garment back on.*)

Tyl.

Four.

All.

Four.

> (*Drumbeat.* TYL *takes* SERAFINA *by the hand.*)

Tyl.

Five.

All.

Five.

> (*Drumbeat.* TYL *snatches the bag of gold from the* RICH MAN, *who makes a noise of protest.*)

Tyl.

You can open your eyes now.

> (*They do. They take in what has happened, roar, and make an angry lunge at* TYL.)

Tyl.

Remember. You promised. No angry words.

Rich Man.

He tricked me again.

> (TYL *holds up a calming hand and smiles. Beat. All smile a broad, saccharine smile. Music.* TYL *and* SERA-FINA *exit jauntily arm in arm. The company holds briefly, then plays the rope out, taking curtain calls off the action. Reenter* TYL *and* SERAFINA *for their call.*)

Starman Jones

A Play for Children

Based on the Novel by Robert A. Heinlein
by Douglas L. Lieberman

PREFACE

I hate fairy tales onstage. This is strictly adult consider-
ation; I loved them as a child, but by age ten they curdled
my stomach, and I avoided the theater (my eventual
profession) for ten years. Fairy tales are for kids.

When Dr. Bella Itkin asked me to write and direct a
new play for the Goodman Children's Theater in Chicago, she wanted a piece for this "lost generation," upper
grade school through junior high. No blue fairies or
dancing panda bears allowed.

Robert A. Heinlein has taught and entertained the
lost generation brilliantly for twenty years. When I wrote
him that I wanted to write a play with low sugar content,
he readily agreed to let me adapt his novel *Starman
Jones*, a favorite of my own school years. The story—a
boy from a backward planet fulfills his deep longing for
space at even deeper personal cost—is thoroughly un-
sentimental, adventurous, and ultimately moving.

The play met Chicago children for two months early
in 1972, and in June was chosen the country's best new
children's adaptation by the National Society of Arts and
Letters.

Lessons from the First Production
The staging included in this text is a record of the first
production. It should *not* be read as the "correct" staging. In fact, when we were done, I felt I had *over*staged,
and that the mammoth effects (including a stunning
6,000-light star field) tended to dwarf the actors, particularly in the complicated and rapid-fire second act.
When the play is done around the country, it will

benefit from the less expensive, more intimate production it is likely to receive.

The actors should be forceful and direct. In our production, the most successful actors were the least subtle. *Starman Jones* is not Chekhov.

The fight scene in Act Two is the only sequence which is difficult to stage. Flashy effects and (yes) violence are in order, but even more important is clarity of event. Sam's death is the pivot of the show, and it must not be masked.

DOUGLAS L. LIEBERMAN

CAST

Maximilian Jones
Sam Anderson
Captain Blaine
Dr. Hendrix
Mr. Simes
Mr. Kuiper
Mr. Giordano
First Crewman (CM-1)
Second Crewman (CM-2)
Eldreth (Ellie) Coburn
Miss Kelly
First Crewwoman (CW-1)
Second Crewwoman (CW-2)
(The Crewmen and Crewwomen will also double the parts of
Monty, **High Secretary**, **Bernie**, **Maw**, **Secretary**, and **Aunt
Becky**.)

Starman Jones takes place in two acts.

> *Imagine a two-story scaffold running the width of the stage,
> various areas set forward or back, connected vertically by
> ladders throughout. Further imagine a large cyclorama or drop
> behind the scaffolding, on which can be wired or projected the
> various star fields called for in the script, and on which lighting
> of various colors can be thrown. Parts of the scaffold will be-
> come a room, a larger chamber, the surface of a planet, a
> farm on earth, all controlled by lighting.*

303

ACT ONE

Scene One

Music. As the house dims, the VOICE *begins, and the curtain opens slowly, revealing a night on Earth, deep purple and black with a few stars. We begin to see* MAX, *backlit, facing the sky, hands high over his head in a private reverie.*

Travelogue Voice.
The planet Earth is a farm planet, long ago left behind in mankind's rush to the stars. A single moon, under it a thin radiation belt, then layer after layer of atmosphere. Somewhere under this lie the farms, and somewhere, once in a while, someone stands on a hill and looks up, through the atmosphere, the radiation, past the moon and the other planets, out at the stars.

Maw.
(*Unseen.*) Maximilian! Max . . . mil . . . yan!

    (MAX *looks around, then does not move.*)

Max! I can see you, Max—you come at once, hear me?

    (MAX *stands. Lights up on* MAW *and* MONTY *in another area.* MAW *is clutching a little bit of lace,* MONTY *is carrying a sack, and a flask protrudes from a shirt pocket.* MAX *moves toward them.*)

Maw.
(*A little loud.*) Max, you remember Monty? Come on, your Maw is talking to you.

Max.
I'm sorry, Maw. I thought . . .

Maw.

Max, honey . . . (*Carefully.*) today is a special day.

Monty.

You bet.

Maw.

Quiet.

Max.

Special?

Maw.

Max, shake hands with your new father.

(MAX *stops.* MONTY *grins, sticks out a paw.* MAX *does not move.*)

Maw.

Maxie!

Monty.

Howdy, son.

(*They shake hands.*)

Maw.

Come on, gimme a big kiss.

Monty.

(*As* MAX *and* MAW *embrace.*) Yep, we just sort of . . . got married, in town today.

(*The embrace breaks, and* MONTY *tosses* MAX *the sack.*)

Monty.

Come on, take this inside.

(MAX *goes into the kitchen.* MAW *and* MONTY *follow, stop at the door.*)

Maw.

Well? (*Giggle.*)

(MONTY *looks at her, then picks her up and carries her in the door.*)

Monty.

I'm starved.

Maw.

Maxie, fix some supper.

Max.

I'm getting it.

Monty.

Honeybun, here we are. (*He looks around.*) Oh boy, another coupla days and we can move out of this dump.

Max.

What do you mean?

Maw.

Quiet, Max.

Monty.

(*Expansive.*) We've sold this stinking little farm, and we are moving to the big city!

Max.

(*Shocked.*) What are you talking about?

Maw.

(*Tightly.*) Fix dinner for your new Paw, Max.

Max.

Monty, this here's our home. You can't . . .

Maw.

Max!

Max.

(*To* MAW.) You promised Dad! You said you'd always live yere! You said . . .

Monty.

Don't talk to your mother like that.

Maw.

I'll get dinner.

Monty.

He'll get it. Let's have a little toast. (*He drinks from the flask, hands it to* MAW. MAX *goes to the stove.*) Here, son. Drink a toast to the bride.

Max.

I've got to get supper.

Monty.

(*Pleasantly.*) Well, the more for us. Son, we gotta get you a job. What do you say? (*No answer.*) Well? (*No answer.*) Max, what can you do besides farm?

Max.

I don't want to talk about it. (*He picks up a bucket and walks to the door.*)

Maw.

Where you going, honey?

Max.

Get some water. (*He exits.*)

Monty.

Punk.

Maw.

Aw, he's a good boy, Monty. (*She pokes around the stove.*)

Monty.

Live and let live, I always say. (*He pinches her; they laugh.*) Boy, look at this junk. Let's sell it all.

Maw.

I hate this place. Max, you know, he's funny about it. He really loved his dad.

Monty.

Well, he's got a new one now. (*He picks up two well-bound books.*) Say, these are pretty things.

Max.

(*At the door.*) Astrogation books. They're mine.

Monty.

What you gonna do in outer space? These'll get us five bucks.

Max.

They're mine! My uncle gave them to me. Tell him, Maw.

Monty.

Nellie?

Maw.

Well, the books did belong to Chet . . .

Monty.

So they're yours now, not his. We sell them.

Max.

Monty, Uncle Chet gave those to *me*.

Monty.

I said we sell them!

Max.

You thief!

Maw.

Max!

Monty.

(*Cold.*) That's far enough. (*He begins to unfasten his belt.*)

Maw.

Monty, please!

Monty.

I'm boss here now. Apologize! You heard me!

(MAX *dives for him and they fall grappling to the floor.* MAW *runs around, squealing. They break and rise, wary,* MONTY *finishes removing his belt and goes for* MAX, *who grabs the bucket of water and douses* MONTY. MAX *picks up the books and flees out the door.*)

Maw.

(*Running to the door.*) Max! Come back here!

(*The lights begin to fade.*)

Maxie!

Monty.

Max!

Maw.

Shut up. Max . . . mil . . . yan!

(*Blackout.*)

Scene Two

Darkness. Crickets. MAX *is walking along the scaffold, very tired. He approaches a glow, which proves to be a small campfire with a pot and a metal cup.* SAM *is squatting in its light, dressed like a tramp.* MAX *stays out of the light.*

Sam.

(*Not looking up.*) Well, don't hide there. Come on down. (*Pause.*) I won't fetch it up to you.

(MAX *comes into the firelight.*)

Howdy. Draw up a chair.

Max.

(*Sitting on ground.*) Howdy.

Sam.

(*Stirring the stew.*) Four days old, just getting good. (*He scoops some up, pulls a spoon from his pocket, hands it to* MAX.) If you're worried about germs, hold it in the fire, then wipe it. If a bug bites me, he dies horribly.

(MAX *does so, then eats hungrily.*)

Sam.

By the way, you can call me Sam.

Max.

Oh, my name is Max. (*He finishes the cup, then smiles.*)

Sam.

Feel better?

Max.

Yes. Thanks. (*Pause.*) Uh, Sam? How did you know I was there?

Sam.

Could see you against the sky. Don't ever do that, kid, or it may be the last thing you do.

(MAX *looks over his shoulder.*)

Sam.

Think your folks'll miss you?

Max.

Huh? How did you know?

Sam.

Done it myself. Go back, kid.

Max.

I won't ever go back!

Sam.

(*Not heavily.*) That bad?

Max.

(*Stares at the fire, then stands.*) Sam, my Maw just

married an old drunk, and he's going to sell the farm!
And he hates me! (*No answer from* SAM.) And he tried
to steal my books!

Sam.

A mouse studying to be a rat. Maybe you did right.

(MONTY *appears in the darkness with a flashlight.*
SAM *sees him.*)

Sam.

He still looking for you?

Max.

Probably. I'd better go. Thanks a lot, Sam.

Sam.

Sit down.

Max.

No, I've got to . . .

Sam.

(*Not ruffled.*) Quiet. Get over there, fast.

(MAX *moves out of the firelight.* SAM *hums, stirs
the stew.* MONTY *approaches, shines the light on* SAM.)

Sam.

(*Suddenly drunk.*) Say, brother! Would you like a
little mulligan stew? Got a drink?

(MONTY *snorts, turns away, prowls on out of sight.*)

Max.

(*Emerging.*) Thanks a lot, Sam. (*He picks up the
books.*)

Sam.

Kid, you're tired and getting a little stupid. He won't be
back. (MAX *hesitates.*) Wait till morning, then you
can find the highway. Got a blanket?

Max.

No, just some books.

Sam.

Say, can I see them? (*Startled.*) Kid, do you know
what you've got here?

Max.

Sure.

Sam.

Max, there are flight tables for a starship! They belong to the Guild!

Max.

That's where I'm going. My uncle was an explorer.

Sam.

No kidding? Sit down. Ever been in space yourself? No, of course not.

Max.

But I'm going to!

Sam.

What? You can't.

Max.

What do you mean?

Sam.

Was your father in the Guild?

Max.

My uncle was.

Sam.

Not good enough.

Max.

How come?

Sam.

I think you're fine. But you're poor, you don't dress fancy, and your father wasn't a starman.

Max.

They won't let me?

Sam.

No.

Max.

I'll make them. Sam, I'm going to the stars.

Sam.

Good luck, kid. (*He looks up.*) Sure is pretty, though.

Max.

Look, there's Alpha Centauri. And Procyon. Uncle Chet was the first man to get there—there's people with two heads!

Sam.

Really? (*Yawns.*) Come on, get some sleep.

Max.

I guess so. (*He reclines, the books next to him.*) Think Monty'll come back?

Sam.

Shh! No. Come on, sleep.

Max.

Yeah. Good night, Sam.

Sam.

Night, kid.

(MAX *closes his eyes. Silence. After a moment,* SAM *rises, very quiet, and slides the books away from* MAX. *He turns to the fire, thinks, then bends down and writes something quickly in the dirt with his finger. Then he slides a little dirt onto the fire, which dims, tucks the books under his arm, stealthily steps over* MAX *and is gone. Silence.* MAX *stirs, reaches a hand toward the vanished books, then sits bolt upright.*)

Max.

Sam? Sam! (*He tosses a couple of twigs into the fire for more light, then scrabbles around, searching.*) Sam, you took my books! (*He sees the note in the dirt, reads quickly.*) "Dear Max. There is more stew in the can. Sorry about the books, but you'll never be an astrogator. Sam." (*He comes forward, yelling.*) Sam! Monty! Maw! I'm going to do it! Do you hear? I'm going to do it! (*He kicks the fire and walks away as the lights fade.*)

Scene Three

Organ music, solemn and grand. A SECRETARY, *dictating.* MAX *appears uncertainly. The music ends as the* SECRETARY *looks up.*)

Secretary.

Young man, this is the Astrogators' Guild. Please leave by the main door.

Max.

No, this is the place I want.

Secretary.

Oh? State your business, please.

Max.

I'd like to talk to someone about joining the Guild.

Secretary.

Joining? I'm afraid that's impossible. (*She works.*)

Max.

But my uncle went into space, and he promised me . . .

Secretary.

Your uncle? What was his name, please?

Max.

Chester Arthur Jones.

Secretary.

Chester Arthur Jones? (*Impressed.*) Just a moment.
(*She speaks quietly into something.*) You're lucky.
The High Secretary will see you. When you go in,
don't sit down, speak only when spoken to, and get out
quickly when he is through.

(*She ushers him into another room where the* HIGH
SECRETARY *is standing, then leaves.*)

High Secretary.

Come in, son. What is your name?

Max.

Maximilian Jones, sir.

High Secretary.

And you are a nephew of Chester Arthur Jones?

Max.

Yes, sir.

High Secretary.

A very famous man. You should be proud.

Max.

I am, sir.

High Secretary.

I've been thinking about you.

Max.

Me?

High Secretary.

You see, you are the *second* Maximilian Jones to come
in today.

Max.
What?

High Secretary.
(*Producing books.*) Are these . . .

Max.
Uncle Chet's books!

High Secretary.
Another man brought these in this morning.

Max.
Sam!

High Secretary.
He left suddenly when we asked for his fingerprints.
Called himself Maximilian Jones.

(MAX *reaches for the books.*)

High Secretary.
Oh, no, you can't keep those. Those tables are Guild
secrets.

Max.
But I know what's in them.

High Secretary.
I'm sorry. Besides, how could you "know" an astrogation table?

Max.
I *read* them.

High Secretary.
(*Doubting.*) Really.

Max.
(*Pacing.*) Listen. "Horst Congruency #472. Beta
Hydrae. Coordinates 6493.50, 4927.83 . . . "

High Secretary.
You mean, you . . .

Max.
I remember everything I read. I always have.

High Secretary.
A perfect memory?

Max.
(*Hopeful.*) Yes, sir. That's why I think I should join
the Guild. I want to go into space, sir.

High Secretary.

Oh, is *that* why you're here. No, that is impossible.

Max.

But Uncle Chet promised me that . . .

High Secretary.

Do you have any record of this?

Max.

(*Sheepish.*) No . . .

High Secretary.

Then I have no choice. That's all, young man.

(MAX *turns to leave.*)

High Secretary.

No, don't go. There is a reward for returning these books. The Secretary has it for you. Buy some clean clothes with it.

Max.

(*Faintly.*) Thank you. (*He returns to the* SECRETARY, *who silently hands him an envelope.*)

Secretary.

I'm sorry.

(MAX *wanders out as the lights fade.*)

Scene Four

MAX *walks despondently. The lights change for Earthport.*

Travelogue Voice.

Earthport is our largest and busiest city. Here are people from all the known planets, and great ships that land to trade goods and messages from the stars. Downtown, the famous Imperial Hotel advertises rooms for all known creatures, where they can order their choice of atmosphere and exotic foods.

(MAX *stops and leans over the edge, watching sadly.*)

But in the center of the city is the Field, and on it spaceships stretching away for miles—military ships, moon shuttles, robot freighters. And if you are lucky, you can see the greatest of all starships, the Asgard. Round as a basketball, with a drive in her base that can pull at space itself, the Asgard travels to the far-thest reaches of the galaxy.

(SAM *appears behind* MAX, *much better dressed.*)

Sam.

(*Gruff.*) Hey, Jack, get away. That's a restricted area!

Max.

Sam! (*He advances, fists swinging.*) I'm gonna . . .

Sam.

Hold it. Hold it! (*He restrains* MAX.) How are you? How'd you make out?

Max.

You ought to be arrested!

Sam.

Shhhhh! We'll *both* get arrested.

Max.

(*Taking a breath.*) You stole my books.

Sam.

Your books? I thought they were the Guild's.

Max.

Well . . . (*He dries up.*)

Sam.

That's better, kid. If you want to turn me in, go ahead.

Max.

Forget it.

Sam.

Thanks. Any luck with Mr. Secretary?

Max.

No. He wouldn't even consider it.

(*They walk.*)

Sam.

So what now?

Max.

I don't know. Be a plumber, maybe. You?

Sam.

Oh, I've got . . . plans.

Max.

They even gave me money to buy new clothes!

Sam.

Money? No, never mind.

(*They halt and look at the ships.*)

Max.

Boy, look at that.

Sam.

She's the Asgard.

Max.

Beautiful. (*A beat.*) Sam, what's on your mind?

Sam.

Nothing. Just an idea.

Max.

I could use an idea right now.

Sam.

(*A beat.*) Max, do you want to be an astrogator, or just go into space? Think about it.

Max.

Well, I guess I'd like to go, any way I can.

Sam.

And your uncle taught you your way around a ship?

Max.

I think so.

Sam.

Max, the Asgard is raising next Thursday, for starside. Would you like to be on her?

(MAX *looks at* SAM, *stunned.*)

Sam.

How much money do you have?

(*Speechless,* MAX *hands over the envelope.*)

Sam.

If I can get you on board, you want to try it?

(MAX *manages a nod.*)

Sam.

(*Walking quickly.*) All right, let's go. (*He elbows* MAX.) Starside, here we come!

Max.

You're coming too?

Sam.

Plans, my boy. Just stick with me! (*They laugh.*)

Scene Five

They enter another area on the scaffold. BECKY *is waiting with a tape measure. She is elderly and a little gross.*

Becky.

This him?

Sam.

Large as life.

(*He spins* MAX *around.* BECKY *measures him efficiently.*)

Sam.

Now, kid, we spread your money around the right places. By next Thursday, you and I will be crewmen on the Asgard.

Max.

But I never . . .

Becky.

Stand still.

Sam.

Use your head! We'll be experienced crewmen, with records to prove it.

(BERNIE *comes in, a pencil over his ear, bent and myopic.*)

Bernie.

Somebody want me?

Sam.

Bernie. How are you?

Bernie.

Ahh, you know. Same old . . . Who's the kid?

Sam.

Max, meet Bernie. You got an identity card?

Max.

It's back at the farm.

Sam.

No matter. (*He hands* BERNIE *money;* BERNIE *counts.*)

Becky.

I'll see what I can do, sweety. (*Exits.*)

Bernie.

What'sya name?

Max.

Maximilian Jones. M-a-x-i-

Bernie.

Some spaceman.

Sam.

M-i-l-i-a-n. You heard him. Full papers for the Asgard, no slips. Understand?

Bernie.

Yeah, yeah. (*He clears his throat.* SAM *gives him more money.*)

Max.

Sam!

Sam.

(*Halting.*) Max, I'll play fair. With this money you can go home, hire a lawyer, and throw Monty off the farm. Want to do it?

Max.

(*A beat.*) Go ahead.

(BERNIE *finishes counting the money, then turns to leave.*)

Sam.

We leave Thursday, understand?

Bernie.

Sam?

Sam.

What?

Bernie.

You're nuts.

(*He exits around* BECKY, *who carries bundles and a makeup kit.*)

Becky.

He giving you trouble?

Sam.

No matter.

(BECKY *peers at* MAX.)

Sam.

How about it? I thought a mustache would help.

Becky.

(*Working on* MAX.) No, that would look silly. Don't flinch, honey duck. Aunt Becky has to work on you. No, we'll move back his hairline, thin it out on top, lay on a few wrinkles. Mustn't overdo it.

Sam.

Max, where's the Worry Hole?

Max.

Huh? That's the control room.

Sam.

What does the Asgard use for fuel?

Max.

Just about anything. It's all the same to a convertor.

Becky.

Think we should kill his hair roots? No, lover, you're too pretty to age prematurely. (*She steps back.*) What do you think?

Sam.

Ugly as sin.

Becky.

(*Handing him a bundle.*) Here, honey, change into this.

(MAX *steps behind a blind. The lights begin to tighten.*)

Becky.

It's awfully quick, Sam.

Sam.

It'll be terrific.

(BERNIE *reenters with the papers.*)

Sam.

Ah. Good.

Bernie.

Where's the kid?

Sam.

Shhh. He'll be out in a second. (*Looking through the papers.*) Max?

Max.

(*Behind blind.*) Yes?

Sam.

You're a member of the Stewards and Cooks Guild. Now listen carefully. When you talk to a spaceman, no matter what ship he served in, you were in a different one. You drink milk on account of your ulcer. Got that?

Max.

I've got an ulcer?

Sam.

And you don't talk much. You can't goof up with your mouth shut. Watch it, kid. If you mess up, it's jail for thirty years. How are you doing?

Max.

I'm done.

Sam.

Well, come on out.

Becky.

(*A beat.*) Don't be afraid. Aunt Becky knows what she's doing.

(MAX *comes into sight. He is in a crewman's uniform. Even his hair is combed differently.*)

Max.

(*Softly.*) Well?

Sam.

(*With a whistle.*) Beautiful. Becky, you're a genius. (*He gives her money, hugs her.*) Let's see you walk.

(MAX *walks around.*)

Sam.
You still walk like a farmer! Get your feet out of those furrows, boy.

Max.
No good?

Sam.
It'll have to do. Grab your bonnet and let's go!

(*They begin to descend from the area.*)

Bernie.
Sam?

Sam.
Yeah?

Bernie.
You're nuts.

(BECKY *throws a uniform jacket to* SAM *as the lights fade.*)

Becky.
Good luck!

Scene Six

SAM *and* MAX *walk along the base of the scaffold.*

Max.
We're going to be late.

Sam.
Who cares? We sign on at the last minute. That way you don't have time to make a slip. Here we are. (*They stop by a ladder.*) Ready, kid?

Max.
I guess so. (*Firmly.*) Yes.

Sam.
Up you go.

(*They climb up. Lights up on* MR. KUIPER *with a clipboard.*)

Mr. Kuiper.
Names?
Sam.
Anderson.
Max.
Jones.
Mr. Kuiper.
(*Taking their papers.*) You're late. That's a bad way to start.
Max.
Yes, sir.
Mr. Kuipèr.
Get your chow and report back. One of you in D-112, and the other in E-009. (*Exit.*)

(SAM *and* MAX *walk down a corridor.*)

Max.
I'm lost already.
Sam.
Just don't let anybody know. We're on C Deck, we can hunt from there.
Max.
Sam, please tell me. You've been in space before.
Sam.
Hush, boy. No questions.

(*A rumble. They grab the scaffolding. The lights falter, then grow bright.*)

Sam.
Feel that?
Max.
(*Puzzled.*) Yes?
Sam.
We made it, kid. We're in space!

(*They stare at each other for a moment, grin, then laugh uproariously as the lights fade.*)

Scene Seven

Lights up on MR. KUIPER *and* MR. GIORDANO *consulting the clipboard with* CM-1.

Mr. Kuiper.
Hydroponics needs some help today.
CM-1.
Yes, sir. First shift?
Mr. Kuiper.
Please.
Mr. Giordano.
I'll look in later.

(CM-1 *exits,* CW-1 *comes down a ladder.*)

Mr. Kuiper.
(*To* MR. GIORDANO.) Check the tanks while you're there. (*To* CW-1.) Ah, Miss Kane, good morning.
CW-1.
Morning sir. Emergency supplies?
Mr. Kuiper.
Correct.
Mr. Giordano.
Have a good time in port.
CW-1.
You bet. We found a great little place . . .

(MR. KUIPER *clears his throat.*)

CW-1.
Right away, sir. (*Exits.*)
Mr. Giordano.
Where's that new boy?
Mr. Kuiper.
Jones? I'd certainly like to . . .

(MAX *approaches in haste, buttoning his shirt.*)

Mr. Giordano.
Sir?
Mr. Kuiper.
(*Seeing him.*) Hmm.

(They watch MAX's *arrival.)*

Mr. Kuiper.
Mister Jones.
Max.
Yes, sir.
Mr. Kuiper.
Mr. Jones, you are late.
Max.
Yes, sir.
Mr. Kuiper.
You were late boarding yesterday.
Max.
Yes, sir.
Mr. Kuiper.
Will you be late tomorrow?
Max.
No, sir.
Mr. Kuiper.
Very good, Mr. Jones. This is Mr. Giordano.
Max.
How do you do, sir.

(They shake hands.)

Mr. Kuiper.
If you are late again, he will also be in trouble. Good
day.

(He turns and exits. MR. GIORDANO *leads* MAX *along
the scaffold.)*

Max.
I'm really sorry, sir.
Mr. Giordano.
It's okay.
Max.
I didn't hear the bell, and I . . .
Mr. Giordano.
Don't worry about it. Kuiper's not as bad as he sounds.
(He stops, hands MAX *a vacuum unit.)* Four decks
each day.

(MAX *stares at the unit.*)

Mr. Giordano.
You know how to handle it?
Max.
Uh, yes, sir.

(MAX *fumbles with the unit, then begins to sweep.*
MR. GIORDANO *watches curiously.*)

Max.
(*Uncertain.*) Doing just fine, sir.
Mr. Giordano.
Hold it.

(MAX *stops.*)

Mr. Giordano.
Don't you want to turn it on?

(MAX *gropes for a switch.* MR. GIORDANO *leans over
and turns it on.*)

Max.
(*Trying to laugh.*) Oh, of course, sir.
Mr. Giordano.
Where were you on your last trip?
Max.
Pardon?
Mr. Giordano.
Your last ship. Where did she fly?
Max.
(*Sweeping.*) Uh, Imperial Survey, sir. I'm not allowed
to talk about it.
Mr. Giordano.
There hasn't been a survey in years.
Max.
Like, I said, sir, this was top secret.
Mr. Giordano.
Sorry. Well, have fun. Oh, don't forget the sandboxes.
Max.
Sandboxes?
Mr. Giordano.
Wake up, Jones. For the cats. (*Exits.*)

Max.

Cats?

Travelogue Voice.

The cats on a starship are full-fledged crewmen, whose job is to catch and eat all the mice that have gone into space with mankind.

(MAX *sweeps. The* TRAVELOGUE VOICE *is continuous over the action described. Lights up on* MR. GIORDANO *and* CW-1, *working in hydroponics.*)

A ship is a tiny kingdom in space. In the hydroponics section, plants grow in giant tanks under an electric sun. Vegetables are picked for fresh food, and the green leaves give off oxygen for the crew to breathe.

(CW-1 *hands* MAX *a carrot as he sweeps by. Faint ship's noises begin to be heard.* MAX *moves on, and lights also come up on* CM-1 *and* CM-2, *working in engineering.* MAX *approaches. Deeper sounds are heard.*)

Pumps, electricity, heat, all are powered from the engineering department. Here men control the atomic reactor that pushes the ship through space. Behind heavy shields, atoms blaze with enough energy to smash a starship into hot gas—or to heat coffee for the captain's table. Engineers know their own importance, and keep to themselves.

(MAX *crunches the carrot. The* CREWMEN *turn and glare. He leaves quickly. Lights up on* SAM, MR. KUIPER *and* CW-2 *checking through several large crates. The sounds increase.*)

Most of the cargo is handled by machine, but every ship carries crates of food and medicine, packed entirely by hand. These supplies can always be gotten open, even if the main power fails. A ship in space is a long, long way from home.

(MAX *stops to talk with* SAM. *The beehive activity increases. Lights up on the* CAPTAIN, DR. HENDRIX, SIMES, *and* MISS KELLY *in the control room.*)

A ship's brain is her control room. Here the astrogators navigate between the stars. The job is tricky and dangerous—this room is known to the crew as the Worry Hole.

(*On the PA.*) Attention, members of watch three. New schedules are now posted outside the chart room.

(MAX *is having trouble with his vacuum unit. He bangs it up and down.*)

And, like any kingdom, a ship has its useless nobility, the passengers.

(*The vacuum unit belches its dirt into the face of* ELLIE, *who is just climbing up.*)

Scene Eight

Ellie.
What are you *doing*?

(*All other areas and sounds blackout.* ELLIE *climbs onto* MAX's *level.*)

Max.
(*Flustered.*) I'm sorry . . . (*He moves to brush her off.*)

Ellie.
Don't touch me. (*She swats at the dirt, but can't reach her back.*)

Max.
I'll get it.

(ELLIE *backs away.*)

Max.
Come on, turn around. (*He brushes her back.*)

Ellie.
Don't you watch what you're doing?

Max.
You're not supposed to be here.

Ellie.

I know that, silly. The other passengers are so boring. (*He is finished.*) Thank you.

(MAX *returns to sweeping. She watches for a moment.*)

Ellie.

Aren't you going to say you're sorry?

Max.

I did.

Ellie.

Oh.

Max.

(*Sweeping toward her.*) Move.

Ellie.

I think I'll go back upstairs, where people are polite.

(*She flounces to a ladder.* MAX *turns in amazement, then moves to another ladder. They both climb down. Halfway,* MAX *sees her paralleling him. He stops. She stops. He goes up a few rungs. She goes up a few rungs. He goes down a step. She goes down a step.*)

Max.

Now what?

Ellie.

You look silly with that thing.

Max.

I was born that way.

Ellie.

Do you play chess?

Max.

What?

Ellie.

Do you play chess? Bet I can beat you.

Max.

I play better than you can.

Ellie.

Fat chance! Meet me in the lounge at four. And get ready to die.

Max.

It's a bet!

(ELLIE *begins to climb.*)

Max.
What's your name?
Ellie.
(*Not stopping.*) Ellie.
Max.
What?
Elllie.
Ellie, you dumdum!

(*She climbs out of sight.* MAX *descends and vanishes.*)

Mr. Kuiper.
(*Amplified.*) Attention all hands. Hydroponics reports
that a crate of their best oranges, repeat, oranges, has
been stolen. Anyone knowing their whereabouts please
report to Mr. Kuiper.

Scene Nine

The CAPTAIN *and* DR. HENDRIX *walk down a corridor,*
SAM *approaches in the other direction. During the lines
below, they pass.*

Captain.
Very good work, Doctor.
Dr. Hendrix.
Thank you. I'm still short a computer man, you know.
Captain.
Train someone new.
Dr. Hendrix.
Captain?
Captain.
We have four hundred crewmen. Find someone who's
good with numbers.
Dr. Hendrix.
The Guild will object.
Captain.
Too bad. Check the records of the new men. You'll
find someone.

(SAM *halts, listening.*)

Dr. Hendrix.

First thing tomorrow. Good idea to know who we have on board, in any case.

Captain.

Let me know.

(*They exit.* SAM *waits a moment, then calls quietly.*)

Sam.

Max! Max!

(MAX *appears, still with vacuum unit.*)

Max.

Sam! What's up?

Sam.

What are you going to do after this trip?

Max.

What? More of the same, I guess.

Sam.

new man on this ship. Tomorrow.

Uh-uh. They're going to check the records of every

Max.

Sam, you said it was all fixed!

Sam.

Put that thing down. Look, I'm phony too, and you don't see me screaming.

Max.

I'll go to jail!

Sam.

Not until we get back to Earth.

Max.

Wonderful.

Sam.

Stop it! There's two things you can do.

Max.

What?

Sam.

You tell me.

Max.

Well, I guess I could confess, tell them everything.

Sam.

Yeah, you could. And I won't stop you. Or you *could* do what I'm going to do.

Max.

What's that?

Sam.

Jump ship.

Max.

You mean . . .

Sam.

On our last stop, I'm going far over the horizon. Just walk out and never say good-bye.

Max.

That's running away!

Sam.

You should know what that's like.

Max.

Oh.

Sam.

So you can choose whichever one you want.

Max.

Either I go to jail, or . . .

Sam.

Picture this. Now listen. By the time they've noticed I'm gone, I'll be lying beside a stream in the wilderness, letting my beard grow and memorizing my new name. Say the word and you'll be next to me, with a fishing pole. (*He lets it hang for a moment, then turns to leave.*) Your choice, kid.

Max.

Yeah. Thanks.

Sam.

Oh, and Max?

Max.

Yes?

Sam.

Would you like an orange?

(*He tosses an orange to* MAX, *then exits laughing.*)

Scene Ten

MAX *puts down his vacuum, leans on the handle.* ELLIE
appears, slowly sneaking up behind him.

Ellie.
Boo!

(MAX *jumps.*)

Ellie.
You missed our date.

Max.
(*Hiding the orange.*) I'm sorry. Besides, I'm not allowed in passengers' quarters.

Ellie.
Phooey. You're chicken.

Max.
I'm also busy. (*He makes a show of sweeping.*)

Ellie.
Something worrying you?

Max.
Look, I can't talk now. Okay?

Ellie.
(*Going for a ladder.*) What's up here?

Max.
(*Not looking.*) The control room.

Ellie.
Hey! (*She climbs.*)

Max.
Wait! Keep out of there! That's the control room!

(*She climbs faster. He goes after her with the
vacuum and she is dragged down, protesting. Swatting
at her, he backs her up several yards, the vacuum
under her nose. They stop, at stalemate.*)

Ellie.
I'm going to sneeze . . .

(*Confused,* MAX *lowers the vacuum, and she dashes
around him to the ladder. As they reach the next level
he grabs her, and she howls.*)

Max.

(*Frantic.*) Shhh! The Captain's in there.

Ellie.

Oh? He's a nice man.

Max.

I've never met him.

Ellie.

Neither have I. Is that where they do that space-warp stuff?

Max.

Shh! Yes it is. And space isn't warped.

Ellie.

Sure it is. That's how we jump between stars. Let's go look.

(*Very quietly they crawl a few feet.*)

Ellie.

Can we get in trouble here?

Max.

I'll say.

(*They huddle like little kids.*)

Ellie.

(*Very quietly.*) How do they do it?

Max.

What?

Ellie.

Jump through space?

Max.

It's kind of . . . do you have a hanky?

Ellie.

Sure. (*She produces a handkerchief.*) Look. It's got the solar system on it.

Max.

"Souvenir of Earth." Here's Earth, here's Mars.

Ellie.

You read it. That's cheating.

Max.

Hush. Now look. How do you get from here to here?

(*The lights begin to cool imperceptibly.*)

Ellie.

(*Running her finger along the drawing.*) Like this.

Max.

Right. What if I fold it up? (*He brings the two points together.*) Now what's the shortest way?

Ellie.

(*Pointing to where the areas are pinched together.*) Across here?

Max.

Right. That's how outer space works. It's folded, like this. Four dimensions. And if your ship gets right up to the speed of light at just the right place, just the right place, just the right direction, you pop across and come out somewhere else.

Ellie.

Wow. What if you do it just anywhere?

Max.

That's why exploring is so dangerous. It's like if you squeeze a watermelon seed, phhht. Out into nowhere.

(*They are both awed for a moment.* ELLIE *shivers.*)

Ellie.

You're smart.

Max.

I guess so.

Ellie.

You must have been in space a lot.

Max.

(*Startled.*) Uh, yeah. Look, I'd better go.

(*He climbs down a ladder.*)

Ellie.

Max! What did I say?

Scene Eleven

At the bottom of the ladder, MAX *sees* SAM, *looking indolent.*

Sam.

Doing pretty well with the ladies. (*He grins.*)

(MAX *moves to swing at him, and* SAM *dances back.*)

Sam.

Hey, hey! Just admiring your taste.

Max.

That's not funny.

Sam.

Okay, I'm sorry. What's eating you?

Max.

What do you think?

Sam.

Oh, that. Yeah, you get into space, then you have to run away again.

Max.

Sam, I just can't decide.

Sam.

Shut up. Where's that old hillbilly bounce-back? When I first met you, you had guts. That's why I teamed up with you. Now you're a scared kid.

Max.

(*A beat.*) I'm sorry, Sam.

Sam.

Accepted. Listen, a word of advice. Don't mess around with rich passengers.

Max.

Rich?

Sam.

You don't know who she is?

Max.

Her? She's Eldreth Coburn.

Sam.

You poor boy. She is also the only daughter of His Supreme Excellency, General Sir John Fitzgerald Coburn, Imperial Ambassador and Resident Commissioner Plenipotentiary.

Max.

Who?

Sam.

Her daddy could buy the Asgard and put it in your front yard. Everybody knows it.

Max.

I didn't.

Sam.

Doesn't matter. A crewman does not mix with money. Ever.

Max.

That's not fair.

Sam.

What was that word?

Max.

Fair.

Sam.

Never heard of it. Just watch yourself, okay?

Mr. Kuiper.

(*Amplified.*) Crewman Jones, report to the Captain's cabin. Crewman Jones, report to the Captain's cabin.

(SAM *whistles, impressed.*)

Max.

That sounds like sourpuss!

Sam.

Trouble already. Think fast, kid.

(MAX *goes up a ladder with his vacuum unit.*)

Sam.

Uh, Max? Good buddy?

Max.

What?

Sam.

Your vacuum?

Max.

Oh.

(*He hands the unit down to* SAM, *who puts it over his shoulder and marches away like a soldier.*)

Scene Twelve

Lights up on DR. HENDRIX, *the* CAPTAIN *and* MR. KUIPER. MAX *enters very hesitantly.* DR. HENDRIX *and the* CAPTAIN *stare at him.* MAX *turns to leave.*)

Mr. Kuiper.
(*Barking.*) Steward's Third Mate Jones reporting, sir.
Max.
(*Sitting in confusion.*) How do you do.
Mr. Kuiper.
Stand up.

(MAX *stands.*)

Mr. Kuiper.
Captain Blaine, and Dr. Hendrix, First Astrogator.
Captain.
Mr. Jones, I'll be brief. We've been looking over your papers.
Max.
Yes, sir.
Dr. Hendrix.
Your past is quite unusual.
Max.
(*A beat.*) Yes, sir.
Captain.
Chester Arthur Jones was your uncle?
Max.
Sir?
Captain.
Mr. Jones, we have an opening in the control room. Would you like to work there?
Max.
What? Would I!
Dr. Hendrix.
(*Smiling.*) I'm afraid you'll just empty ashtrays for a while.
Max.
I'd love that, sir!

Captain.
Your uncle was one of my teachers. I owe him this much.
Dr. Hendrix.
(*Producing Guild books.*) These are astrogation books. Study them.
Max.
I don't have to, sir.
Dr. Hendrix.
But you . . .
Max.
I know them by heart.
Mr. Kuiper.
Mr. Jones, that's impossible!
Captain.
That will be all, Mr. Kuiper.

(MR. KUIPER *exits.*)

Captain.
Young man, the control room is no place for silly stories.
Max.
Try me.
Captain.
Very well.
Dr. Hendrix.
This had better be good, Mr. Jones.

(DR. HENDRIX *takes a book to the corner of the room, the* CAPTAIN *holds another copy.*)

Captain.
(*Reading.*) Horst Congruency #853.
Max.
Alpha Centauri.
Captain.
Coordinates?
Max.
9472.58, 7492.87, 8423.50.

(*The* CAPTAIN *looks at* DR. HENDRIX, *who nods.*)

Captain.
Jump figures. Approaching central route.
Max.
3850.
Captain.
3702.
Max.
8404.
Captain.
Add gravity correction.
Max.
Negative .04 per cent.
Captain.
Dr. Hendrix?

(*He nods. The* CAPTAIN *turns a page, then begins rapidly.*)

Captain.
One minute to transition. 3840.
Max.
(*Tense.*) 4791.
Captain.
Faster. 8542.
Max.
7490.
Captain.
3693.
Max.
4190.
Captain.
3782.
Max.
Correction, 3783, sir. You misread.

(*Startled, the* CAPTAIN *looks at* DR. HENDRIX.)

Dr. Hendrix.
I'm afraid he's right, sir.
Captain.
(*After a beat, smiling.*) Dr. Hendrix, he's all yours.
(*He moves to exit.*)

Max.

You mean I can do it?

Dr. Hendrix.

I'd like to talk to you for a moment.

(CAPTAIN *nods to* DR. HENDRIX, *then exits.*)

Dr. Hendrix.

Max, that's quite a trick.

Max.

Thank you, sir.

Dr. Hendrix.

Wait. (*He picks up a folder.*) What is this?

Max.

It's my flight record, sir.

Dr. Hendrix.

Then these are your past trips into space. Anything you'd like to say about them?

Max.

(*Faltering.*) Does this affect whether I get the job?

Dr. Hendrix.

Yes.

(MAX *moves slowly to the end of the room, then spins around.*)

Max.

Sir, it's phony from one end to the other. It's all lies.

Dr. Hendrix.

Good. If you'd said anything else, I'd have thrown you off the ship.

Max.

You knew.

Dr. Hendrix.

Yes. The Captain does not.

Max.

You didn't tell him?

Dr. Hendrix.

No.

Max.

But I can still . . .

Dr. Hendrix.
Report to the Worry Hole tomorrow at 11.
Max.
Thank you, I . . .
Dr. Hendrix.
Don't thank me! I don't like this at all. But you may
have the talents I need.
Max.
Yes, sir. (*He moves to exit.*)
Dr. Hendrix.
Max? (*Suddenly warm.*) I was about your age when
I started. Good luck to you.
Max.
Yes, sir.
Dr. Hendrix.
(*Business again.*) That is all.

(MAX *retreats in confusion.*)

Scene Thirteen

Under the TRAVELOGUE VOICE, MAX *meets* MR. GIOR-
DANO, *who brings him a new uniform jacket of visibly
higher rank.* MAX *changes into it, then* MR. GIORDANO
shakes his hand and departs with the old jacket.

Travelogue Voice.
The control room is the brain, ears, and eyes of a starship. Here cameras take pictures of the stars outside,
and automatically compare them to the ship's star
charts. Here are Dopplerscopes to calculate relative
velocity, radar for landing on a planet, dials and gauges
to help find the way through deep space, and the instruments needed to make the big jump between the
stars.

(MAX *approaches the control room, which lights to
reveal* DR. HENDRIX, SIMES, *and* MISS KELLY *at work.*)

And most important, a giant projection screen where
one can see—the stars.

(*The cyc lights, and infinity of stars.* MAX *just entering, staggers back from the view and stands transfixed.*)

Simes.
Hey! You!

(MAX *awakens.*)

Simes.
Come here. Don't you know enough to report in when you come on duty?

Max.
Sorry, sir. Jones here.

Simes.
Simes.

Kelly.
Kelly.

Simes.
Make us some coffee.

(MAX *steps back, lost, and* KELLY *points to a corner, where* MAX *produces several paper coffee cups, hands them around.*)

Max.
(*To* DR. HENDRIX.) Morning, sir.

Dr. Hendrix.
(*Warm.*) Good morning, Max.

Simes.
Jones, this isn't a tea party. Dust off those cabinets.

Dr. Hendrix.
Prepare for course reading. (*Pointedly to* SIMES.) Mr. Jones will assist.

(KELLY *and* MAX *work side by side,* SIMES *on another panel.* DR. HENDRIX *observes; all have open books before them.*)

Simes.
Scopes ready.

Kelly.
Computer ready.

Max.
Uh, computer assistant ready.
Simes.
Just say, "Ready," Mr. Jones.
Dr. Hendrix.
First reading.
Simes.
(*Reading from his console.*) 4826.30 4728.95, 4726.-
31.

(MAX *and* KELLY *punch into the computer.*)

Kelly.
8472.
Max.
9470.
Kelly.
7387.
Max.
8406.
Dr. Hendrix.
Compute.
Kelly.
(*After a moment.*) First approximation, on course,
sir.
Simes.
7493.57, 7251.94, 4693.49.

(DR. HENDRIX *walks around, observing.*)

Kelly.
8473.
Max.
8361.
Kelly.
7490.
Max.
3848.
Dr. Hendrix.
Compute.

Kelly.

(*After a moment.*) Second approximation, slightly off, sir.

Dr. Hendrix.

Jones and Kelly, switch places.

Simes.

You're not going to . . .

Dr. Hendrix.

This is my control room, Mr. Simes.

(MAX *and* KELLY *switch.*)

Simes.

8473.47, 2839.49, 8922.43.

Max.

8473.

Kelly.

2369.

Max.

9748.

Kelly.

7803.

Dr. Hendrix.

Compute.

Max.

(*After a moment.*) Third approximation. We *are* off course, sir.

Dr. Hendrix.

Jones and Simes, switch places.

(SIMES *spins around, amazed, then reluctantly stands to move.*)

Dr. Hendrix.

Prepare course corrections.

Simes.

(*Exploding.*) You can't let him con this ship. I'm the astrogator here.

Dr. Hendrix.

You are the *second* astrogator. I am the first.

Max.

Dr. Hendrix, if he doesn't . . .

Dr. Hendrix.
Mutiny already? (*Smiling.*) Let me worry about it.

(MAX *sits at* SIMES's *console.*)

Dr. Hendrix.
Prepare course correction.
Max.
(*A little unsure.*) 7894.42, 3552.82, 4729.56.

(*The* CAPTAIN *enters and stands, observing.*)

Simes.
8763.
Kelly.
4792.
Simes.
6489.
Kelly.
7738.

(MAX *looks around, frightened.*)

Max.
Do you want to . . .
Dr. Hendrix.
Do your job, Max.

(*Reluctantly,* MAX *speaks to a grill in the panel.*)

Max.
Engineering, this is . . . Mr. Jones speaking. Fire 43 for 2.6 seconds.

(*A faint rumble.*)

(*Walking.*) Course correction complete, sir.
Dr. Hendrix.
Resume stations. Projection off, please.

(*The stars vanish. All take their original seats.* KELLY *gives* MAX *a thumbs-up sign.*)

Dr. Hendrix.
Good work, Max.

Max.
Thank you.
Dr. Hendrix.
That is all until the next watch.

(MAX *stands, nods to the* CAPTAIN *and exits.*)

Captain.
(*Taking* DR. HENDRIX *to the side.*) Well, Doctor, how did he do?
Dr. Hendrix.
Jones? (*Smiles.*) He's brilliant, Captain. Brilliant. (*To crew.*) Prepare jump for Halcyon.

Scene Fourteen

Travelogue Voice.
Halcyon is a tiny whistle-stop between great stars. Ships stop for fuel and then move on—in Halcyon's case it is iron ore, shoveled from the hills straight into the ship's tanks. The natives are three-legged canni-bals, but luckily for man they are awake only at night, and by then the great ships are gone.

(*The cyc lights, an oddly colored sky with perhaps two moons near the horizon.* MAX *is walking outside with* MR. GIORDANO.)

Max.
(*Morose.*) Lonely, isn't it.
Mr. Giordano.
Gives me the creeps. How're you doing upstairs?
Max.
In Worry Hole? All right.
Mr. Giordano.
All right? Kelly tells me you're hot stuff.
Max.
We'll see.

(*They arrive at a ladder.*)

Mr. Giordano.
Going up?
Max.
I think I'll walk around a little.
Mr. Giordano.
Get in before dark. (*He climbs out of sight.*)

(MAX *looks out for a moment, then* SIMES *arrives, a little drunk.*)

Simes.
Well, well, if it isn't smart boy.
Max.
Good evening, Mr. Simes.
Simes.
Oh yeah? I think the same thing about you, only worse.

(MAX *says nothing.*)

Simes.
Aren't you going to ask me to sit down?
Max.
Have a seat, sir.
Simes.
There's no chair, smart boy. (*He leans on a ladder.*) Smart boy, do you know why I'm sitting with you?
Max.
No, sir.
Simes.
To tell you something, that's why. Ever since you did those fancy tricks with the computer, you've been Dr. Hendrix's fair-haired . . . fair-haired boy. Fair-haired . boy.

(MAX *moves away.*)

Simes.
Get back here!

(MAX *stops.* SIMES *lurches to him.*)

Simes.
Get this straight. You go buddy-buddying up to Dr.

Hendrix, I'll throw you out of the control room. You understand? *You understand?*

(SAM *has come up behind* SIMES. *He puts a hand on* SIMES's *shoulder.*)

Sam.
Good evening, Mr. Simes.
Simes.
(*Off stride.*) Well, if it isn't Sam. Do you know smart boy here, with the rich girl friend?
Sam.
I've seen him around.
Simes.
Yeah. Have a drink.

(SAM *takes the bottle, turns away a few steps, and pours it on the ground.*)

Simes.
(*To* MAX.) Say, how *is* your little chickie?
Sam.
(*Holding up the bottle.*) Mr. Simes, there's nothing in here.
Simes.
What? Give it to me. (*He looks.*) Gotta get some more. (*He goes to a ladder, then points at* MAX.) *He* took it. You watch out for him. That's an order. (*He climbs away.*)
Sam.
(*After a moment.*) I like an officer who acts like an officer. Give you a bad time, kid?
Max.
Sort of.
Sam.
He like that in the control room?
Max.
Sometimes.
Sam.
Beautiful. Got any friends up there?
Max.
Dr. Hendrix seems to like me.

Sam.

No kidding. He's the greatest. Listen, kid, if you've got Hendrix on your side, you're all right. Pretty soon you'll be captain.

(MAX *smiles weakly.*)

Sam.

What's wrong, Max?

Max.

Sam, our plans. I can't run away now. (*He plucks at his uniform.*)

Sam.

So that's it. Kid, I was fending for myself before you were born. Stay on board, and if you ever need me, you'll know where to find me.

Max.

You mean it?

Sam.

Yes, sir.

(MAX *smiles.*)

Sam.

Say, here comes your girl friend. (*He moves to the ladder.*)

Max.

But Sam . . .

(ELLIE *approaches, and* SAM *climbs out of the light.*)

Ellie.

Spooky, isn't it?

Max.

Yes, miss.

Ellie.

I'll "Yes, miss" you!

(*She growls at him like an animal. He growls back. They repeat this more actively, then both are laughing loudly.*)

Ellie.

Hey, that's the first time I've seen you laugh.

Max.

(*Still laughing.*) Be quiet. (*Suddenly very straight.*)
You know you shouldn't be out here now.

Ellie.

(*Laughing.*) Why?

Max.

Because of the natives.

Ellie.

(*Faltering.*) Natives?

Max.

Cannibals, you know. With three legs.

(ELLIE *looks around. The sky is darker.*)

Max.

And there's nothing they'd like more than a nice bowl
of human-being *soup.*

(ELLIE *shrieks, then laughs.*)

Ellie.

Max, you're terrible!

(MAX *makes gross gobbling noises. They giggle. A
whistling sound is heard.*)

Ellie.

Max, look! A shooting star! (*She points, and they gaze
at it for a moment.*) Make a wish, Max. Make a wish.

(MAX *closes his eyes.*)

Ellie.

Now don't tell anybody what you wished.

Max.

Come on, it's getting late.

(*They climb on board.*)

Scene Fifteen

Ship's noises are heard. At the top, they meet MR.
KUIPER *for once without his clipboard.*)

Mr. Kuiper.
Mr. Jones, the Captain wants to see you.
Max.
Oh. Good-night, Ellie. I have to run.

(MAX *and* ELLIE *leave in different directions.* SAM *climbs down from above, having overheard.*)

Sam.
What's up?
Mr. Kuiper.
(*A beat.*) Dr. Hendrix is dead.

(*He moves away and begins to walk, close to tears.* SAM *follows.*)

Mr. Kuiper.
I don't know. I just don't know. I saw him before dinner—he seemed all right. But Kelly found him dead in his bunk, like a heart attack. Just keeled over. I don't know what's going to happen.
Sam.
What do you mean?
Mr. Kuiper.
Mr. Simes is now First Astrogator.
Sam.
(*Nods his head.*) What about the Captain?
Mr. Kuiper.
(*Looking straight at* SAM.) The Captain is a very old man.

(SAM *puts his hand on* MR. KUIPER's *shoulder, then exits.*)

Captain.
(*Amplified, slowly.*) This is the Captain speaking. The body of Dr. William A. Hendrix will now be passed through Airlock 42 for burial between the stars. All hands will observe silence.

(MR. KUIPER *stands alone. One by one the ship's noises shut down. Silence.*)

Captain.
Rest in peace.

   (*Fade to blackout as* MR. KUIPER *turns wearily and walks away.*)

Scene Sixteen

The control room. KELLY *and* MAX *are on computer,* SIMES *is at the scope, the* CAPTAIN *is "on books."*

Kelly.
Two minutes to transition.
Captain.
Check course.
Simes.
4378.52, 1463.43, 5589.37.
Kelly.
4785.
Max.
3261.
Kelly.
2139.
Max.
8625.
Captain.
Compute.
Kelly.
(*After a moment.*) A little off course, sir.

(*The* CAPTAIN, *looking very tired, does not answer.*)

Kelly.
Captain!
Captain.
Yes. Prepare course correction.
Simes.
4789.32, 3188.52, 4890.5.

   (*Tension is mounting.*)

Kelly.
8043.
Max.
4875.
Kelly.
3451.
Max.
8472.
Captain.
Compute.
Kelly.
(*A beat.*) Error is increasing. Thirty seconds to jump.
Captain.
Simes! Check the course.
Simes.
4782.75, 1499.36 . . .
Max.
.37
Simes.
Quiet.
Max.
It's 1482.37 seconds. You misread!
Kelly.
Twenty seconds.
Max.
Captain.
Simes.
Get off the board, Jones. *Get off.*

(MAX *stands and moves away.* SIMES *quickly takes his chair, the* CAPTAIN *sits at the scope.*)

Kelly.
8131.
Simes.
4753.
Kelly.
8016.
Simes.
3148.

Max.

Captain, it's *wrong*!

(*The* CAPTAIN *stands, confused.*)

Kelly.

Ten seconds.

(*Grabbing the book,* SIMES *moves to the speaker grill.*)

Simes.

Engineering. This is Simes. Emergency correction fire #43 for . . .

(*A low whine is heard, rapidly rising in pitch. All freeze. Abruptly the noise stops.*)

Simes.

(*Very quietly.*) Jump completed, Captain.

Captain.

Projection, please.

(*The sky lights, a field of stars, new and unfamiliar.*)

Simes.

(*A long beat.*) I've never seen that sky before.

Kelly.

Captain, we're lost.

(*All stand staring at the stars except* MAX, *who looks out at us, frightened.*)

CURTAIN

ACT TWO

Scene Seventeen

As the curtain parts, the cyc is glowing an unpleasant color, with perhaps an ominous, steamy motion in it.

We hear a strange scraping noise, metal moving slowly against metal.

Travelogue Voice.

Lost in an unknown galaxy, her fuel running low, the Asgard limped to the nearest star. It had only one planet, and there the Asgard set down in an ocean of deadly methane and ammonia, a stormy atmosphere of poison gas. This terrible place was deadly to man, but it too could provide fuel for the Asgard. The planet had no name, but Ellie called it . . . "Charity."

(*Under the voice we see* SIMES, *in silhouette, sneaking into the Worry Hole and rummaging around. As the voice finishes,* MAX *appears at the door, and flicks on the light.*)

Simes.

Turn that off!

Max.

What are you doing?

Simes.

Working.

Max.

In the dark?

Simes.

Get out of here.

Max.

I asked you what you were doing.

Simes.

This is my control room. Turn that light off.

Max.

(*Cuts around him to a console.*) These are ship's records.

Simes.

Shut up.

Max.

(*Picking up tape spools.*) These are records of the jump. You're taking them so nobody will know *you* got us lost.

Simes.

(*Dangerous.*) Give me those.

Max.

Get out of my way.

Simes.

Give me those!

(MAX *breaks around him to the door.*)

Simes.

Hold it, smart boy.

(MAX *falters.*)

Simes.

I know something about you. A little secret, shall we say? About a little boy on a farm? (*Advancing.*) And you're going to forget all about this, right now, because if you don't, I'll tell every man on this ship about you.

(*They stand face to face. Slowly* MAX *hands over the tapes.*)

Simes.

Thank you. (*Smiling.*) Oh, turn on the lights as you leave.

(SIMES *exits.* MAX *watches him go, stands a moment, then slams a fist against a wall. The lights fade out. Another scraping noise in the darkness.*)

Scene Eighteen

Lights go up on a crew meeting. KELLY, MR. GIOR-
DANO, CM-1, *and* CW-1 *are sitting on the floor or on stools. Standing are* MR. KUIPER *and the* CAPTAIN.
SIMES *enters.*)

Captain.

Is everyone here?

Mr. Kuiper.

(*Checking off* SIMES.) Yes, Captain.

Captain.

Good. (*Very gray, very quiet.*) Look around you. In this room are the most trusted members of my crew. Our passengers have been told that we are making an unscheduled stop. With you I will be more blunt. The Asgard is lost. (CREW *reaction.*) No passenger ship, having once left its course, has ever reported back to Earth. We are on our own. (*A beat.*) Miss Kelly, your report?

Kelly.

Right now we're floating on the ocean, drawing in fuel. As soon as we can, we'll lift into space again. There are two nearby stars, and if we're lucky, one of them will have a planet we can call our home. If not, I don't know what we'll do. (*She sits.*)

Captain.

Thank you. Mr. Kuiper?

Mr. Kuiper

If we find this planet . . .

Captain.

(*Softly.*) When.

Mr. Kuiper.

Beg your pardon, sir?

Captain.

(*Stranger.*) *When* we find this planet . . .

Mr. Kuiper.

Yes, sir. When we find this planet, I will be in charge of building a colony. We can live on emergency food for a time, but we will have to build homes and grow our own crops. We will be there for the rest of our lives.

CW-1.

So we're Adam and Eve?

Mr. Kuiper.

That is correct.

Captain.

Thank you. Questions?

Simes.

(*Standing.*) Captain, I think we should talk about how we got lost.

Captain.

Does that matter now?

Simes.

I think so. If I didn't have that new kid in the control room, we might be okay right now.

CM-1.

What do you mean?

Simes.

It was *his* fault.

Mr. Giordano.

You mean Jones?

Simes.

That's right. If he had . . .

Mr. Kuiper.

Sit down.

CW-1.

I think we should know.

Simes.

We should. I think we should have a trial.

Captain.

(*Suddenly very powerful.*) Mr. Simes. There will be order on my ship.

(SIMES *sits. A grim silence.* CM-1 *and* SIMES *whisper.*)

Captain.

Any . . . useful questions?

CM-1.

Captain, ever since we set down in the ocean, I hear noises sometimes. Kind of . . . scraping.

Kelly.

I've heard it too, underneath us.

CM-1.

Like something's trying to get in.

CW-1.

Something?

CM-1

What is it?

Captain.

Mr. Giordano?

Mr. Giordano.

(*Stands.*) We've all heard it. All I can say is, this is a strange planet.

CM-1.

(*As the* CREW *reacts.*) And we're sitting here, while something is out there?

Mr. Giordano.

I didn't say that.

Kelly.

We've got to get fuel.

CM-1.

(*Standing.*) We've got to get out of here. What if it . . .

Mr. Kuiper.

Shut up.

CM-1.

But it's trying to get in! It'll kill us! You're going to let it kill us!

(MR. GIORDANO *slaps him once, very hard. He shuts up, then sits.*)

Captain.

(*Strong but almost defeated.*) Gentlemen, this must never happen again. There are three hundred people on this ship, all counting on *you*. Do you understand? (*A beat.*) Mr. Giordano will investigate the noises. Work sheets will be posted tomorrow. In the meantime speak to *no one* about this. (*A beat, then wearily.*) That is all.

(*As the* CREWMEN *fan out across the set and exit* CM-1, CW-1 *and* SIMES *are in intense conversation. They see* MAX *and* SAM *and move on in a huddle.*)

Scene Nineteen

Sam.

Well, it's all messed up now.

Max.

Sam, aren't you scared?

Sam.

Scared? I've been in worse scrapes than this.

Max.

In space?

Sam.

That would be telling. (*He smiles.*) You know, kid, I may get my wish yet.

Max.

How?

Sam.

Suppose we find a green planet. Remember the stream? the fishing pole? You just wait.

Max.

(*Softly.*) Sure.

(*After a moment* SAM *exits.* MAX *sits on the edge of the scaffold, his legs dangling.* ELLIE *appears behind him. He does not look up. She sits next to him, and silently swings her legs in rhythm with his. He stops. She stops. He swings; she swings. Finally he looks at her.*)

Ellie.

(*Not loud.*) Hi, Max.

Max.

H'lo Ellie. (*He swings his legs.*)

Ellie.

Is it true?

Max.

Is what true?

Ellie.

That we're lost?

Max.

(*Stops swinging.*) Who's lost?

Ellie.

Us. The ship.

Max.

Don't know what you're talking about.

Ellie.

Max. Everybody says we goofed up in the last, whatya-macallit, transition.

Max.

(*Formally.*) I was in the control room during the last jump, and I can assure you that everything looked fine to me.

(*He stands as if to exit. Another scraping sound.*)

Ellie.

What was that?

Max.

What?

Ellie.

Oh, Max, cut it out.

Max.

Ellie, I'm not allowed to talk about it.

Ellie.

But it sounds like the whole ship is cracking.

(MAX *stands mute.*)

Ellie.

You're scared, aren't you?

(MAX *nods.*)

Ellie.

(*More gently.*) Can I help with the unpacking?

Max.

(*Surprised.*) What do you know about it?

Ellie.

Emergency stores, three hundred persons, twenty-eight days.

Max.

Where'd you hear that?

Ellie.

Daddy's an ambassador. I've been on ships plenty of times.

Max.

You know all about space jumps too?

Ellie.

That's right.

Max.

Then why'd you make me go all through it?

Ellie.
'Cause boys don't like girls who are smart.
Max.
Thanks a lot.
Ellie.
I'm sorry.
Max.
You didn't tell me you're rich, either.
Ellie.
So what? I've got a boyfriend too.
Max.
What?
Ellie.
A boyfriend. That's why I'm here. I'm traveling to see him.
Max.
You *were* traveling to see him.
Ellie.
(*A beat.*) That's not funny.
Max.
I'm sorry. I gotta go.
Ellie.
Max!
Max.
If you're so smart, you can do fine without me. (*He grabs a ladder and climbs.*)
Ellie.
Max, please!
Max.
(*Returns.*) Ellie, promise me something. Until we take off, stay in your room. Stay *inside*, away from the hull of the ship. Please. Promise me.
Ellie.
I promise.

(MAX *exits on ladder.*)

Ellie.
Bye, Max.

(*She exits.*)

Scene Twenty

The cyc darkens a bit. Faint noises, very strange. SIMES, CM-1, *and* CW-1 *appear in the darkness.*

SAM *appears unseen.*

Simes.
Ten minutes.
CM-1.
Check.
CW-1.
How about the others?
Simes.
They'll be here.

(SAM *turns away quietly.*)

CM-1.
Hey!
Simes.
Stop him!

(*They grab* SAM *and pull him forward.*)

Sam.
Let go!
Simes.
What did you hear?
Sam.
Nothing.
Simes.
(*Slaps him.*) What did you hear?
Sam.
Mutiny. (*He spits.*)
CW-1.
That's right.
Simes.
Lay off.
CM-1.
We're taking over.
Sam.
You'll have to kill the Captain!

Simes.

Shut him up!

CW-1.

Wait a minute . . .

> (SAM *jerks free and runs.*)

CW-1.

Get him!

Simes.

He's going for the alarm!

> (*They scuffle.* SAM *breaks free again and runs. Reaches a girder and pulls a lever. An alarm sounds, very loud. Stand off.* MR. GIORDANO *and* CM-2 *drop into sight and close in. They fight.* MAX, ELLIE, *and* CW-2 *add themselves to the melee.* MAX *and* SAM *team up. The fighting is deadly serious but* SAM *has found his element.* SIMES *falls, rises again, arm broken.* SAM *is pulled away and nearly goes under.* MAX *goes after him. A terrible scraping noise, then another. The lights falter. A siren goes off. The participants grab for supports.*)

Mr. Kuiper.

(*Amplified.*) General Quarters. We are under attack. General Quarters. Prepare to stand off invasion through the hull.

> (*Lights also up on* MR. KUIPER *and* KELLY *in the control room, frantically punching into the computer. Smoke billows out from under the set. More scraping and crashing. Shouts and coughing as* CREWMEN *run for cover.* SIMES *falls and is still.* ELLIE *and a* CREW-MAN *are trapped.* SAM *wades in and pulls* ELLIE, *choking, up to* MAX, *then goes back into the smoke against* MAX's *protests. He hangs oddly to a ladder, doubles over, and falls out of sight.* ELLIE *and* MAX *try to go for him, are driven back. Others are crawling or running from the gas.*
> *A different siren sounds.*)

Kelly.

(*Amplified.*) Secure for takeoff. Secure for takeoff.

(*The ship's torch roars. The cyc fades, is replaced by the strange stars. Gradual fade to silence and lingering smoke.*)

Max.

(*On the ladder where* SAM *was last seen.*) SAM!

(*He moves toward the smoke with* ELLIE. *All areas' lights fade out except on* MAX *and* ELLIE.)

Ellie.

Max! Be careful!

Max.

Sam! (*No answer.*) Sa—am!

(*After a moment, all lights dim to blackout.*)

Scene Twenty-one

MR. GIORDANO *and* MAX *are on an upper level near a block and tackle.* MR. GIORDANO *making notes on a clipboard.* ELLIE *is at the bottom of the rope below* MAX. CM-2 *carries a crate across the stage to* ELLIE, *she slips it to the rope, and* MAX *pulls it up to be recorded and stacked by* MR. GIORDANO. CM-2 *has exited, and returns with another crate.*

CM-2.

Pressed beef, thirty pounds. (*Exits.*)

Max.

(*Craning the box up.*) This is the last of the beef. How long will it last?

Mr. Giordano.

Maybe forty days. Should only last thirty, but with only half the crew . . .

Max.

Yeah.

Mr. Giordano.

Sorry.

CM-2.

(*Another crate.*) Medicine and first-aid. (*Exits.*)

Max.

Send this over to sick bay.

Mr. Giordano.

No kidding. Say, Max, I just want to say I'm really sorry about your buddy.

Max.

Sam?

Mr. Giordano.

(*Nods.*) With the Captain, Simes, everybody getting killed, I don't know if anyone said anything to you.

Max.

Thanks.

CM-1.

(*Calling from the side of the stage.*) We've got a lot of vegetable seeds, for planting. You want 'em?

Mr. Giordano.

(*Calling back.*) Leave 'em there. The only way we can fly to another planet is if we wave our arms. (*He does so.*)

Ellie.

Max?

(*No answer.*)

Mr. Giordano.

Ellie's calling you.

Max.

I know.

CM-2.

(*Another crate.*) Yeast and flour, twenty pounds.

Max.

(*Leaning over to* ELLIE.) Why don't you stay with the passengers where you belong?

Mr. Giordano.

Jones!

Ellie.

the crate to the rope.)

Mr. Giordano.
She's right.

Max.
I'm sorry. (*He pulls the box up with energy.*)

(CM-2, *having overheard, exits.* MAX *and* MR. GIOR-
DANO *unclip the crate, then* MAX *returns to the edge.*)

Max.
Ellie? (*No answer.*) I really *am* sorry. Sam being . . .
dead just . . .

Ellie.
(*Warmer.*) I know.

Max.
I promise, I really mean it, I'll never, ever be like that
again.

(ELLIE *grins, and they wave okay signs at each
other.* CM-2 *appears pushing a very large crate.* ELLIE
*runs to help him, and they laboriously move it beneath
the pulley and hook it.*)

CM-2.
Torches and metal—repair.

Mr. Giordano.
Good. That we need!

(MAX *starts to pull it up.* MR. GIORDANO *moves to
help him but* MAX *nods "no" and very slowly gets it to
the top by himself,* ELLIE *cheering him on. He and*
MR. GIORDANO *unclip it.*)

Mr. Kuiper
(*Amplified.*) Mr. Jones, report to the Captain's cabin.
Mr. Jones, report to the Captain's cabin.

Mr. Giordano.
That's you, Max.

Max.
We don't even *have* a captain.

Mr. Giordano.
Take off.

(MAX *exits.* CM-2 *appears with another large crate.*
ELLIE *again moves to help him. Lights fade on* MR.
GIORDANO.)

CM-2.
Having some trouble with your boyfriend, eh?

(ELLIE *drops her end, and the crate falls on his foot. He howls, and* ELLIE *stands and watches him with her arms crossed.*
Blackout.)

Scene Twenty-two

KELLY *and* MR. KUIPER *are in the* CAPTAIN'S *cabin.* MAX *enters.*

Mr. Kuiper.
Come in, Mr. Jones. Sit down.
Kelly.
Coffee?
Max.
Uh, yes. Thanks. (*He takes a cup.*)
Mr. Kuiper.
What shape are you in, Mr. Jones?
Max.
All right, I guess, sir. Tired maybe.
Mr. Kuiper.
I'm sorry to disturb you. Do you know what shape we're in?
Max.
(*Puzzled.*) Well, we took off from Charity because of those . . . things . . .
Kelly.
Burned to a crisp.
Max.
(*Smiles a moment.*) And there's very little food, half a crew, no planet, and not enough fuel to go anywhere.
Kelly.
But we *could* get back to where we first came out.
Mr. Kuiper.
Miss Kelly feels that we could return to the point of

transition, and try to pass through it in the other direction.

Kelly.

Get out through the door we came in.

Max.

Can I help, sir?

Mr. Kuiper.

You can do more. Did you know that every copy of the astrogation books has been destroyed?

Max.

No, sir. But I know them by heart.

Mr. Kuiper.

So Kelly insists.

Max.

Wait, do you want me to be astrogator?

Kelly.

More than that.

Mr. Kuiper.

(*With feeling.*) Max, a ship is not just steel. Like a body, it must have one head, of flesh and blood. Do you understand me?

(MAX *shakes his head.*)

Kelly.

Max, you must be captain.

(*Several beats.* KELLY *hands* MAX *a captain's jacket.*)

Max.

I can't do that.

Mr. Kuiper.

You must.

Kelly.

(*Softly.*) You can take us back, Max!

(MAX *comes forward, clutching the jacket, stands a moment. Abruptly he slips into the jacket and turns around.*)

Mr. Kuiper.

What are your orders, Captain?

Max.

Stop all unpacking. Reduce power except where need-ed. Prepare for transition. We jump in two days. We're going to try . . . (*He takes a breath.*) to go home.

(*Blackout.*)

Scene Twenty-three

Control-room noises are heard in the darkness, and voices below, all amplified. Nothing can be seen.

Kelly.

One minute to transition.

Max.

4782.40, 3572.51, 7489.55.

Kelly.

3467.

Mr. Kuiper

8426.

Kelly.

9643.

Mr. Kuiper.

1467.

Max.

Check me.

Kelly.

(*A beat.*) Your memory's still holding, Max.

Max.

Good. 4318.40, uh, 5790.13, 4465.27.

Kelly.

7563.

Mr. Kuiper.

6790.

Kelly.

7532.

Mr. Kuiper.

5668.

Max.

Check me.

Kelly.
(*A beat.*) Drifting slightly. Thirty seconds to jump.
Max.
Here we go. 8751.38, 5627.16, 957 . . . 7, uh . . .
Kelly.
Repeat.
Max.
9573.27.
Kelly.
4669.
Mr. Kuiper.
9725.
Kelly.
1385.
Mr. Kuiper.
4613.
Max.
Check me.
Kelly.
(*A beat.*) Still drifting. Give us a correction. Fifteen seconds.
Max.
483 . . . 5 . . . 4835 . . .
Kelly.
Max!
Mr. Kuiper.
4835.47, 8574.13 . . .
Max.
(*Without transition.*) . . . 8735.04
Kelly.
2579.
Mr. Kuiper.
8873.
Kelly.
6806.
Mr. Kuiper.
1423.

(*A low whine begins.*)

Max.
Transition!

(*The whine rises unbearably in pitch, holds, then, gone.*)

Max.
(*A beat.*) Projection, please.

(*The cyc lights, the old, familiar stars. Area lights begin to come up on* MAX, KELLY, *and* MR. KUIPER *in the Worry Hole, also on* MR. GIORDANO, ELLIE, CM-2, CW-1, CW-2 *scattered across the set, all facing the stars.*)

Kelly.
(*Quietly.*) That's the Big Dipper.

Ellie.
We're home!

(*General jubilation as lights and cyc fade to blackout.*)

Scene Twenty-four

Travelogue Voice.
The planet Earth circles around a star which its inhabitants simply call the "Sun." It is a pleasant place, with chlorophyll plants and fur-bearing mammals, the largest of which is the race known as "Man."

(*The cyc has begun to glow, blue sky with clouds. Somewhere a bird is chirping. We see* MAX *in silhouette, watching the clouds. He moves to the "tree" and leans against it as the lights come up. He is holding an astrogation manual with a large sheet of paper inside, and he is dressed in uniform. He takes out the paper and reads.*)

Ellie.
(*Amplified.*) Dear Max, How are you, dummy? Daddy told me the Astrogators' Guild finally let you in. They

sort of had to, didn't they, after you brought their ship back. I hear you're a real astrogator now, on the Elizabeth. Terrific. I suppose you heard I'm married now. We all gotta go sometime. Anyway, you'd love him. I know I do. Absolutely best of luck. Love, Ellie.

(MAX *smiles and climbs down a ladder. At the bottom, he glances at the letter again and grins.*)

Officer's Voice.
(*Amplified.*) Mr. Jones, report to the control room. (MAX *looks up.*) Mr. Jones, report to the Control Room.

(MAX *snaps the book shut in his hand, and on the snap the cyc switches to the stars. He tucks the book under his arm and climbs up another ladder, as . . .*)

CURTAIN

The Riddle Machine

by Beth Lambert

PREFACE

The Riddle Machine was first produced at Holiday
Theatre in Vancouver, in 1966, with a primarily unpro-
fessional (and unpaid) cast of teenagers; only Robot was
played by a professional actress. I had been asked to
write a children's stage play—my first—by Miss Joy Coghill, a remarkable woman who is responsible for so much
innovative work in Canadian children's theater. I began
with some vague idea of monster children and the general
theme of growing up—and was working out conventional
plots, with castles, fairy godmothers, witches, and so on.
Miss Coghill said, "Make it new!" and so, in the end, I
came up with a play which, Miss Coghill says, broke
almost every rule of children's theater at that time. I
think even she was rather taken aback by my unreliable,
and obviously existential, universe, but she valiantly stood
up to doubtful members of the board, as well as to those
parents who, after the first performance, canceled their
season's tickets. Critics were equally dubious. One review
in a local newspaper maintained that the play would
never be a success because it simply did not have any of
that magic which children need and demand in theater.
In general, the adult reaction was: it's an interesting idea,
but certainly not an idea for a *children's* play.

Children's reactions to the play were certainly unusual:
they would sit quite still, grasping the backs of the chairs
ahead of them. Sometimes they called out messages of
warning or encouragement, but otherwise they seemed
such an attentive—such a "good"—audience that, a
year later, when *The Riddle Machine* played at *Expo*, one
critic commented that she could not believe the children

enjoyed the play; they were all so rigid! (Later, the same critic admitted that perhaps a restless audience is a bored one.)

As for Joy Coghill and myself, I think we knew that something unexpected had happened on that first Saturday afternoon. It was the moment in the play when the space children, having just entered the atmosphere of the destination planet, come to the viewing port and cry out, "There it is, the new world!" In one silent and absolutely simultaneous movement, the entire audience of children turned in their seats to look to the back of the old movie theater in which we were playing. It was an incredible, and *very* magical, moment for us.

A year later the play went on a fully professional four-month cross-Canada tour under the aegis of Canada's centennial celebrations. And, a year after that *The Riddle Machine* was performed at The Jack and Jill Theatre in Chicago.

I remember two marvelous comments by children: One girl on returning home from the play was asked by her mother, "Well, what was it about?" "Oh, I dunno," said the girl evasively and then, turning to the adult who had taken her to the play, murmured, "I can't very well say it's about *her*." (The charge that the play was an attack on motherhood was obviated the next year by having Robot played as a man.)

After one performance a boy came up to me and said, "How did you know it was like that?" Of all the nice things that have been said about the play, I think I value that the most.

BETH LAMBERT

SOME NOTES ON THE CHARACTERS

Robot:
1. a mechanical human. The world which sent these children out so many hundreds of years ago was more developed than our own; thus Robot is not a crude mechanical contrivance but rather a pretty highly developed human replica. Still, there is a certain stiffness, an inflexibility in Robot's movements. If you can imagine never having relaxed into laughter, you may get an idea of his/her physical rigidity.* If you worked out all the synapses and circuits in the human brain, you would find that these correspond with those of Robot's. But none of the circuits leads to the making of a question; only to the making of answers.

   Confusion is registered physically—a little like a seized-up car engine or a washing machine that shakes and shivers when it is instructed to wash and rinse at the same time. These moments lead to an Emergency, for which Robot is provided with the synaptic safety valve of Making a Decision. Unfortunately, the inventors of Robot didn't realize that without laughter all incongruity is an Emergency. One incongruity concerned the formulas: Robot dutifully fed the children both formulas until it struck her as incongruous that she herself needed only *one.* Incongruity led to confusion, confusion led to the Making of a Decision: there were two possibilities— either Robot herself should take both formulas, (for wasn't she a humanoid?), or else the children really needed only one. As Robot's circuits do not lead to the making of questions, Robot has never asked herself if she was totally adequate. Self-doubt has not occurred to her. She decided that whatever is sufficient and good for the replica is sufficient and good for the model, and the diet was changed.

   Making a Decision is freedom of choice, and freedom of choice is human; and like all humans Robot is, to the degree that she is free, open to folly. Robot is equipped with a built-in abdominal computer for the answering of questions.

   * Robot has been played by both an actress and an actor.

Some people are a bit like Robot: they forget the purpose of the routine, until routine is the only end. A little like a mother who, intent on making a proper home for her family, becomes more concerned with the home than with the people who make it one; whereas all children know that cupboards are for hiding in and beds for bouncing on, mothers sometimes appear to think that cupboards are only for putting away winter blankets and beds are only for sleeping in.

Dove:

2. a rather mouldy, moth-eaten bird, who mocks folly in any form; who has lived five hundred years, if not longer. Who remembers why he has been put on board, even if no one else does. Who is perhaps a little sad with memory and knowledge, but who knows also about hope and laughter. Dove, too, or rather the unaccountable inclusion of Dove on board the spaceship, has been an incongruity. But Dove has managed to keep out of the way for five hundred years and the incongruity has not yet led to Emergency confusion and the Making of a Decision.

Ug:

3. who is to be king. Ug isn't very bright and power makes him dangerous—not because he is basically mean but because he likes to get his own way, and when he doesn't becomes a bit of a bully. Really, he wants to be liked but tends to go about it in the worst possible way. Ug lived on our street. His mother told him he was the best boy in the whole wide world, and he had to learn the hard way.

Polly:

4. Polly too lived on our street. She always reported us to our mothers when we fought, instead of letting us settle things sensibly by bashing each other and forgetting it. She was always threatening to "tell" if we did something adults thought dangerous or immoral. She allied herself with authority and suffered dreadfully for it, being called "tattle tale" or "teacher's pet." The adults thought she was a perfect little lady, which didn't help matters at all.

Casper:

5. who is a peacemaker. When he grows old, he'll probably think a lot and maybe write a history of the trip to the new world. He is kind and generous, without the violence to be a leader, but too bright to be merely a blind follower. Although he is ready to believe the best of everyone, he is too perceptive not to notice the worst when it pops up. He is much more intel-

ligent than Hap, but his intelligence makes him question too much—long past the time for action.

And then there is . . .

Cara:
6. who is different and ashamed of her difference, and . . .

Hap:
7. who is different, and who is not ashamed.

CHARACTERS

Hap
Cara
Ug
Casper
Polly
Robot
Dove

SET

A spaceship with five sleeping cells, one of which has already been ruptured. A staircase leads to Robot's quarters and workshop. There is a disposal unit, an ejection hatch, a viewing port. The Riddle Machine is a large computer-type instrument, with a sign on it saying, "DON'T TOUCH!" A formula cupboard contains two bottles labeled Blastium Fixate *and* Halcyon Pixate. *This cupboard is also used for storing Cara's feather duster Robot's wooden spoon and medical kit, etc.*

When the play opens, CARA *is dusting the spaceship.* DOVE *watches cynically. This is one of the useless tasks* ROBOT *assigns* CARA *to keep her out of mischief. Because* CARA *is not allowed to touch anything, the duster never comes in contact with the spaceship apparatus.* CARA *is trying very hard to believe in what she is doing.*

Cara.

(*Dispiritedly.*) There! That looks *much* better.

(DOVE *comes over and, with a wing tip, tests the top of one of the cells for dust. Looks at it with mock horror and holds out his wing tip for* CARA's *inspection.*)

Cara.

What do you mean, dusty? How could it be dusty? You *know* there *really* isn't any dust on a spaceship! Oh! You're making fun of me again. You mustn't make fun of me, Dove. Even if it *is* just pretend-dusting, it's very good practice for the new world. There'll be real dust there and I'll really be able to dust. In the meantime, I've got to be kept busy or I'll Get into Mischief. (*Dusts busily.*)

Robot.

(*Calling from her quarters.*) Cara?

Cara.

Yes, Robot?

Robot.

What are you doing down there?

Cara.

I'm dusting, Robot, just like you told me.

Robot.

That's a good girl. You're not touching anything, are you?

Cara.

Oh no. Just like you said, Robot. I'm just pretend-dusting. I'm not really touching anything.

Robot.

That's a good girl.

(DOVE *grabs the duster and dusts* CARA.)

Cara.

Now you stop that! Dove, please, please don't Get me into Mischief. Dove, please. I've got to be good for *some*thing, even if I am a Mistake. (*She grabs the duster from* DOVE *and goes on, pausing in front of her own cell.*) Oh dear. It's dreadful to be a Mistake. I do wish I'd waited until I was Ready. It'd be so nice to just crawl back and get up with everybody else. It's lonely to be a Mistake. (*Dusting.*) But there's no use crying over spilt milk. Still—(*looking about at the gleaming sterile spaceship.*)—I will be glad when there really is some dust or something to really clean up.

(DOVE *shrugs then pulls out some tail feathers and scatters them all over the floor.*)

Cara.

Oh! (*Quite pleased.*) Now look what you've done. You really are a naughty old bird. Robot's quite right about you, you're just a bother. (*Happily brushing up the feathers with her duster into a dustpan.*) If Robot catches you . . . ! (*Empties the dustpan into the disposal unit, which flares up satisfactorily.*) There! Now, that *really* does look much better.

(DOVE *shrugs and shakes his head at* CARA.)

Cara.

(*Comes to the viewing port and looks out.*) It's almost

time. It's almost time, Dove. Soon they'll be getting
up. I'll hear them yawn.

(HAP *yawns in his cell.*)

Cara.
And, then I'll hear them moving.

(*Hap grunts and moves.*
DOVE, *startled, looks at* HAP's *cell. Tries to attract*
CARA's *attention.*)

Cara.
It'll be nice. There'll be someone to talk to. And maybe . . .

(HAP *sleepily ruptures his cell.*)

Cara.
(*Not noticing.*) . . . maybe they won't notice the way
I am. They'll say, "Hello."
Hap.
Hello?
Cara.
That's right. And I'll say, "Hello." Stop it, Dove, I'm
busy. And they'll say, "Which one are you?"
Hap.
(*Over.*) Which one are you?
Cara.
And I'll say, "I'm Cara. Did you have a good sleep?"

(HAP *looking about.*)

Cara.
And then they'll say, "Yes, thank you very much."
Hap.
(*Over.*) Hey, where is everybody!
Cara.
(*Turns.*) Oh!
Hap.
(*Getting out, begins to bang on the sleeping cells.*)
Hey, get up, get up. Everybody out. Time to get up.
Hey!

Cara.

But it's not time! You're not supposed to be up yet. Stop that! Oh it's all my fault. I was making too much noise. I was Getting into Mischief!

(DOVE *excitedly comes up to* HAP.)

Hap.

Hey! Is it you, Dove? Hey, remember me?

Cara.

It's not time to get up! You're not Ready!

Hap.

I'm the one who brought you on board, remember? But you were just a little thing then.

Cara.

Was it *you*? Are you to blame for Dove? Oh dear!

Hap.

Just a tiny bunch of feathers then, now look at you, poor old thing. (*Scratches* DOVE'*s head.*) Someone gave you to me, just before they put us in the spaceship. Someone, some old guy, and he said I was to remember, something about doves . . . but I've forgotten.

Cara.

Oh dear, Robot's going to be so upset!

Hap.

Robot? Oh yeah, the machine. Is it still around?

Cara.

Oh shh!

Robot.

(*Calling.*) Cara?

Cara.

See?—Yes, Robot?

Robot.

What are you doing down there? You're not touching anything, are you?

Cara.

Oh no, Robot.

Robot.

You're not touching the Riddle Machine, are you?

Cara.

(*Turns to see* HAP *approaching the* RIDDLE MACHINE. *Runs and slaps his hands.*) Oh *no*, Robot, I wouldn't.

Hap.

Hey, cut that out!

Cara.

You're not to touch it. Didn't you hear Robot?

Hap.

I'm not afraid of any old Robot . . . just a bunch of nuts and bolts anyway. (*He starts to inspect the* RIDDLE MACHINE *but* DOVE *mimes caution, pointing upstairs and shh-ing with wing tip.*)

Cara.

Oh, Robot's coming! Robot's coming. You've got to get back. (*Pushes* HAP *desperately.*)

(DOVE *also begins to pull and tug at* HAP *to get him back into his cell.*)

Hap.

Hey, quit pushing. Hey! I'm not afraid of your old Robot. Hey, quit that.

(*But they succeed in getting him into the cell,* DOVE *crawling in after him and trying to hold the pieces of the cell skin together.*)

Hap.

Hey, your feathers . . . they're tickling me! (*Laughs.*)

Cara.

Oh please shhh! (*Runs to the formula cupboard and stands to attention.*)

Hap.

What's the matter, aren't we supposed to laugh either?

Cara.

Of course not. Don't be silly.

Robot.

(*Coming down the stairs.*) Ah, there you are, Cara. Are we all ready? It's feeding time.

Cara.

Yes, Robot.

(As if by solidly established routine, CARA *opens the cupboard and takes out the Blastium Fixate and a long wooden spoon. This she hands to* ROBOT. *Together they go to each of the cells,* CARA *pouring the formula into* ROBOT's *spoon and* ROBOT *feeding each of the cells through a little opening in the top.)*

Robot.

(Over.) Tsk, tsk. Poor little Cara. It's a shame. Well, mistakes *will* happen. Waste not, want not, I always say. Mistakes will happen, and one can always find *some* use for everything, even for a Mistake. Yes, indeed, there'll be plenty for you to do on the new world.

Hap.

(From within the cell.) Boy, you sure think you're somebody!

Robot.

I beg your pardon!

Cara.

I didn't say anything!

Robot.

I thought you said something.

Cara.

No. I . . . I coughed. *(Coughs to prove it.)*

Robot.

Coughed? You can't cough on a spaceship. There are no germs to cause a cough on a spaceship. It's impossible to cough.

Cara.

I'm sorry.

Robot.

Well, see that it doesn't happen again. I wouldn't like to see you become an Emergency, Cara.

Cara.

No, Robot.

(ROBOT is now feeding HAP, and he reacts.)

Hap.

Uyukkkk.

Robot.

What was that?

Cara.

(*Coughing.*) Just a tickle. In my throat. Maybe I'm allergic?

Robot.

Nonsense. You can't be allergic on a spaceship, there's nothing to be allergic *to*.

Cara.

I'm so sorry. I won't do it again.

Robot.

See that you don't.

Cara.

Yes, Robot.

Robot.

(*Ends by giving* CARA *her formula.* CARA *makes a face. Then* ROBOT *takes her dose.*) Delicious! Eh?

Cara.

Oh yes, delicious.

Hap.

Yeackk.

Robot.

I beg your pardon?

Cara.

(*Covering.*) Uh, Robot, when are we going to get there?

Robot.

Were you spoken to?

Cara.

No, Robot.

Robot.

You mustn't speak until you're spoken to. You know that, Cara.

Cara.

Yes, Robot, I'm sorry.

Robot.

(*Spotting a stray feather overlooked by* CARA.) What's this? A feather. A feather! That bird. That bird's been at it again. Oooooh. That scrawny, scraggy, scruffy,

squatter-squab has been messing up my spaceship
again!

Cara.

I'll take care of it, Robot. (*Takes the feather and disposes of it.*)

Robot.

(*Whirring and seizing up.*) Ooooooh. What *good* is
a bird on a spaceship! What's it *for*! You can't even eat
it, it's so old and stringy. Making a mess all over the
place. I won't have it, do you hear? That bird is getting to constitute an Emergency, and in an Emergency
I am empowered to Make a Decision. It's almost time,
and everything must be *ready* . . . I really am going to
have to Make a Decision about that bird.

(CARA *replaces the formula bottle and the spoon in
the cupboard while* ROBOT *begins to search for* DOVE.)

Robot.

Come out, come out, wherever you are . . . (*Low.*)
you nonfunctional featherbrained . . . fowl, you!

Riddle Machine.

(*Rings, as if an alarm clock. Then says.*) It is time to
get up.

Robot.

Oh my, oh my. Did you hear that? It's time. It's time.
Oh what a moment. Get up, get up my lovelies.
Ahhhhh. (*As the* CHILDREN *emerge sleepily.*) There
you are. Ah. Look, look, Cara, aren't they . . . beautiful! (*Beautiful they are not. Gray, uniform automatons, they lean together like straw men, and* HAP,
*with a mocking smile, leans too, assuming their dopey
expression.*) For five hundred years I've cared for them
—cared for them like a mother. Better than a mother
because *I* never make a Mistake and now, now they're
getting up. (ROBOT *reviews them.*) Perfect. Absolutely
perfect. You see—(*To* CARA)—what proper care and
attention will do? You see what a good diet and a strict
upbringing can accomplish? Hap, and Casper, and
Polly, and Ug . . . ah Ug!

(UG *slumps forward.*)

Robot.

(*Catching him.*) My pride and joy . . . look, Cara, look at Ug. Isn't he splendid? Come come, Ug, that's no way for a king to behave. There. (*Leans him against the others.*) Don't you think Ug will make a perfectly splendid king, Cara?

Cara.

(*Weakly.*) Oh yes, splendid.

Robot.

He's just a little sleepy, that's all. What you need is a few warming-up exercises. Come along now. One, two, three, four, one, two, three, four.

(ROBOT *leads them in an exercise pattern. The* CHILDREN *react with wooden movements, like baby robots.* HAP *follows, mocking them, but without catching* ROBOT's *eye.* ROBOT *manipulates their arms and legs until everyone is working in clocklike order, expressionless and stone-eyed.*)

Robot.

Very good, very good. Excellent. One, two, three, stop. Now, children, in a very few moments you will be put to the test. In a few moments, the Riddle Machine is going to ask you a very important question, and you must be ready for that question. So if there's anything you'd like to know, now's the time to find out. Come, come, we're on a very tight schedule, you know. If there's anything you'd like to know, I have all the answers here in my computer. (*Indicating her abdominal computer.*) No questions? No questions. Well, of course. You're all absolutely perfect. There's really no need to ask questions at all. You already know all you need to know. One, two, right turn—(*To face the* RIDDLE MACHINE.) Attention!

Hap.

I've got a question.

Robot.

Ah. A question. (*Punching her computer buttons in readiness.*)

Hap.

When do we get to the new world?

Robot.

Ah yes, a very good question. Your question, Ug? Yes, of course, it must be Ug's question, such an intelligent question. (*Presses the computer buttons.*) When do we get to the new world? (*The computer ejects a piece of paper, rather like a ticker tape.* ROBOT *reads.*) "We shall arrive at our destination in exactly twelve hours, our earth time." (*Disposes of the slip of paper in disposal unit.*) There. Got to keep things tidy. Now, anything else? An excellent question, Ug. (*Starts to turn again.*)

Hap.

I've got another. Who gave you the say-so anyway?

Robot.

Ah yes. (*Pressing buttons.*) A question. And every question has an answer. Who gave you the say-so ...anyway????? Who said that? Who asked that question? Which one of you—?

Riddle Machine.

Attention.

Robot.

Oh my. Yes, pay attention now. Straighten up there. Shhh! Shh! Quiet. The Riddle Machine is going to speak!

Riddle Machine.

(*A quiet contrast to* ROBOT'*s excited voice.*) Good morning, children. I say "Good morning" because it *is* morning for you and for the new world you are about to enter. For five hundred years my voice has been waiting for you. In a short while the spaceship will reach your destination—an unknown planet far beyond our stars. But, before you will be allowed to enter that new world, you must answer a riddle. You will have three chances only. Listen carefully. And think. Here is the riddle:

> When all of space has yielded to travel
> And is as simple as A, B, and C,
> What will still be left to unravel,

The puzzle, the mystery, the final key?
What is the greatest riddle of all?

Robot.

Well, go on, answer the riddle. It's perfectly simple.

Casper.

Think.

Polly.

Answer.

Ug.

The riddle.

Robot.

Come along, Ug, you're to be king. *You* answer the riddle. The greatest riddle of all is . . . the greatest riddle of all is . . . ?

Ug.

The greatest riddle of all is—the greatest riddle of *all*.

Robot.

Right!

Riddle Machine.

Wrong. You are not ready.

Robot.

Wrong? But it was perfectly logical!

Hap.

Oh boy, how dumb can you get!

Robot.

Who said that? Who *said* that? You! Come here. Come here at once!

Hap.

(*Goes to the* RIDDLE MACHINE.) Hey, this is quite a rig. What's this for?

Robot.

Don't touch, don't touch. Can't you read? You must not touch the Riddle Machine. Oh my nuts and bolts. Something's gone wrong. You're not right at all.

Hap.

I don't look like them, if that's what you mean. Who wants to! Eyeackkk.

Robot.

You're cheeky.

Hap.

Aw, go bust an electrode.

Robot.

Don't touch!—You're disobedient.

Hap.

I'm not hurting anything.

Robot.

You're naughty. And you're bad. (*Musing.*) You're a bad, naughty, cheeky, disobedient boy. This constitutes an Emergency. And in an Emergency I am empowered to Make a Decision. *You* are going to have a checkup. Checkup time. Cara?

(CARA *scurries for the cupboard and extracts* RO-BOT's *medical kit.*)

Robot.

Just sit here.

Hap.

I don't need a checkup, I feel fine.

Robot.

I'm the best judge of that.

Hap.

Couldn't catch a cold if you ran for it.

Robot.

(*Grasps him and sits him down firmly. Begins to check him with various complicated-looking instruments.*) It just so happens . . . that I am a competent practitioner in all the medical arts . . . I have my degrees in biology, zoology, psychology, mineralogy, archaeology, and paleontology.

Hap.

All the same, you're just a machine.

Robot.

(*Warningly.*) I am also a specialist in *surgery.* (*Sticking an instrument in his mouth.*) Now, we shall see. You're obviously an error of some kind. (*Pushing computer buttons as the investigation proceeds.*) You're either overdone or underdone, but something is dreadfully wrong. And now we'll see precisely what the matter is. (*Computer tape comes out.*) Why, you're not finished! You're not done at all. You got up early, didn't you? You didn't wait to be told. That's why you're a bad, naughty, cheeky, disobedient boy. This constitutes an Emergency, and in an Emergency I am empowered to Make a Decision. Now, what do we do with bad, naughty, cheeky, disobedient boys, children?

Casper.

Something nasty.

Polly.

Lock him in a closet where it's dark.

Ug.

Give him a spanking?

Robot.

Nooo, noo, I'm not programmed to harm a human . . . but you're quite right, children, bad, naughty, cheeky, disobedient boys must be punished.

Hap.

(*Disentangling himself from the medical apparatus, which* CARA *picks up and puts away.*) I'd like to see you try!

Ug.

I think you ought to be spanked.

Hap.

I've got a few ideas for you too, Ugly.

Polly.

Put him in a closet where it's dark.

Casper.

It's *al*ways something nasty.

Robot.

A closet, a nice dark closet . . . yeees. I've got just the thing. Children!

(CHILDREN *come to attention.*)

Robot.

Catch the bad, naughty, cheeky, disobedient boy.

Hap.

Ya, ya, ya ya yaa, can't catch me! (*And they chase him, stiff and incompetent, blundering about.*)

Robot.
Come, come, on your toes, please.

> (CHILDREN *obediently go up on their toes.*)

Robot.
No, no, you're chasing Hap, remember?
Hap.
Yeah, you're chasing me, remember?
Robot.
Come along now, pull yourselves together.

> (*They try to do so literally.*)

Casper.
(*Stopping to think it over.*) I don't really think I'm coming apart, Robot.
Robot.
There! He's right in front of you. Follow your nose!
Hap.
(*As* CASPER *and* POLLY *literally attempt to follow their noses,* HAP *catches* UG's *nose and pulls him about.*) Like this, here, I'll show you . . . follow your nose!
Robot.
Oh my goodness, will you please use your heads!

> (UG *uses his head as a battering ram and bowls* HAP *over, sitting on his chest to hold him down.* POLLY *then grabs his arms, and* CASPER *grabs his legs.*)

Robot.
Ah! Excellent, Ug, excellent. Not every king can use his head the way you can. Now, children, put the bad, naughty boy in the ejection unit. It's not as good as a closet, but it will have to do.

> (*They drag* HAP *to the ejection unit.*
> ROBOT *waits until the breathless* HAP *is deposited, then flicks the switch and he is enclosed in a space lock.*)

Cara.
You're not going to *eject* him, are you, Robot?

Robot.

Why, Cara, I hadn't thought of that. Eject him. Yes, that's a very good idea. Space is much darker than a closet, and colder too. It would teach him a lesson. (*Moves for the switch.*)

Cara.

Oh no! I mean, if you eject him, won't he . . . explode?

(HAP *has regained his breath and is feeling the walls of the ejection unit.*)

Robot.

A question. And every question has an answer. If Hap is ejected into space—(*Punching computer buttons.*) —will he explode? (*The answer comes back on a long, long tape. Reading.*) "The internal pressure of the human body, not being equal to the complete lack of pressure in space, will . . ." hum, hum, hum, hum, yes, it certainly seems likely that he will explode. Well, that's human beings for you. A *machine* wouldn't explode! No, no, I can't eject him, I'm not programmed to harm a human being, you see. He'll be perfectly all right in there though, until he learns his lesson. And until the air runs out.

Cara.

Until the *air* runs out?

Robot.

Oh my, yes, the air's running out, you know. Hap will have to learn his lesson soon. Or he'll choke to death.

Polly.

But we won't let you out till you're good. So there.

Casper.

It's much nicer to be good.

Ug.

I'm the king of the castle, and Hap's the dirty rascal.

Robot.

Now, there was something I had to do, now what was it?

(HAP *is kicking the walls of the ejection unit.*)

Polly.

I'll tell. Robot? He's kicking.

Robot.

Yes, yes, but you must be quiet now. There's something I have to do . . .

Polly.

But he's kicking, Robot, he's kicking and he's banging.

Robot.

Ooooh . . . do be quiet. Uh . . . do your exercises or something.

(*They immediately go into their exercises.*)

Robot.

Now, what was it . . . That boy has upset the entire routine. Ah! the riddle. I've got to find you the answer to the riddle, or you'll never get to the new world at all. Yes. The Riddle. Well, a riddle's only a question, and every question has an answer. Be good now. I'm going to my quarters to make an answer. (*Starts up the stairs.*)

Cara.

Robot? You won't forget, about the air?

Robot.

Forget? A machine never forgets. I'll let him out, as soon as he's learned his lesson. Now, be good, and don't Get into Mischief.

(HAP *signals to* CARA *to come and let him out.*)

Cara.

Oh, I can't. I've got to be good. (*Joins the* CHILDREN *and tries to do the exercises, but stumbles.*)

Polly.

(*As* CARA *makes a mistake.*) You're not doing it *right*. I'm going to tell. (*Calling.*) Robot!

Cara.

I'm *try*ing.

Robot.

Now what is it?

Polly.

Cara's not being good.

Robot.
Oh for goodness' sake, *will* you be quiet down there!
Cara.
I'm *try*ing to be good.
Polly.
Shh! Be quiet.

> (DOVE *emerges from* HAP's *cell and watches the* CHILDREN. *Then begins to do an absurd step which throws them off.*)

Ug.
That silly bird's making me lose my step.
Casper.
Don't pay any attention.
Polly.
Sh!!

> (HAP *is beginning to feel the lack of air.*
> DOVE *continues to mock the* CHILDREN *until he catches sight of* HAP. *Quickly, he goes to the ejection unit, grasps the situation, and goes to get Cara.*)

Cara.
Please Dove, don't, you'll get me into Mischief.

> (HAP *begins to pound desperately, but with gathering weakness, on the wall of the ejection unit.*
> DOVE *tugs frantically at* CARA.)

Cara.
Oh Dove, what is it? (*Sees.*) Oh. (*Goes to* HAP.) What's the matter.
Hap.
(*Mouths.*) No . . . air.
Cara.
Oh . . . I can't hear. What is it? Robot! Robot!
Robot.
Are you being a good girl, Cara?
Cara.
Yes, but—
Robot.
You're not touching anything, are you?

Cara.

Oh no, Robot, but—

Robot.

Then, for goodness' sake—be quiet!

Polly.

Shhhhh!

Cara.

Oh what will I do . . . he's choking. He's used up the air. (*To the* CHILDREN.) Please help me. I'm sure he's used up all the air, and now he's choking!

Ug.

Don't bother us.

Casper.

We're being good.

Polly.

Hap's a bad, naughty, disobedient boy, and he's got to be punished.

Ug.

And I'm the king of the castle.

Cara.

Oooooooh.

(HAP *slumps to the floor.*

DOVE *pulls* CARA *toward the ejection-unit control board.*)

Cara.

But I can't. I haven't been *told*. Robot hasn't *said*. (*Looks at* HAP.) But I don't know which one. "Open exit hatch"—no, not that one. "Close ejection unit"—no. "Open ejection unit"—I really shouldn't. (*Closes her eyes.*) Now I'll never be good! (*Pulls the lever. The ejection-unit door swings open and* HAP *falls onto the floor of the spaceship.*)

Polly.

I saw what you did. I'm going to tell! Robot! ROBOT!

Robot.

Now that's enough. Go back to your cells. You're all being very naughty.

Polly.

(*To everyone.*) Shhh!

(*They go to their cells.*

DOVE *is fanning* HAP *with his wings.* CARA *kneels beside him.*)

Ug.

(*From his cell, whining.*) I'm hun*grey.*

Polly.

Shh!

Hap.

(*Sits up dazedly.*) I'm out . . . whew!

Cara.

I did it. I let you out.

Hap.

(*Disgusted.*) Yeah, you sure took your own sweet time about it. Didn't you see me dying in there? Now what's the matter!

Cara.

It's just that, now I'll never be like them. I was going to try and try, but now I'll always be a Mistake. And you too.

Hap.

Oh, stop that. You don't want to be like them . . . they're Mistakes if anyone is. Where are they anyway?

Cara.

In their cells.

Hap.

And It? The machine?

Cara.

Robot's up in her quarters. Making an answer to the riddle.

Hap.

But it's our riddle!—We've got to do something about that machine.

(DOVE, *excited, mimes that* HAP *is to get up.*)

Cara.

Oh, please don't do anything else. Don't get into any more trouble.

Hap.

No, they're the Mistakes, Cara. We're all right, or I am, and you'd be all right too if you'd stop sniveling. But Robot's done something to them . . . they're not right at all.

(DOVE *listening, encouraging* HAP, *nods his head.*)

Hap.

See? Dove thinks so too, don't you, Dove—They'll never be able to answer the riddle the way they are. Yes, yes, Dove, that's a good fellow, but I'm trying to figure out something now. (*Brushes* DOVE *away.*)

Cara.

No, *we*'re the ones who aren't right. *Robot* said—

Hap.

"Robot said, Robot said!" That machine's been feeding you a bunch of malarkey.

(DOVE *reacts strenuously to this idea, but* . . .)

Hap.

All right, Dove, but I can't play with you just now. Let me try to think. Cara, you were up before me. Did Robot do anything to the others? You know, did she do anything special to their cells?

Cara.

Noo. Nothing much at all. Of course, Robot *fed* you every day. But that's all really.

(DOVE *jumps up and down and claps his wings.*)

Hap.

It's no time for games, Dove. We're being serious.

Cara.

Poor Dove. I think he's been lonely, all these years. And Robot hates him so. He's missed having company, I think. And then, it *was* you who brought him on board.

Hap.

Okay, old fellow. Yes, yes, I'll play with you in a while. But not just now. If only there was someone who'd been here all along, someone who could tell us—

Cara.

Dove! Dove's been here all along, for five hundred years!

Hap.

Oh sure. That's a big help. Doves can't talk.

Cara.

No, but . . . (*Looks at* DOVE.) I think he can *show* us. Hap, that's what Dove's trying to say. Isn't it, Dove? You can *show* us.

(DOVE *nods vigorously.*)

Hap.

Can you show us, old fellow? Is that it? Yes? Good! Go on then, quickly, before the machine gets back. What happened? What did Robot do to them?

(DOVE *mimes eating.*)

Hap.

Something to do with . . . eating?

(DOVE *flaps his wings and nods.*)

Hap.

With eating . . . but we didn't *eat* . . .

(DOVE *mimes going to the cupboard . . . mimes the walk of* ROBOT *. . . taking down a bottle, pouring the formula into a spoon.*)

Cara.

The feeding formula. That's how Robot always fed you.

Hap.

The formula. Did Robot do something to the feeding formula?

(DOVE *shakes head.*)

Hap.

Then *what* did Robot do? It's no good, I don't understand you, Dove.

(DOVE *goes to the feeding-formula cupboard and indicates both jars.*)

Hap.

Yes, yes, there were two jars of formula . . .

(DOVE *mimes that* ROBOT *used only the Blastium Fixate.*)

Hap.

Robot used this one? But *not* that one? Not *that* one?

Cara.

That's right! Robot never used the Halcyon Pixate. Only the Blastium Fixate. I asked her once, why, but she got very upset.

Hap.

That's it then! Robot changed the feeding formula. That's it, isn't it, Dove?

(DOVE *indicates with great relief that* HAP *has got it.*)

Hap.

Then *they*'re all suffering from vitamin deficiency or something. We've got to feed them the other formula too. Come on, Cara, you hold the spoon . . . (*Getting the bottle of Halcyon Pixate.*)

Cara.

Oh dear, I don't know if I should . . .

Robot.

(*Calling.*) You're all very quiet down there. Are you Getting into Mischief?

Cara.

Oh dear.

Robot.

You're not touching anything, are you? You're not touching the Riddle Machine?

Cara.

Oh no, Robot. (*To* HAP.) We can't! It would be wrong. It can't be the formula. That's all *we* had, and we aren't like them. And besides, I've got to be good.

(DOVE *indicates that* ROBOT *is coming.*)

Cara.

Robot's coming. Hap! Put it back. Please.

Hap.

(*Replaces the bottle.*) Then it's up to you, Cara. If Robot sees me, she'll *know*. But you can do it... I'll hide. (*Goes to his cell.*) It's up to you now, Cara.

Cara.

No, no, I mustn't.

Robot.

(*Appearing with a tool kit.*) No answer! No answer at all. That's human efficiency for you. I've gone through my computer from Riddle to Reason, but there's not an answer anywhere. A riddle's only a question, and every question has an answer, and that answer must be *some*place. (*Eyes the* RIDDLE MACHINE. *Then sees* DOVE.) Aha! I've caught you now. (*Pounces on* DOVE.) Haven't I enough to do without mouldy, mangy, misbegotten... mudhens! on my spaceship? See! There! You've dropped a feather. You're *al*ways dropping feathers. I won't have it, I tell you, I won't have mess on my nice, clean spaceship. You've been an Emergency right from the beginning, and in an Emergency I am empowered to Make a Decision.

(DOVE *after a scuffle, manages to escape* ROBOT*'s grasp and dodges awkwardly about the spaceship, finally waddling behind the* RIDDLE MACHINE. ROBOT *pursues but is brought up short by recall of the larger Emergency.*)

Robot.

Come here! Catch it, Cara!—Ooooh. If it isn't one thing, it's another. (*Stops at* MACHINE.) But, first things first. You can wait. I'll deal with you later. (DOVE *waddles off to a safe vantage point.*) Right now, I've a much more important Emergency to deal with. (*Sets down the toolbox. To* RIDDLE MACHINE.) You're a machine, and I'm a machine. A riddle is only a question and every question has an answer. *You*'ve got that answer, inside you. (*She begins to unscrew the panel of the* RIDDLE MACHINE.)

Cara.

(*Shocked.*) Robot!

Robot.

Eh? What? Oh, it's only you, Cara.

Cara.

You're touching the Riddle Machine!

Robot.

Now that's a good girl, go on about your business.

Cara.

But the sign says "DON'T TOUCH."

Robot.

Good little girls should be seen and not heard.

Cara.

But, you're being disobedient.

Robot.

Cara? You want to be good, don't you?

Cara.

You're not being good!

Robot.

Just go on about your dusting.

Cara.

I won't. There's nothing *to* dust.

Robot.

Cara, if you're going to be naughty, I'll have to punish you. You wouldn't want that, now would you? (*Has got the panel off now.*)

Cara.

(*Glances at the ejection unit.*) Noooo . . .

Robot.

I'm only doing this for your own good. You'll understand when you're older.

(CARA *simmers, but takes up her duster.*)

Ug.

(*From inside the cell.*) Row-bot. I'm hun-grey.

Casper.

Me too. I'm hungry.

Robot.

In a minute.

Polly.

I'm starving!

Robot.

In a *min*-ute!

Ug.

(*Grumpily.*) Aren't I supposed to be king? Didn't you say I'm supposed to be king?

Robot.

You're not king yet. You have to get there first.

Ug.

Well, if I'm supposed to be king, then I want my lunch. What's the good of being king, if you can't have your lunch when you want it?

Robot.

You can't be king at all unless you get to the new world, and you can't get to the new world unless you answer the riddle . . . (*Gets a screwdriver and begins to poke about inside the* RIDDLE MACHINE—*Lights flicker dangerously and* ROBOT *and* CARA *glance up uneasily.*) And you can't answer the riddle unless I find the answer . . .

Ug.

(*Over.*) But I'm starving to death!

Robot.

. . . Oh, all right! I'm coming. (*Puts down the screwdriver and goes to the formula cupboard.*) If it isn't one thing, it's another. Cara?

Hap.

Cara? Now!

Cara.

(*Looks from one to the other, then puts away her duster.*) Yes. I . . . I'll try. (*Signals to* DOVE *and they go into a huddle while* ROBOT *fusses about at the cupboard.*)

Robot.

(*Taking out the wooden spoon.*) Cara?

Cara.

Yes, I'm coming.

(*Reaches up to get the Blastium Fixate, then* DOVE *goes into action, distracting* ROBOT *by awkwardly bumping into her, upsetting the routine, even causing* ROBOT *to drop the spoon.*)

Robot.
Get away. Get away, you horrid bird. Stop that. Oh, my nuts and bolts, it's going to be one of those days!

(CARA *switches the bottles.*
DOVE *waddles away hurriedly.*)

Robot. . . . .
You wait. You just—wait. I'll get my digitals on you yet.

Polly, Casper, and Ug.
(*Over.*) I'm hungry!

Robot.
Cara? Where are you? Get the formula.

Cara.
Yes, Robot. (*Takes down the Halcyon Pixate and pours it into* ROBOT's *spoon.*)

Robot.
Here we are! (*Gives a spoonful to* UG, *who sticks his head out obediently.*) Robot's own special formula.

Cara.
Your own special formula, Robot?

Robot.
Yes, of course. (*To* UG.) Isn't that nice now, doesn't that taste good?

(*As* CARA *pours the next spoonful.*)

Ug.
Mmmmm-MMM!

Cara.
Then you *did* change the diet.

Robot.
Of course I changed the diet. The things they gave you. Tch.

Ug.
Peanut brittle!

Robot.
Yes, precisely . . . (*As she feeds* CASPER.) . . . things like peanut brittle . . .

Casper.

Ice cream?

Robot.

. . . and ice cream. Absolutely unheard of, a diet like
that. All *I* need is right here in the Blastium Fixate . . .
(*Feeds* POLLY.)

Cara.

But, Hap and me, we were fed the same formula, and
we didn't turn out . . . like them.

Robot.

Well, a good formula doesn't always take with human
beings, they're funny that way. (*Counting the cells.*)
. . . That reminds me . . . (*But* CARA *is ready to pour
out her own dose.* ROBOT *feeds* CARA.)

Polly.

Strawberry pie!

Robot.

Strawberry pie! Yes, that's the sort of stuff *they* would
have given you. Peanut brittle, ice cream, strawberry
pie. It certainly was a good thing I was here to Make
a Decision. After all, all I needed was the Blastium
Fixate, and I decided that what's good enough for a
robot, is certainly good enough for a . . .

Cara.

A gingerbread man.

Robot.

A *what*?

Cara.

Mine tastes like a gingerbread man.

Polly.

Oh no. Strawberry pie.

Casper.

Tutti frutti. (*Contemplating.*) Maple walnut . . .
chocolate fudge . . . whipped cream . . . and a cherry
on the top. Definitely ice cream.

Robot.

Ice cream? Peanut brittle? Strawberry pie? Nonsense
. . . Blastium Fixate always tastes like . . . (*Tasting
spoon.*) . . . Halcyon *Pix*ate? Halcyon Pixate! Oh my
nuts and bolts! (*Takes the bottle from* CARA *and reads*

label.) You stupid girl! You've used the wrong formula! (*Keeps bottle until next needed.*)

Hap.

(*Emerging from his cell.*) Hey, how about me? I'd like some too.

Robot.

You! (*Whirls to check ejection unit.*) How did you get out?

Hap.

I don't want strawberry pie or peanut brittle or even ice cream. What I want's a hot row-bot . . . ha . . . and I think I've got one too!

Robot.

It was *you*! You did this. You did it on purpose.

Cara.

No. It was me. I did it. And I don't think I even care. Ooooh . . . I feel so funny . . .

Robot.

But we've given them a massive overdose. There's no telling what will happen now. (*Goes to the* RIDDLE MACHINE *and turns her back on them all.*) Well, I've done *my* best. You'll see. You're just like all human beings . . . you can't leave well enough alone. It's not my fault.

Hap.

But you're all right, aren't you, Cara? Cara?

Cara.

Oh Hap, I feel so . . . queer . . . but, it's . . . nice too.

(*The* CHILDREN *emerge from their cells, wondrously changed. They look about themselves in dazed wonder.*)

Hap.

Oh look, Cara, look. They're all new. Robot, look.

Robot.

(*Steals a look, then turns away again.*) It's not my fault, whatever happens.

Ug.

What's happening? I feel very odd.

Casper.

I've got the most interesting feeling . . .

Polly.

I'm sure I should tell on somebody, but I can't remember who to tell.

Cara.

Oh, you're all so beautiful! And me, I'm beautiful too. I'm not a Mistake anymore. Now I'm just like everybody else. Oh, I feel like dancing and singing . . .

Ug.

Yes. I shall sing a song!

Casper.

I think I might dance.

Polly.

I'm going to fly!

Robot.

(*To* HAP.) Now see what you've done!

Hap.

But they're wonderful. They're really perfect now.

Robot.

You wait.

(*The* CHILDREN *are beginning to move about.* CARA *begins to sing.*)

Cara.

(*To "In and Out the Window."*)
      I've got a funny feeling,
      It's really quite appealing,
      If something doesn't happen,
      I'll simply blow my cork!   Whee!

Casper.

(*To "All Around the Mulberry Bush."*)
      Everything is turning around
      And nothing is familiar,
      Down is up and up is down,
      I'm feeling most peculiar . . .

Polly.

(*To "See Saw Margey Daw."*)
      Hee, haw, folderol,
      Come and dance with me, Casper . . .

I'll show you how to dance and sing . . .
Oh can't you go any faster?!

(*She grabs* CASPER *and begins to pull and push him about the spaceship, whirling him faster and faster.*)

Cara.

I've got a funny feeling,
It's almost got me reeling,
If I don't make it happen,
I'll simply blow my cork!

(*And she grabs* DOVE *and begins to dance about with him.* DOVE *gets away as fast as possible, his dignity impaired.*)

Ug.

I'm not sure a king should do anything silly, but . . .
(*Leaping, to "Three Blind Mice."*)

Whizz, bang, whoo!
I've got an itch in my shoe.
I know it'll never go away
Until I kick up my heels and say
Whizz, Bang, Whoo!
Got an itch in my shoe!
Zip, Zap, Zot!
An itch is what I've got!
I've got to dance the itch away,
C'mon Robot, whadd'ya say?

(*Grabs* ROBOT *and dances with her, dragging her about.*)

Whizz, Bang, Whoo!
Zip, Zap, Zot!

(*Everything becomes confused and chaotic. Everyone is singing his or her own song, dancing faster and faster in a frenzy of excitement.* POLLY *grabs* DOVE *now, and* ROBOT *is passed from one* CHILD *to the next. Finally,* ROBOT *extricates herself [and the bottle of Halcyon Pixate] from the clutches of* UG. *She limps over to sit beside the* RIDDLE MACHINE.)

Robot.

Now see what you've done. You've gone and loosened a screw.

Ug.

(*Laughing.*) Robot's got a screw loose, Robot's got a screw loose!

Children.

(*Panting, take up the refrain.*) Robot's got a screw loose!

Cara.

Ah, poor old Robot. Here, I'll fix it for you. (*Gets the screwdriver and tightens the screw.*)

Robot.

Hmmph! (*Flexing leg.*) It'll never be the same again.

Cara.

Ug didn't mean any harm.

Robot.

Humans never do.

Ug.

C'mon, what'll we do now?

Polly.

Yes, let's *do* something.

Casper.

Hide and go seek?

Polly.

I'll be *it*.

Casper.

I'll be *it*. I thought of it first.

Ug.

I'm king. I'll be *it*. (*Hides his eyes.*) One, two, three, four, no hiding behind the goal . . .

Polly.

I'm not going to play if I can't be *it*.

Casper.

Me neither. Nobody ever lets me have any fun.

Hap.

Oh, don't be silly. We can all play. We'll take turns.

Casper.

You keep out of this. Who asked you?

Polly.

Yeah, who asked you to butt in?

Ug.

Buttinsky!

Cara.

Oh, who wants to play anyway. (*Wanders to viewing port.*) When are we going to get to the new world?

(*They wander over listlessly and look out, like children peering out of a window on a rainy day.*)

Hap.

(*Baffled.*) What's the matter?

Ug.

Oh, we're never going to get there.

Polly.

There's nothing to do on this stupid old spaceship anyway.

Casper.

I wish I had a good book to read.

Hap.

But you were so happy! You were all having so much fun!

Cara.

Well, we're not having any fun now.

Polly.

I want to go ho-ooome!

Riddle Machine.

Attention! Attention! You are about to enter the atmosphere of the new world.

(*The spaceship begins to rattle and shake. Everyone shudders under the impact.*)

Hap.

Hold on, everybody!

(*The lights blink, the tremors subside.*)

Polly.

Ooooooh.

Cara.

There it is, the new world!

Hap and Robot.

Come to LOOK. (*Everyone sighs.*)

Hap.

We're almost there. It's only a few hundred miles away.

Cara.

It's so beautiful . . . look at the oceans . . .

Casper.

And the mountains . . .

Ug.

And the rivers . . .

Robot.

My brand new world!

Hap.

Our brand new world!

Riddle Machine.

You will now be able to see your destination, the new planet, but you will not be allowed to enter that new world until you answer the riddle. This is your second chance. If you are unable to answer the riddle correctly, the spaceship will remain in the atmosphere until your third and final chance. Now, listen carefully.

Hap.

Sh! Everyone be quiet.

Polly.

I'll answer the riddle. It's my turn.

Ug.

No you won't. I'm king.

Casper.

If everyone will just be quiet and let me think, *I'll* answer the riddle.

Ug.

I'll answer the riddle.

Polly.

You did it last time, it's my turn now.

Casper.

Nobody ever lets me have any fun.

Hap.

Sh!

Cara.

Oh, you're always so bossy!

Riddle Machine.

When all of space has yielded to travel,
And is as simple as A, B, and C,
What will still be left to unravel,
The puzzle, the mystery, the final key?
What is the greatest riddle of all?

Ug.

I've got it, I've got it!

Hap.

Are you sure? Be careful.

Ug.

The greatest riddle of all is . . . the greatest riddle of all
is . . .

Polly.

He's just making it up, he doesn't know at all.

Ug.

I do too. The greatest riddle of all is: What has ten
legs, feathers, and no eyes at all? Ha ha. You'll never
get it.

Riddle Machine.

You—are—not—ready.

Hap.

Oh Ug! For crying in the sink!

Robot.

Wouldn't listen to *me*! Oh no.

Ug.

Well, *I* think that's a pretty good riddle.

Hap.

Not that kind of riddle!

Casper.

(*Pondering.*) What *does* have ten legs, feathers . . .

Ug.

And no eyes at all? You'll never get it . . . give up?
Five ostriches, with their heads in the sand. Ha ha.

Polly.

Five ostriches? Boy, what a dumb riddle. Boy, Ug, are
you ever dumb.

Hap.

You've wasted our second chance. And there's only
one more. Now we've all got to really think, or we'll
never get to the new world at all.

Polly.

Robot? What can we do now? What can we play now?

Hap.

You're not to play anything. We've got to be serious.
We've got to find the answer to the riddle.

Ug.

Oh, don't worry about the riddle, Hap. Robot can
answer it, can't you, Robot?

Cara.

That's right. You were going to answer it anyway,
weren't you, Robot?

Casper.

Sure. What have we got a robot for anyway . . . let
her answer the riddle.

Robot.

Hmmph! Oh yes. Human beings all over. You've all
done exactly what you pleased. You've all been
naughty, bad, disobedient and cheeky . . . loosened
my screw and hurt my feelings and now *I'm* supposed
to answer your silly old riddle. Now *I'm* supposed to
take care of everything.

Hap.

Robot can't answer the riddle. It's *our* riddle, and
we've got to do it ourselves.

Cara.

But I don't really feel like worrying about the riddle,
Hap. I'm feeling, I don't know, sort of sad . . . maybe
if I could have some more of the Halcyon Pixate,
Robot.

Ug.

Yes, let's have some more peanut brittle.

Polly.

Strawberry pie.

Casper.

Tutti frutti maple walnut chocolate fudge ice cream!

Robot.

Oh no you don't! You have quite enough already.

Hap.

That's right. It just makes you silly. Silly little babies, that's all you are. Now grow up, and answer the riddle.

Ug.

Aw, Hap, don't be such a spoilsport. Robot can answer the riddle.

Hap.

Robot can't answer the riddle, Robot's just a machine!

Robot.

Oh, is that so? Is that so? Just a machine, am I? Let me tell you, young man, it's very fortunate for you I *am* a machine. Yes, indeed, children, I'll answer your riddle for you. Robot will take care of everything. But first you must be very good, and do exactly what Robot tells you to do.

Polly.

Can we have some more strawberry pie?

Robot.

Yes, yes, anything your little hearts desire, only you must promise to be very very very good, and do just what Robot says.

Polly.

Oh, we will, we will.

Robot.

Very well, then, just a little taste, not too much, we don't want to spoil your supper, do we? (*Starts to pour the formula into the spoon, the* CHILDREN *crowding about . . .*)

Hap.

What are you doing? It's dangerous for them, you said so yourself!

Robot.

Don't pay any attention to Hap, children; he's an awful old spoilsport, isn't he? Here, Cara, just a teensy-weensy taste . . .

Hap.

(*Knocks the spoon away and grabs the formula bottle from* ROBOT.) No! You're not going to get any more.

You're going to answer the riddle and go to the new world. We'll make our own food, nobody has to spoon feed us. We're not babies! (*And he pours the bottle down the disposal unit.* ROBOT *grabs the bottle away, but it is too late.*)

All.

OOoooooh!

Polly.

Is it all gone?

Hap.

Yes, it's all gone, so grow up!

Children.

OOOoooooooooh!

Robot.

Never mind, children. I *do* think I've got just enough bits and bobs up in my quarters to make you all some nice new formula. Would you like that?

Hap.

What? *New* formula? What are you trying to do? What are you up to now?

Robot.

Never you mind about Hap, sweeties, he's just an old party pooper, doesn't want anyone to have any fun.

They.

Hap is a party pooper, Hap is a party pooper.

Hap.

Can't you see what Robot's up to? She just wants to be the big boss of everything. Forever and ever. Even on the new world.

Robot.

Oh, don't listen to Hap, dearies. Just so long as you have lots of fun and can laugh and dance and sing all you like—you let Robot worry about the serious things. That's what you *want*, isn't it?

(*The* CHILDREN *pause.*)

Ug.

That's right. I don't mind being king so long as I don't have to worry about anything.

They.

Yes, let's just have fun!

Robot.

And you will, my pets, lots and lots and lots of fun.
I'll make you a lovely new formula, peanut brittle and
strawberry pie and ice cream, anything you like, but
you must do everything that Robot says, and be very
very very good. You will be good, won't you?

(*They nod.*)

Hap.

Not me, not in a zillion years! I'll never be good.

Robot.

All right. Now we're going to have a nice little game.
And then I'll make the formula. Are you ready?

(*They nod.*)

Cara.

(*To* HAP.) Oh, come on, Hap, it's only a game. Don't
be such a worrywart.

Robot.

Attention! That's right. That's very nice. You're coming along nicely, Cara. Now—I want you all to—
catch the bad naughty cheeky disobedient boy!

Hap.

(*As they begin to circle him.*) No—don't do it. She's
not on our side.

Ug.

Aw, come on, Hap, it's only a game.

Polly.

We're just going to *catch* you, that's all.

Cara.

And then we'll catch someone else, won't we, Robot?

Casper.

It's just in fun, Hap.

Hap.

No, it isn't in fun and it's not a game. Look! (*Points
to* ROBOT *who has gone to the ejection-unit panel and
has her hand on the lever.*)

Casper.

(*Doubting.*) But . . . it *is* only a game, isn't it, Robot? You can't hurt a human, can you?

Robot.

A question. And every question has an answer. (*Presses her computer buttons: answer comes out.* ROBOT *reads as if for the first time.*)—No, I am programmed never to harm a human. (*To herself.*) But I *am* empowered to Make a Decision in the case of Emergency.

(DOVE *hearing this flaps down and into the fray. The* CHILDREN *blithely chase* HAP, *who is really terrified this time, but in the confusion they capture* DOVE *instead. At the right moment . . .*)

Robot.

(*Shouts.*) In here!

(*They heave* DOVE *into the ejection unit and* ROBOT *closes the ejection-unit door.*)

Cara.

(*Laughing at the mistake at first.*) Oh, we've got Dove!

Casper.

(*Laughing too.*) Where's Hap?

Polly.

All right, Dove, don't worry, we'll let you out. (*Goes to the panel, but* ROBOT *keeps her hand on the lever.*)

Robot.

Yes, indeed. We *do* have Dove, don't we? Well, waste not, want not, I always say.

Hap.

(*Who has escaped to the stairway, now cries out.*) You let Dove out! You let him out!

Robot.

Why should I? It's only a moth-eaten messy old bird, been nothing but trouble since the moment we left the launching pad. I may not be programmed to harm a human, but there doesn't seem to be any rule about nonfunctional feather dusters!

Cara.

Oh Robot, you can't eject Dove!

(*They react. The game has turned very serious.*)

Robot.

Why can't I? I can, and I will . . .

They.

Oh no!

Robot.

Yes, I will, *unless* . . . that bad naughty cheeky disobedient boy promises to be good!

Cara.

Oh Hap, promise, promise. Robot's going to eject
Dove!

Hap.

(*Coming down to the ejection unit.*) Dove, oh Dove.
You're a funny old thing . . . but . . . I brought you
on board myself. That old man, he told me—remember something about doves . . . but I can't remember
. . . you may not be good for anything, but I can't let
Robot do it . . . all right, all right, I'll promise. I'll
be g—

(DOVE *inside the unit, shakes his head furiously at*
HAP.)

Hap.

But she'll eject you . . . you'll fall out!

(DOVE *indicates vehemently that* HAP *is not to give in.*)

Hap.

Oh Dove, you're right, I can't give in, but . . . Dove!
Good-bye, old fellow.

Cara.

Hap, no!

Hap.

(*Turns to* ROBOT.) I'll never be good. Not the way
you mean "good." Never never never.

Robot.

Very well!! (*Ejects* DOVE.)

(*The* CHILDREN *react, rush to the viewing port, but* DOVE *is gone.* HAP *simply stares at the now empty ejection unit.*)

Ug.

(*To* ROBOT.) You said it was only a game.

Casper.

He's gone, he's really gone.

Polly.

(*To* ROBOT.) Oh, I wish I could tell somebody on *you*!

Cara.

How could you, Hap, how could you?

Hap.

Because I had to. Because Dove knew ... don't you see? We'll all have to grow up now ... and answer the riddle ... and go to the new world. By ourselves.

Cara.

If that's growing up, I don't want to grow up, ever!

Robot.

That's all right, children. Robot will make you all some nice new formula, and you'll all feel much much better. (*Goes to the staircase.*) You've all been very very good. (*Goes up.*)

Ug.

I don't feel very good.

Polly.

Me neither. (*They start toward their cells.*)

Casper.

I—really—don't think—that was necessary, at all!

Cara.

(*At viewing port, turns to* HAP.) Maybe I am growing up, after all. I seem to have some growing pains, right *here*. (*Puts her hand over her heart and begins to cry.*)

BREAK *or* CURTAIN *is possible here.*

ROBOT *comes down the stairs, humming busily to herself, puts the new formula into the cupboard, checks*

the CHILDREN: *they are all quiet and despondent.* CARA
is still looking out the viewing port, HAP *slumps by the
ejection unit.* CASPER *is thinking, rather out of sight by
the* RIDDLE MACHINE. POLLY *and* UG *are curled up in
their cells.*

Robot.

There! Now everything's nice and ready. Everybody
being good? Ah, that's right. Now—(*Cautiously,
checking to make sure that no one is looking,* ROBOT
crosses to the RIDDLE MACHINE, *takes out the screwdriver, and begins to investigate* RIDDLE MACHINE's
interior.) You're a machine and I'm a machine. Together there's nothing we can't do. A riddle is only a
question, and every question has an answer, and you've
got that answer somewhere inside you. Now, now,
don't make a fuss. (*Pats the* MACHINE *as disturbing
sounds and flickering lights occur.*) I'm only doing
this for your own good.

Casper.

(*Darts to* HAP.) Hap, Hap. Robot's taking the Riddle
Machine apart.

Hap.

I know. She was doing it before too.

Casper.

But the sign says, "DON'T TOUCH!"

Hap.

What does *she* care?

Casper.

But it's not right. Robot might break it, and then
where will we be?

Hap.

We'll be right where we are now—up in the air forever. Maybe Robot's right. I've been thinking and
thinking and *I* can't get the answer to the riddle. Maybe we should let Robot take care of everything . . .

Casper.

No, Hap, you were right before. I've been thinking
about it too. You were right, it's *our* riddle.

Hap.

Everything I do seems to turn out wrong. I got Cara to change the formula bottles, and all it did was make you so silly, you couldn't answer the riddle. And then I threw it all away, and Robot ejected Dove. I can't do *any*thing right.

Cara.

(*Noticing* ROBOT's *activity, comes over.*) Hap, you've got to *do* something. Robot's taking the Riddle Machine apart! If she breaks it, we'll never get to the new world.

Hap.

Oh what's the use? It probably isn't a good world anyway. How do we know?

Cara.

How do we know anything? Hap, I'm ashamed of you. Yes, truly I am. You're giving in.

Hap.

I didn't give in before and look what happened. Now Dove's gone.

Cara.

I know. I would have given in, I think, but you didn't, and Dove didn't want you to give in either. You didn't give in, and now Dove's gone, and now you're giving in!

(*The* RIDDLE MACHINE *begins to flicker and buzz in earnest.*)

Robot.

Aha! The memory bank! This is it!

Cara.

Hap! You've got to do something.

Casper.

Look! She's breaking it!

Hap.

(*Half-rising.*) But what can I do? I'm only one person.

Casper.

We'll help. Tell us what to do. We'll all help.

Cara.

Yes, I'll get the others. (*She runs to the cells and shushes* POLLY *and* UG, *who crawl out carefully and join* HAP *and* CASPER.)

Robot.

Yes, the memory bank, it's here somewhere, the answer to the riddle.

(*She pulls out the memory bank, the lights flicker and flash furiously, and the* RIDDLE MACHINE *goes dead.*)

Robot.

It's not here! The answer's not here! It's not here, it's not there, it's not anywhere! OOOooooOOh! (*Kicks the* RIDDLE MACHINE.) You're not a good machine at all! You're on their side! (*Kicks it again.*) I'll fix you, you traitor, you—you're a bad, naughty, cheeky, disobedient machine . . . and bad naughty cheeky disobedient machines have got to be punished! (*Kicks it again.*)

Ug.

What is it?

Polly.

What's happening?

Casper.

Robot broke the Riddle Machine.

Hap.

Sh. Be quiet. We've got to get the memory bank back. Just follow me. Do everything I do—Robot? Robot, I've made a decision.

Robot.

Grrrr! Rrrrrrowow!—Eh? Eh? *You*'ve made a decision? *You*'ve made a decision, that's a laugh, if a robot could laugh, which I can't. *I'm* the one who makes decisions around here.

Hap.

But I've decided to be good.

Robot.

Have you now? Have you indeed? Well, it's about time.

Hap.

And we were just thinking, if you'd put us through our exercises, we'll all be so very very good, you'll hardly know us.

Robot.

(*Pocketing the memory bank.*) Put you through your exercises? Oh, all right. If it isn't one thing, it's another. Attention! One, two, three, four . . . etc.

(ROBOT *leads the* CHILDREN *about the stage in a marching exercise. During this* HAP *bumps into* ROBOT *and snatches the memory bank away.*)

Robot.

Don't be so clumsy!

Hap.

Sorry. (*Passes the memory bank to* CARA, *who passes it to* CASPER, *who passes it to* POLLY, *who passes it to* UG.)

(UG *slips away to the* RIDDLE MACHINE *and, after a little trouble, manages to get the memory bank back in place. The* RIDDLE MACHINE'S *lights go on—it is working again.*)

Robot.

Eh? Eh? What's that? (*Turns to see.*) Whatever are you doing! Can't you read? The sign says "DON'T TOUCH!" Oh! (*Feels in pocket. Realizes what has happened.*) You tricked me!

Ug.

But I had to put the memory bank back, Robot.

Polly.

Yes, he had to, or the Riddle Machine wouldn't work.

Ug.

And we wouldn't be able to hear the riddle . . .

Polly.

Or answer the riddle . . .

Casper.

Or get to the new world.

Robot.

Ug! You were my pride and joy, and to think you've turned on me like this.

Ug.

But I've got it working again, Robot . . . see?

Robot.

Oh yes. You've got the Riddle Machine working again. What good is that going to do? You can't answer the riddle anyway, can you?

(*They look at one another and hang their heads.*)

Robot.

Well, I wash my hands of you, yes I do. I'm not going to find your answer for you now. And you, Ug—you're much too bad to be king. No, you can't be king now.

Ug.

Well—I don't really want to be king anyway. Let Hap be king. Kings have too much worry for me, and Hap seems to like to worry. I'd rather . . . *fix* things, like I fixed the Riddle Machine. I did that all right, didn't I?—I'll fix you too, Robot, if anything goes wrong with your insides.

Robot.

Fix me? Fix *me*!

Ug.

Well, I meant, when we get to the new world, maybe you'll need to be fixed up now and then . . .

Robot.

You're not going to *get* to the new world! Do you hear? You're all far too naughty to get to the new world. Oh, yes, I know—you'll just get there and then you'll do exactly what you please. Yes, maybe it's just as well you can't answer the riddle. I can keep a much better eye on you right here, in the spaceship. A spaceship is just as good as a new world anyway. I can keep my eye on you here . . . I can make sure you don't Get into Mischief. I can make sure you don't ever trick me again.

Cara.

I will—Yes, I will. I'll trick you all the time!

Ug.

That's right. I'll trick you too. I'll be horrid and mean
and naughty and do everything bad I can think of.

Casper.

So you'd better let us go—you'd be well rid of us
really. We'll just make your life a perfect misery.

Robot.

Oh, I'm used to that.

Polly.

And I'll tell on you too—if I can think of who to tell.

Hap.

We'll never do anything you say.

Robot.

Oh, I think you will. I think you'll do everything I say.
(*Goes and stands in front of the formula cupboard.*)
Human beings are very imperfectly designed. Not at
all like a machine. Now, a machine can go without
fuel for a very long time. But human beings seem to
need to eat quite regularly. All I have to do is—wait.
You'll get hungry. Then you'll come to me. You'll
have to come to me. Then you'll do exactly as I say.—
You're getting hungry now, aren't you? Yeeees. Peanut brittle, little Ug? Lovely crunchy munchy peanut
brittle?

Ug.

(*Tempted but.*) Nope, don't want any. Peanuts get
into your teeth.

Robot.

You're *ly*ing in your teeth . . . And strawberry pie,
little Polly? Lovely strawberry pie, with real strawberries . . . (*Takes the formula bottle down and pours
some of the formula into the wooden spoon. Tasting
it.*) Mmmm, lovely real strawberries.

Polly.

Strawberries make me sick to my stomach.

Robot.

Poor little Polly, you must be *so* hungry. And . . .
(*Tasting.*) . . . chocolate fudge, maple walnut tutti

frutti ice cream, Casper, with whipped cream and a
cherry on the top . . .

Casper.

No thank you, all the same.

Robot.

Gingerbread for you, Cara, all the gingerbread men
you can eat . . .

Cara.

Gingerbread's for babies!

(*But they are being tempted.*)

Robot.

Mmmmmm . . . peanut brittle and strawberry pie,
chocolate fudge sundae, so good you could die . . .
(*Waves the formula bottle in front of their noses.
They sway toward it.*)

Ug.

I'm hungry . . .

They.

No, Ug, no, you're not!

Ug.

No I'm not. I just *feel* hungry, I'm not really.

Hap.

That wouldn't, by any chance, taste like hot dogs,
would it?

Robot.

Hot dogs? (*Tastes.*) Why yes, yes it does.

Hap.

With onions and mustard and a pickle on the side?

Robot.

Oh my yes, a great big pickle on the side.

Cara.

Hap! You wouldn't!

Hap.

Well, you've had two feedings since we got up, but
I haven't had a thing.

They.

Hap! No!

Robot.

Lovely onions and lovely mustard and lovely lovely pickle! (*Inspired.*) French fries on the side!

Hap.

I don't believe you.

Robot.

(*Waving the bottle in front of his nose.*) There's only one way to find out!

Hap.

Well, maybe just a little taste . . .

They.

No, Hap, no!

Hap.

(*Taking the formula bottle.*) Are you sure about the pickle?

Robot.

Absolutely positively sure!

Hap.

That's good, because pickles give me the hives! (*And he throws bottle and all down the disposal unit.*)

They.

Hurrah!

Robot.

(*Ominously calm.*) I see. You've done it again, have you?

Hap.

We told you we would. We said we'd never be good. We'll starve to death first!

Robot.

You, my young man, have become an Emergency. And in an Emergency, I am empowered to Make a Decision. For the good of the spaceship, for the good of all the children, I have decided that you, Hap, have got to go! (*And she points toward the ejection unit.*)

Casper.

Oh no, Robot, that's not right. You're not allowed to harm a human.

Robot.

I can, and I will!

(*And she begins to chase* HAP. *The* CHILDREN *put up a struggle, but* ROBOT *gets* HAP *and drags him toward the ejection unit. It is difficult, however, to manipulate the lever, the* CHILDREN, *and* HAP, *and, in all the confusion, as* ROBOT *leans to grab the lever,* HAP *kneels down to make a tripping block . . .*)

Hap.

(*As* ROBOT *pulls the lever.*) Now! Push!

(*They all push and* ROBOT *stumbles over* HAP *into the ejection unit.* HAP *scrambles out, and* CASPER *pulls the lever which shuts* ROBOT *up in the unit.*)

They.

Hurrah!

Robot.

Let me out! Let me out, oh you bad naughty children, let me out! Oh my nuts and bolts, oh dear oh dear. Is this how you treat me, after all I've done for you? I was only doing it for your own good. Let me out!

Polly.

We won't let you out till you're good! (*And they all laugh.*)

Cara.

We've done it, we're safe!

Polly.

Yes, now we can go to the new world.

Casper.

But we've got to answer the riddle first.

Ug.

I'm hun-grey!

Hap.

So am I. I'm starved.

Casper.

Well, we can eat all we want once we get to the new world. Come on, thinking caps everybody, what is the greatest riddle of all?

Hap.

I'm too hungry to think . . .

Ug.

Me too.

Polly.

I want to go home . . .

Robot.

You see? You can't do without me, can you?

Cara.

Oh, it'll be time soon to answer the riddle and we won't be able to . . . (*Wanders to the viewing port.*) There it is, our new world, just down there . . . but we'll never get there, never.

(*They wander over and look out. Suddenly.*)

Hap.

What's that?

Cara.

What?

Hap.

Down there, something coming toward us . . .

Cara.

I can't see! I . . . oh Hap! It's Dove . . . !

They.

It's Dove, it's Dove . . .

(DOVE *flies up the aisle, wings spread, with a branch of the new-world fruit in his mouth. He no longer seems old and moth-eaten, but beautiful and shining and new.*)

Hap.

I remember, now I remember what the old man told me about doves . . . they can fly. Doves can fly!

Cara.

Dove's not dead at all . . . he can fly!

Robot.

(*As* DOVE *comes up to the ejection unit.*) Dove? But you're supposed to be dead!

(CARA *runs to the ejection-unit panel and levers the door open.* DOVE *flies in.*)

Casper.

Watch out for Robot!

Robot.

(*Stumps in after* DOVE.) If you think *I'm* going to help any of you ever again, you've got another think coming.

Cara.

Oh Dove, you're alive! (*Hugs him.*)

Robot.

You'll never answer the riddle, *you*'ll never get to the new world . . . you and your silly old Dove, what good's he going to do, eh? (*Sulks off in a corner.*)

Cara.

Look, Hap, Dove's brought us something, from the new world . . .

Casper.

What is it? I've never seen anything like that before.*

Hap.

I think it's some sort of . . . fruit. Did you bring these for us, old fellow?

(DOVE *nods.*)

Robot.

Don't eat it, it's poison!

Hap.

Is it for us to eat? Is it, Dove? (DOVE *nods.*)

Cara.

Oh it must be to eat, Dove knew we'd be hungry.

Casper.

I think—we've got to take the chance, Hap. Maybe it is poison, but—I think we've got to eat something or we'll never be able to think, and if we aren't able to think, we won't be able to answer the riddle, and if we don't answer the riddle . . .

Hap.

Okay, okay, we've got to try it.

Casper.

On the other hand, if it *is* poison, and we do eat it, then I think we'll die, and we'll never answer the riddle anyway, and I think—

---

* Of course we can recognize the fruit.

Hap.

Casper, you think too much. (*Takes a bite.*)

Cara.

Is it all right?

Hap.

Well, I haven't dropped dead—*yet.* (*Takes another bite.*) If I do, you'd better not eat any, I guess. (*Laughs. Eats.*)

Riddle Machine.

Attention! Attention!

Hap.

Okay, this is it! Here, it's all right, it's wonderful. Go on, everybody. Eat. Okay, Riddle Machine, fire away. We still don't know the answer, but now at least we can think . . .

Casper.

(*Eating.*) And if we can think, we can try, and if we can try . . .

Hap.

Quiet!

Robot.

Hmph! (*And turns away.*)

(*The* CHILDREN *eat and listen.*)

Riddle Machine.

Listen carefully. This is your third and final chance to enter the new world. If you cannot answer the riddle this time, the spaceship will never land. You have sixty seconds.

> When all of space has yielded to travel,
> And is as simple as A, B, and C,
> What will still be left to unravel,
> The puzzle, the mystery, the final key?
> What is the greatest riddle of all?
> (*Tick, tick, tick, etc.*)

(*The* CHILDREN *think very hard.*)

Hap.

Come on, now, everybody, we've got to begin.

Cara.

You try, Hap.

Hap.

You'll have to help me. But I think it has something to do with the new world . . .

Casper.

Yes, and I think it has something to do with us—with being ready for the new world.

Cara.

Yes, that's it. We had to be ready.

Ug.

With growing up?

Hap.

Yes, I think so.

Casper.

But, I'm not sure I really understand about growing up at all . . .

Cara.

Except, it hurts sometimes . . .

Polly.

But if the riddle is growing up, we'll never answer it, because I don't know what growing up is, do you?

Hap.

But we're only supposed to say what the greatest riddle of all *is* . . .

Cara.

As far as I'm concerned, the greatest riddle of all is *me*. (*Hopelessly.*)

Polly.

And me . . .

Ug.

And me . . .

Casper.

And me! I think, Hap, I think—that's it!

Hap.

Yes! We're the greatest riddle of all . . . because, because even if we know all about space and . . .

Casper.

. . . and even if we know everything about everything in the whole universe . . . there'll still be *us* . . .

Cara.

. . . to figure out!

Hap.

The puzzle—the mystery—the final key!

Riddle Machine.

Five, four, three . . .

Hap.

A human being! The greatest riddle of all is . . .

They.

(*All say quietly.*) . . . a human being.

Riddle Machine.

You—are—ready.

Robot.

Oh! But that's silly. Human beings are very simple to figure out . . . now, a machine, a machine is what you might call—complicated.

Cara.

Oh Robot, do shut up!

Hap.

Here we go! We're going dooooooo-oown!

(*The spaceship descends to the new world. The* CHILDREN *lean together and hold on. The spaceship lands.*)

Polly.

Are we there? Are we really there? (*They go to the ejection unit.*)

Robot.

Go on then, go! You and your silly old Dove. Who cares about me. I can just rust away in here. Go on. I don't need you.

Hap.

But we need you, Robot. If you'll just be . . . well, if you'll be just a machine.

Robot.

Hmph!

Casper.

I don't know, Hap, she'll be nothing but trouble.

Robot.

Oh please take me with you. I won't be any trouble,

really I won't. And I can be useful, you know. I can
do all sorts of things, really I can. Don't leave me all
alone.

Hap.
Yes. You can be useful . . . and you can be trouble
. . . but I guess maybe we'll have to get used to trouble.
(*Grins.*) Come on, Robot. (*And he pulls the ejection-
unit lever so that the door to the new world now stands
open.*) Ready everybody?

Ug.
What's out there? Can you see anything?

Hap.
(*Stepping out.*) I can see . . . creatures.

Polly.
Oh! Are they bug-eyed monsters?

Cara.
(*Stepping out.*) Oh, now I can see them too. No, no,
they look sort of—like *us!*

Polly.
It's scary!

Casper.
(*Takes her hand.*) Come on, Polly. Don't be scared.
I think—they're friendly.

(*They all take hands,* DOVE *joins his wing tip to*
CARA's *hand and* ROBOT *takes his other wing tip . . .
and they begin to come out.*)

Polly.
It's *still* scary.

Cara.
Yes, it is. But maybe we'll have to get used to that too.

Hap.
Come on, just take one step at a time.

(*And they greet the* CHILDREN *of the new world.*)

CURTAIN

Five Minutes to Morning

*A Play
for Young People
in Three Acts*

by Mary Melwood

PREFACE

I was born in a Nottinghamshire village which was still unspoiled and where several generations of my mother's family had lived. There was an enormous sense of belonging there—used to feel that it was *our* village. Although I never go back because it has been completely spoiled, it is the vision of this village as it was during my childhood which distills into everything I write.

For years, as a young teacher in the village school, my mother supplied the concerts or plays for the community —she used the children of the village, and their performances were usually held in the school. In the house there were trunks full of fancy dresses left over from productions of years past, and my sister and I were always dressing up and acting. I wrote plays from childhood.

I married in 1939 and had two sons. I gave up writing and never thought to begin it again—much too absorbed in the two boys and family life. When the children were in their teens, my husband persuaded me to write a radio play for a competition organized by the B.B.C. The play, *It Isn't Enough*, didn't win a prize but was singled out for a bit of praise. Later, it was broadcast, and then televised.

I never wrote anything for children until *The Tingalary Bird* which won the first Arts Council Award to a play for children. It was translated into Polish and German, has been produced and televised in Canada, and was presented all over the U.S.A. as well as in Australia. *Five Minutes to Morning*, my next play, also won an Arts Council Award.

In 1970 I was asked by the Nottingham Playhouse

Company to write a play to be performed outside at the city's first festival. The play, *A Masquerade in the Park*, was performed during the run of the festival before as many as twelve hundred children at a time.

I have just completed my first novel—about childhood—once again on the borderline somewhere between an adult and a children's book. It will be published next spring by Andre Deutsch.

MARY MELWOOD

CHARACTERS

Tom Skinch, an English farmer
Jolyon, a young man
Mrs. Venny, a retired schoolmistress
The Squirrel
The Cat
The Dog ⎬ Mime Characters
The Hen
The Wild White Pony

Five Minutes to Morning was given its first production by the Unicorn Theatre for Young People at the Arts Theatre in London, England, in April 1966.

ACT I

Scene One

Before the curtain rises a small blue light appears over the proscenium. It moves about, disappearing in one place and reappearing in another until the curtain goes up; then it disappears again. Now disclosed is a backdrop of autumn-tinted hills dotted about with stony heaps which show where cottages once stood. There is a stone heap at the right side of the stage. The blue light appears again, hovers about, then disappears at the same time that three shots are heard from backstage. Immediately follows a commotion of galloping hooves, the sound of a whinneying horse and ejaculation in a man's voice. JOLYON *runs onstage from the right and* TOM SKINCH *from the left. They collide,* JOLYON's *spectacles fall off.* SKINCH *begins to disentangle himself from the coils of a rope which he has been throwing. He is encumbered by a gun, a full shooting bag, and a number of dead birds and animals whose bodies are festooned about his person.*

Skinch.

Hey! Look out, can't you? (*His voice changes as he recognises* JOLYON.) Oh, it's you. Didn't expect to see you up here.

    (*Birds and rabbits are dropping around him.* JOLYON *is groping about on the ground for his spectacles.*)

Skinch.

You remember me, eh?

(JOLYON *finds his spectacles and puts them on.*)

Skinch.

You know. Tom Skinch. We met this morning at the
lawyer's.

Jolyon.

I'm afraid I—of course, Mr. Skinch.

Skinch.

Changed me clothes. Bit more sporting in the afternoon when I'm looking for a bit of supper. (*Puts his
gun and bag on the stones.*) It's a wonder you weren't
knocked down just now, though.

Jolyon.

Knocked down?

Skinch.

Didn't you see it?

Jolyon.

Oh yes. That's what I was looking at when I didn't
see you. It got in my eyes.

Skinch.

Got in your—

(*He breaks off at a loss.* JOLYON *takes off his spectacles and polishes them.*)

Jolyon.

At first I thought it was these. New pair, you know.
(SKINCH *looks slightly bewildered.*) Always having
trouble. I'm glad you saw it too. (*Puts spectacles
firmly on.*)

Skinch.

I'm always seeing it. It's always around here.

Jolyon.

I suppose it's a sort of marsh gas . . . like a will-o'-the-
wisp, only blue.

Skinch.

Will-o' . . . Blue! Just what are you talking about?

Jolyon.

The blue light. Rather odd, wasn't it . . . I've been
watching it all the way up from the village.

Skinch.

I'm talking about the white pony that nearly knocked
you down. Surely you—

(*Breaks off. Sound of galloping hooves in the distance. Full of excitement* SKINCH *pushes* JOLYON *aside
and scrambles to the top of the stones, brandishing his
rope.*)

Skinch.

Quick! Move out of the way . . . Here he comes! (*Loud
noise of hooves.* JOLYON *scrambles up beside* SKINCH
who shouts and waves the rope about.) Who-o-oa!
Whoa! Who-o-oa! (*Laughing, he throws the rope like
a lasso.*) Got you, you brute . . .

(*Sound of hooves fades into the distance.*)

Jolyon.

No. (*Pause.*) You missed him. (*Pause.*) Too slow.

(SKINCH *looks daggers at him.*)

Skinch.

If it hadn't been for you—(*He changes his angry tone
somewhat.*) You should have kept out of my way.
There he goes, drat him.

Jolyon.

Where?

(*From the top of the stones they look offstage.*)

Skinch.

Straight over to the old woman's wood, sure enough.
(*Mutters.*) Just as if she's got him on a string.

Jolyon.

Is he yours?

Skinch.

Mine? (*Laughs.*) He is when I can catch him. No . . .
he belonged round here somewhere . . . (*Waves his
arm in direction of ruined cottages.*) Lots o' things get
left behind as people kept going away . . . Hens . . .
. . . Cats . . . (*Laughs*) . . . old woman herself . . . come
to that.

Jolyon.

Who?

Skinch.

Why, Mrs. Venny, of course . . . still up there, all by
herself . . . and a wood full of cats. I'll *cat* 'em . . .
(*Catches* JOLYON's *arm.*) Look . . . d'you see those
trees over there? That's where he's gone. Thinks he's
safe there but—(*Shouts angrily.*)—he'd better look
out for himself. That'll be Skinch's wood after tomorrow. There'll be a little surprise in store for him
and a few others as well.

(*Climbs down from stones winding up the rope.
Sits down on top of the stones.* JOLYON *remains standing and looking out.* SKINCH *reaches for his gun and
begins to polish it with a rag from his pocket.*)

Jolyon.

So that's—my wood. (SKINCH *looks up sharply.*) Well,
it is.

Skinch.

I like that . . . you've sold it to me, don't forget.

Jolyon.

No I haven't, yet. We haven't signed anything.

Skinch.

That's all arranged for tomorrow.

Jolyon.

Perhaps I ought to think it over . . . look around a
bit . . .

Skinch.

There's nothing to look at. A few old thorn trees—
(*He rides over* JOLYON's *interruption.*)—a bit of stony
ground . . . (*He picks up a piece of stone and drops
it.*) I'm doing you a good turn in taking it off your
hands.

Jolyon.

(*Coming down from stones.*) Why did he want me to
have it though?

Skinch.

Who?

Jolyon.

My grandfather. He never even knew me. I wonder why he left it so that it couldn't be sold until I'm eighteen.

Skinch.

Don't ask me. People are always doing silly things.

Jolyon.

Everything else was sold.

Skinch.

Aye . . . to me . . . farm, fields, I bought the lot.

(*Stands up. Holding gun with one hand, he pulls* JOLYON *up beside him with the other. They stand on stones looking off.*)

Skinch.

You see that wood . . . well, that's my land to the north of it. (*Pause,* SKINCH *pointing.*) And there, to the south, that's my land. And it's my land to the east of it, and there again it's my land to the west . . . it's *all* my land, except for that bit in the middle where the old woman lives. That's just because your grand-dad tied it up to you years and years ago before you were even born. Ridiculous.

Jolyon.

I don't see why—

Skinch.

I don't see why *you* should have it when you don't want it and *I* shouldn't have it when I do. Anyway, now you're eighteen and you can sell it to me and at last it'll be all my land. I'll shoot wherever I like all over it—and no interfering old woman's going to stop me neither. (*He raises his gun.* JOLYON *moves away.*) Hey, hold on a bit! It won't go off.

Jolyon.

It had better not . . . or I won't be able to sign those papers tomorrow.

(*Begins to move away.* SKINCH *does not want to lose him and quickly begins to gather his things together.*)

Skinch.

Wait—I'll walk with you. (*A sheep bleats.*) Get off
with you, Grr—or I'll have the wool off your back—
(*As* JOLYON *moves in opposite direction.*) Hey. This
way. Where are you going?

Jolyon.

I thought I'd look at the little school my grandfather
built—

Skinch.

All closed down, long since. No kids about here now.
(*Laughs.*) That's where I got my odd—education.

Jolyon.

. . . and see Mrs. Venny. I'll have to tell her I'm selling
the place.

Skinch.

Tell *her*! It's nothing to do with her. Just because she
lives there, it doesn't mean she owns it, though I dare-
say she thinks she does. (*Laughs.*) *She*'s got a few
surprises in store. Oh, come on, look how dark it is.
(*Wind rises.*) There's a wind getting up as'll blow you
into next week if you don't look out.

(*Sound of school bell ringing faintly.*)

Jolyon.

Listen. (*Pause.*) I've heard it before this afternoon.

Skinch.

Just another of *her* tricks. She does it for spite to scare
off the birds when she sees me out shooting. Well,
O-U-T spells "out"—doesn't it?

Jolyon.

Yes, but—

Skinch.

Thought it did. Well, O-U-T she goes. As soon as I
own that place—and it won't be long now . . . I'll be
up there pushing it all down. Won't take five minutes.

Jolyon.

But—

Skinch.

(*Almost to himself.*) Always interfering. Can't leave

things alone, spoiling my sport, meddling with my snares—and those cats of hers—they're forever after my pheasants. (*He mimics old woman's voice.*) "It's cruel to rear birds just to shoot 'em," she says. "It's cruel of your cats to eat 'em," I says. "It's cat's nature to eat birds," she says. "Well, it's my nature to shoot 'em," I says. (*Looking at* JOLYON, *suddenly wary.*) I'm thinking of her own good, of course, poor old thing. Living all alone, all those cats tisn't right, is it? She'll be much better off when I've got her moved out. Hey —you're not really going up there... (JOLYON *is moving off.*) You're making a mistake... she'll shut the door in your face... she won't like it... you'll wish you hadn't... don't say I didn't warn you... and mind that pony... he's as wild as... (*He has gathered all his possessions up.*) And don't forget tomorrow... ten o'clock sharp at the lawyer's. The sooner it's all signed up the better—

(*They go off opposite sides,* SKINCH *singing.*)

> I'll have him live,
> I'll have him dead—
> A pony to ride—or
> A rug for my bed.

Scene Two

No curtain. Sound of wind. The stage darkens. The little blue light reappears and plays over the backcloth, which slowly begins to rise, revealing, wrapped in mystical blue light, Mrs. Venny's home with the thornwood behind it. JOLYON *appears at the side of the stage and stands watching. The building now revealed was the school of the ruined hamlet and is so dilapidated as to be almost a ruin itself. The wall facing the audience has a gothic-type window with latticed panes, many broken. In the right wall is a door with a step down. As* JOLYON *stands aside this side door opens and* MRS. VENNY *comes out to throw out food for the*

*birds. She goes in again closing the door. It is like a
dream scene which* JOLYON *is waiting to enter. Now
the blue light which bathes it begins to filter away.*
JOLYON *steps forward to knock at the door when there
is a sudden cackle and scurry and a rush of wings. He
ducks, putting an arm over his head so that his spectacles fall off. As he begins to search for them around
the doorstep his attention is caught by the sight of a
huge striped furry tail which waves in an exaggerated
way around the back of the building. He stops searching and stares. As he does so the backdrop forming the
front wall of the school slowly goes up to reveal the
interior with* MRS. VENNY *inside.* JOLYON *cannot see
this but the audience can. He drops on his knees to
grope about for his lost spectacles around the doorstep.*

   *Disclosed to the audience is an old-fashioned school-
room. In the back wall is a door, leading into the wood.
To the left of this is another gothic window through
which is hinted the thornwood behind, also a glimpse
of the ruined schoolhouse. Some of the broken dia-
mond-shaped panes are stuffed with old exercise
books. Through others, brambles have grown and hang
down into the room like a curtain. There are a few
school benches. Near the door at the back is the
teacher's desk and stool, an easel and worn-out black-
board. Various tattered music sheets of the old-fashioned tonic sol-fa hang on the walls. To the right of
the door at the back is a harmonium, piled with books
and papers. At the right side of the room is an iron
stove with pipe going up through the ceiling. On it
stands a frying pan and large copper kettle, brightly
polished—a treasure. A long-handled toasting fork
hangs nearby. Baskets of wood are near the stove. In
front of the stove is an old pressed-down-looking easy
chair. There is a shelf on the wall near the stove, and
on it are various photographs and ornaments, notably
a large shell. Also on the shelf are bags of seeds, jars
labeled "Jam," "Pickles" and "Wine." Also at the right
side of the room there is a large hole in the ceiling. A*

stepladder stands beneath it with an opened umbrella on the top step. There are damp patches on the walls and mushroomlike shapes growing on them. On the window ledges tomatoes and gourds have been put to ripen, and there are rosehips and twigs in jam jars. Hanging from the ceiling are bunches of carrots, herbs, and strings of onions. Cluttered about in corners are various pipkins, pails, brooms, and household paraphernalia. At the side of the room opposite to the stove an apple tree has poked in through a hole in the wall. On its branches there are still a few withered leaves and one small green apple at the top. Underneath the tree is a hamper of sour-looking crabs. The branches of the tree are used for hanging things on; there are a lighted storm lantern (now the only light in the room), a shabby carpetbag and an old tweed travel cape with a tartan lining. Candles stuck in old-fashioned sticks are here and there. At the front of the stage, right, only partly in view, is a truckle bed made up of a straw palliasse and red wool blankets. Front stage is a hole in the floor, lightly covered with a piece of cardboard and with a danger sign near it.

MRS. VENNY *is sitting at the teacher's desk. She is sturdily dressed in coat and skirt and wears a respectable hat. Attached to her jacket by a thread is a pair of pince-nez which she clips onto her nose as she sorts through piles of papers, checking and counterchecking as she is distractedly searching for something.*

The wind becomes louder and it rattles about the place in such a way that she raises her head and listens. JOLYON *outside the door makes a scratching sound as he gropes about.* MRS. VENNY *listens, then resumes her search through the papers.*

Mrs. Venny.
A is for Ann . . . B is for Beatrice . . . But where is the third one? It's on the tip of my tongue. To think I could forget such a thing as my own name! (*She breaks off as her ear picks up the sound of* JOLYON *groping out-*

side. She calls out.) Come in, whoever you are. The door is never locked. Everybody's welcome. (*Pause.*) Unless . . . (*An idea strikes her and she looks extremely alert and putting down her papers, tiptoes across the room.*) unless . . . (*She reaches the side door and flings it open so suddenly that* JOLYON *falls into the room.*) . . . It's you, TOM SKINCH!

(*With a cry of triumph she pounces on* JOLYON *and drags him into the room by the back of his collar.*) Aha! I've caught you, Tom Skinch. Up to your old tricks again, eh? (*With surprising strength she heaves* JOLYON *further into the room, and dances him up and down.*) What are you up to this time, eh? Blowing up my house, eh? Battering down my door . . . eh? Come on, heave ho! (*She pulls him up.*) First we'll turn out your pockets and see what you've got. Matches, bombs, dynamite. (*With a final heave she hoists* JOLYON's *face in view.*) Bless my boots! (*She lets him go so suddenly that he sinks down again.*) It isn't— You're not Tom Skinch!

Jolyon.
Oooh! Ouch!

(*Disheveled, hat on floor.*)

Mrs. Venny.
You're . . . no . . . Tom . . . Skinch. (*She puts on her pince-nez.*)

Jolyon.
I know I'm not. (*Recovers his breath.*) I never said I was.

Mrs. Venny.
You never said you weren't.

Jolyon.
I'm sorry.

Mrs. Venny.
(*Suspiciously.*) Sorry. Why?

Jolyon.
I'm sorry you thought I'm Tom Skinch—and I'm not.

Mrs. Venny.
You should be glad you're not Tom Skinch. I'd make

you sorry if you were, I can tell you! Creeping undei
doors, looking through keyholes! I'll keyhole him—
and you too.

Jolyon

Keyholes! I was looking for my spectacles, that's all.
They're outside somewhere.

Mrs. Venny.

H'm. (*Walks to the open door and looks out.*) Where?
Why should THEY be out when you're in?

Jolyon.

(*Following her.*) I was just going to knock at the
door—

(*Pause. The scene darkens. He hesitates, then steps
outside, looking around.*)

Mrs. Venny.

(*Standing on the doorstep.*) Yes. Go on.

Jolyon.

I was just going to knock when there was an odd sort
of noise, and something—

(*The wind is blowing now.*)

Mrs. Venny.

Yes. Go on.

Jolyon.

Something flew at me—or the wind blew—or something.

(*The wind is blowing harder. He breaks off, hesitates and looks around the darkening scene. Farther
away, from the wood, there is a long-drawn-out sound,
"Ahoo! Ahoo! Ahoo!" JOLYON jumps inside the room
with one leap, MRS. VENNY steps back and the door
closes with a bang. JOLYON gasps.*)

Jolyon.

What's that?

Mrs Venny.

One of your "somethings," I suppose. (*As JOLYON
stands just inside the room and stands peering about.*)
But come in. (*He steps further in. She walks to the*

teacher's desk.) If it's spectacles you require—(*She rummages in a drawer and comes back to him holding several pairs.*) Try these. I made 'em myself.

(*She puts a pair on his nose and the scene is immediately plunged into dark green.*)

Jolyon.
Oh! No!

(MRS. VENNY *changes them for another pair. The scene becomes deep purple.*)

Mrs. Venny.
How's that? Better?

Jolyon.
Not better. Just different.

(*He takes them off, the scene returns to its original lighting.*)

Mrs. Venny.
I don't see why one should require everything always to look the same, do you? (*Putting another pair on his nose.*) But you'll like these—(*The scene becomes rose-colored.*) Well?

Jolyon.
Different again. But . . . rather nice.

Mrs. Venny.
I thought you'd like these . . . at your age. Now, welcome to my little home.

(JOLYON *takes a step and stumbles against the stepladder. Righting himself he nearly puts his foot into the hole in the floor.*)

Mrs. Venny.
Just be careful where you put your feet, that's all.

(JOLYON *takes off the spectacles and gives them to her. The lighting returns to normal.*)

Jolyon.
I think I can manage without them, thank you.

(*He stumbles backward into her armchair and sprawls into it.*)

Mrs. Venny.

It seems like it . . . but make yourself at home. (JOLYON *stares around the room.*) I can see you like it. So educational, isn't it . . . and yet so cosy. (*Pause.*) Have you lost your tongue or are you dreaming?

Jolyon.

Dreaming . . . is that what I'm doing?

Mrs. Venny.

I don't know. We'll soon see. (*She picks up the toasting fork and gives him a prod.*)

Jolyon.

Ouch! (*Jumps up out of chair.*)

Mrs. Venny.

If you felt that, you're still awake. (*Pause.*) Let me take your hat. (*Holding out her hand.*)

Jolyon.

(*Holding on to it.*) Oh no! I must go!

Mrs. Venny.

Go? But you've only just come.

Jolyon.

I've only come . . . (*At a loss—looks around.*) I'm sorry. I *must* go!

Mrs. Venny.

If you've *come* merely to *go*, you couldn't blame me if I asked you *in* just to send you *out* again, which I wouldn't dream of doing—so—your hat please.

(*She peremptorily holds out her hand.* JOLYON *gives her his hat. He is ill at ease.*)

Jolyon.

What I mean is . . . I only called to tell you something —to mention that Tom Skinch and I—(*He breaks off.*)

Mrs. Venny.

Ha! Tom Skinch. So he *is* in it.

Jolyon.

In what?

Mrs. Venny.

In everything, it seems. (*Taking his hat she goes to the apple tree and hangs it up as a hatstand. Seeing* JOLYON's *stare she explains.*) The apple tree used to be ALL outside, then it came in. It's very convenient, especially as I'm so fond of apples. (*She is moving away from the tree when she stops, thinks, then says with the air of one presenting a luxury.*) Go on, take one. Help yourself. (JOLYON *hesitates then moves to take an apple from the hamper.*) Stop! Stop! Not those! They're my Best Selected—for apple pies, apple puddings, apple—(*She stops as if she had forgotten the word.*)

Jolyon.

Apple Dumplings?

Mrs. Venny.

No. Not Dumpling. It's on the tip of my tongue but I just can't remember what it is.

Jolyon.

Can you eat it?

Mrs. Venny.

Of course you can—but not until you've picked it. Go on. Pick it from the tree.

(*She points to the apple at the top of the tree.*)

Jolyon.

That! Up there?

(MRS. VENNY *nods, a mischievous expression begining to glint in her eye. He looks up at the apple, makes a gesture of attempt, then gives up.*)

Jolyon.

I can't. It's too high. I can't reach.

Mrs. Venny.

Nonsense. Try. Throw you hat at it.

Jolyon.

But I don't even *want* an apple—oh—all right! (*He breaks off, and taking his hat from the tree, in exasperation he throws it up at the apple. Now both hat*

and apple are high up on the tree.) Now see what's
happened.
Mrs. Venny.
That's nothing.

(*She stands beneath the tree and looks up with a
winning expression as if she can charm the hat down.
She makes a wheedling sound with her lips as if to
a bird. She claps her hands . . . and the hat falls down
into them. It looks like an act of magic.* JOLYON
certainly looks as if he thinks it is. He stares at MRS.
VENNY, *and at the hat from which she is daintily
brushing off bits of leaf—then up at the tree. Smiling,
and with her tongue in her cheek she gives him his
hat with a flourish.*)

Mrs. Venny.
You look surprised! Things do as you wish them to,
sometimes, you know. (*Pause.*) Aren't you going to
eat your apple?
Jolyon.
Apple? But I didn't—I haven't one.
Mrs. Venny.
Oh yes, you have. (JOLYON *looks inside his hat. She
looks on smiling.*) Now your pockets. (*He puts his
hat aside and begins to turn out his pockets.*) That's
right. Now the other one. *All* of 'em.

(*She stands over him as he goes through all his
pockets; she is very much the schoolmistress. Now, on
the pretext of helping in the search, she comes closer
and begins to go over his front with rapid fingers.
Suddenly with a cry of triumph she rolls out an apple
from under his chin.*)

Mrs. Venny.
Voilà. What did I tell you! (*Her face is alight with joy
in her achievement. She holds the apple up high deli-
cately poised between conjurer's fingers.*)
Jolyon.
(*Abashed.*) I swear—I never. I don't see how.

Mrs. Venny.

Not your fault. (*Carelessly throwing the remark away.*)
Just a bit of magic, that's all.

Jolyon.

Magic?

Mrs. Venny.

Catch! (*She tosses the apple to him.*) School-treat
tricks. We used to have school treats when I was a
teacher here. Buns and races. You know the sort of
thing . . . and conjuring tricks after tea. *I* did the
tricks. I thought I'd forgotten 'em but bless me, I'm
as good as ever. Aren't you going to eat it?

Jolyon.

I don't feel very hungry. (*He looks at the apple
dubiously.*)

Mrs. Venny.

Take it home if you like. Make a pudding of it. Or a
pie. Or . . . (*Her memory begins to worry her again.*)
. . . or a . . . I've forgotten that word again, the one
that reminds me of something. Never mind. It'll come
by itself, presently.

(JOLYON *moves to look at the objects on the shelf.
He picks up a photograph.*)

Mrs. Venny.

You may look at the photographs if you wish. That
was our cricket team.

Jolyon.

(*Peering.*) Nineteen-o'-something. Cricket! But there
aren't eleven players here . . . there's only seven of 'em.

Mrs. Venny.

We played our own kind of cricket, up here, of course.
(*She looks at the photograph and sighs.*) Heyday. All
parents and grandparents now. (*He takes up another
picture. She gives him a sharp look.*) Careful. There's
something particular about that—now what, I wonder?

(JOLYON *looks from her to the picture.*)

Jolyon.

I know. They were yours . . . your children.

(*She looks at the picture then turns away.*)

Mrs. Venny.
Mine—or other people's. They've all grown and gone.
Put it back but . . . carefully. (*She takes up the large
shell.*) The brave Captain Venny gave me this.

Jolyon.
Captain Venny?

Mrs. Venny.
Captain and Mrs. Venny. There they are. There's a
picture of 'em.

(JOLYON *picks up another photograph and looks at
it.*)

Mrs. Venny.
The brave sea captain and his young little missus. Go
on, have a look—and then—guess!

Jolyon.
It's very faded. (*He looks at it closely.*)

Mrs. Venny.
The sea journeys and travels, the wonders and marvels
that couple were going to see together.

Jolyon.
Why . . . *She* is You.

(MRS. VENNY *comes close to look.*)

Mrs. Venny.
Captain and Mrs. Venny. Oh, very faded. (*Thrusts
it back on the shelf.*) Go away! Go on the shelf! All
lost. The brave Captain—and his ship . . . and where
are our years together, eh? All at the bottom of the
sea? (*She puts the shell to her ear.*) One fancies one
can hear the sea in a shell. (*Different voice.*) When I
came to teach in this little school. The first teacher and the last. Now everybody's gone. Parents, pupils,
teachers, all gone away, except me. (*She holds the
shell to her ear and says so suddenly that* JOLYON
jumps.) Are you there?

Jolyon
Yes.

Mrs. Venny.

Ssh. Not you. (*Pause.*) Captain Venny, Captain Venny. (*Pause.*) Typhoons and Tempests and tussles in store. Tricks, Trials, and Trespassings—and troubles galore. What is best to do, I wonder? (*She waits, listening intently, then taking the shell from her ear she smiles and speaks in an ordinary manner to* JOLYON.) It's nice to hear the sound of the sea in a shell, isn't it? (*She returns the shell to its place on the shelf. When she turns back, she sees that he is staring at the window.*) What is it?

Jolyon.

That's what I was going to ask *you*. There's something outside—and it's got six tails. (*Pause.*) Look!

(*Across the window on the outside moves the same large striped tail seen earlier. It travels slowly across like a moving question mark and it is followed by a family of tails, varying downward in size but all peculiarly large.*)

Mrs. Venny.

Tt—Tt—Haven't you seen a cat with kittens before?

Jolyon.

Cat! Kittens!

(MRS. VENNY *opens the back door and calls from the step.*)

Mrs. Venny.

Cat-a-puss! Cat-a-puss! (*She closes the door.*) She won't come in. She's rather cattankerous. You understand the word, I suppose.

Jolyon.

Oh yes . . . except that I've always thought it's—CANtankerous.

Mrs. Venny.

So it is. But *I* prefer cattankerous when it's about cats.

Jolyon.

But—

Mrs. Venny.

You don't agree?

Jolyon.

Yes. I was only going to say, I was thinking—

Mrs. Venny.

Well?

Jolyon.

(*Trying to get it out.*) Wouldn't you . . . wouldn't you perhaps like to live somewhere else, more convenient?

Mrs. Venny.

(*At a loss.*) More *convenient.*

Jolyon.

Nearer the town, perhaps, where you wouldn't be so lonely?

Mrs. Venny.

(*Amazed.*) I? Lonely? Live near a town?

Jolyon.

In a nice little house . . . with bay windows?

Mrs. Venny.

Bay windows? (*Amused.*) Whatever next?

Jolyon.

I mean, this isn't really a house, is it?

Mrs. Venny.

It's home. That's much more important.

Jolyon.

And you could have gas . . . and electricity . . . and water.

Mrs. Venny.

Water! Goodness, young man, I have all the water I want. (*Looks at hole in roof.*) Sometimes, more.

Jolyon.

I should think so. It must be like a shower bath when it rains.

Mrs. Venny.

Shower bath! (*The word hits home.*) I never thought of that. (*Looks thoughtfully up at the hole and goes to stand beneath it.*) I suppose it could . . . I suppose it would . . . (*Pause—she silently thinks the matter over measuring with her hands and eyes.*) I believe you're right. (*Entranced.*) Why didn't I think of it before? I'll do it. Bless my hammer and nails, I will.

(She gleefully rubs her hands together. The wind is blowing very loudly now. There is a strange, hollow, reedy note blown through the room. Pause.)

Jolyon.
What's that?

(Silence, except for the wind.)

Mrs. Venny.
Do you mean the wind? *(With her hand to her ear, listening.)* We're going to have a night of it, I do believe. Oho! I shouldn't be surprised at—*(She breaks off.)*

Jolyon.
Surprised at—what?

Mrs. Venny.
Oh, nothing. Or anything.

(The note comes again.)

Jolyon.
That's it. That's what I meant.

Mrs. Venny.
Oh, that! It's only the wind blowing through the old harmonium. It's a wind instrument, you see. You have to blow wind into it . . . like this. *(She moves to harmonium and puts feet on the pedals.)*

Jolyon.
Can I try it? Does it play?

Mrs. Venny.
Does *IT* play indeed! *I* play. *It* is played upon—and *YOU* MAY play it if you can.

(Pause. He tries to blow and play it, not very successfully. MRS. VENNY *turns up some sheets of music.)*

Mrs. Venny.
Do you know your Doh me Soh Doh? *(*JOLYON *looks blank.)* But I suppose all that's gone out of fashion. *(She points to the tonic sol-fa music sheets hanging up. Then she sings making the appropriate signs in the old-fashioned way.)* Doh, Me, Soh, Doh. That should

be high but *I* sing it low because my voice isn't as good
as it was, so I'll play and *You* sing.

Jolyon.

(*Aghast.*) Me! Sing!

Mrs. Venny.

Why not? Here's the song. (*She gives him a piece of
music, then sits down at the instrument and plays a
few notes, pedaling furiously.*) You begin when I say
"Go."

Jolyon.

But I don't know the first thing about singing.

Mrs. Venny.

The first thing is to open your mouth—like this. Now
—one, two, three, go.

(*She pedals and plays and to his surprise* JOLYON
*finds himself striking an attitude and singing the fol-
lowing verse.*)

Jolyon.

Dreamer, they call me and dreaming's a
pleasure
I have to admit that I cannot forsake
Youth's dreams must end at the sound of the
Morning,
Five minutes to morning, 'Tis time to Awake!

Mrs. Venny.

Mumble, mumble. Lift up your chin and open your
mouth wider, like this. Now, try again. Are you ready?
Go!

(*JOLYON takes a deep breath, gives* MRS. VENNY
a meaningful look, and addresses the next verse to her.)

Jolyon.

Dear Mrs. Venny.

(*She stops playing and turns to him.*)

Mrs. Venny.

Stop! Stop! (*He looks at her.*) You'll have to enunciate
better than that. Now, once more . . . Go! (*She plays
again.*)

Jolyon.

> (*Singing.*)
>> Dear Mrs. Venny, I've something to tell you.
>> Somehow I must tell you before I depart.
>> My message is this, you must leave your poor
>>> dwelling—
>> I hope you won't mind, that it won't break your
>>> heart.

> (MRS. VENNY *stops playing. Silence. She slowly gets up from the instrument and looks at* JOLYON. *He looks at her as if his heart is in his mouth. Silence.*)

Mrs. Venny.

I hope you'll never have to sing for your living, that's all. Never mind. Just sit down in the chair and get your breath back while I think about our next lesson.

> (*She stands thinking, has an idea, and with an exclamation goes out.* JOLYON *sinks into the armchair in front of the stove.*)

Jolyon.

It's no good. I can't get it out. I've tried to say it. I've tried to sing it. What can I do now? Write it, I suppose.

> (*He begins to feel through his pockets for a pen and brings one out. He is looking for a bit of paper upon which to write.*)

Kettle.

> (*Softly.*) Huff-uff-uff-uff-uff-

Jolyon.

> (*Looking up.*) What's that? What did you say? (*Looking all around. He sits back at last and begins to scribble.*)

Kettle.

> (*More loudly.*) Huff-uff-uff-uff-uff-uff-OUCH!

> (JOLYON *springs to his feet with a loud cry just as* MRS. VENNY *comes in rattling a tray of tea things, and sets down the tray.*)

Mrs. Venny.

Our next lesson begins with a T. (*Pause, during which she looks at the disturbed* JOLYON.) Hm. Tremors—Tremblings and Trepidations—(*Pause.*)—or something.

Jolyon

There's something—

Mrs. Venny.

Thought so.

Jolyon.

Something in the room.

Mrs. Venny.

Of course there's something in the room. The room's *full* of things.

Jolyon.

But—

Mrs. Venny.

Ssh. Quiet. (*Silence.*) Quieter still. (*Intense silence.*)

(KETTLE *slowly then with increasing speed:* "HUF, HUF-FUFF-FUFF-FUFF-FUFF.")

Mrs. Venny.

It's the kettle. Haven't you heard a kettle singing before?

Jolyon.

But it *shouted*!

Mrs. Venny.

You'd shout if you were sitting on a hot stove, wouldn't you? (*Settles the kettle firmly.*) It's merely singing that it'll soon be ready to make tea. Do you like tea?

Jolyon.

(*Hopefully.*) Very much.

Mrs. Venny.

Chamomile tea? (*Reaching up for a bunch of herbs.*)

Jolyon.

(*Cast down.*) I don't know.

Mrs. Venny.

(*Flings some leaves into teapot.*) You soon will. What about toast?

Jolyon.

Oh *yes*!

Mrs. Venny.

Mm. *I'm* very fond of toast myself. That's why I keep
such a good toasting fork. (*She shows him the toasting fork then hangs it up again.*) But there isn't any
bread. Do you like cake?

Jolyon.

Of course.

Mrs. Venny.

So do I. (*Pause.*) And I like hot-cross buns, scrambled
eggs, and kippers. (*She ticks them off on her fingers.*)

Jolyon.

So do I.

(*Pause. They look at each other.*)

Mrs. Venny.

The most convenient thing to be fond of here is—
mushrooms!

(JOLYON'*s eyes follow hers up to the funguslike
growth on the damp patches on the walls. He jumps
up suddenly.*)

Jolyon.

I don't think I'll have tea, thank you.

Mrs. Venny.

There probably won't be time.

(*Loud blast of wind.*)

No, I'm sure there won't. Get your hat. Quick. You'll
need it.

(JOLYON *finds his hat, rather surprised at her tone.*)

Mrs. Venny.

You're fond of travel, I hope?

Jolyon.

Yes, I am.

Mrs. Venny.

By air?

Jolyon.
I don't see why not.

Mrs. Venny.
Bravo. Have you a good head for height—and space —and particularly speed?

(*Noise outside.*)

Jolyon.
I don't see what—

Mrs. Venny.
Save your breath. It's time.

(*Increasing noise of wind outside.* MRS. VENNY *darts across to the tree, takes down her travel cape and wraps it about herself with an air of urgent preparation.* JOLYON *shouts to her over the increasing wildness of the wind.*)

Jolyon.
Good-bye, Mrs. Venny.

(*She shouts back over the noise.*)

Mrs. Venny.
Good-bye? What d'you mean? I'm going too.

(*He stares at her in surprise and begins to make his way to the door but he finds it difficult to walk properly, and stumbles about as if he is on a ship. Now everything about the place that can be made to rattle and shake does so. The wind whistles and howls. Things inside and out clatter and bang.* MRS. VENNY *is swaying from side to side.* JOLYON *is still trying to stumble to the door.* MRS. VENNY *shouts as if the wind is in their ears.*)

Mrs. Venny.
Better hold on to something—till you're used to it. Get your air-legs bye and bye.

Jolyon.
(*Holding on.*) What's happening?

Mrs. Venny.
(*Above the din.*) Keep calm! Keep calm!

Jolyon.

(*Shouting.*) I *am* calm!

Mrs. Venny.

Don't be so nervous. (*Pause. Noise.*) We're off! We're off!

(*She generates such a feeling of hilarity, there is such an illusion of movement and speed that* JOLYON *is gradually drawn into it in spite of himself. He begins almost to give himself up to the excitement of the noise of the wind, the flashing and changing of the lights that go streaking past the window.* MRS. VENNY *is holding on to her hat and looking through the window in a downward way, as if from an airplane.*)

Mrs. Venny.

(*As if coaching the pilot.*) Gently, gently now. Watch those trees. Carefully . . . we're up. We're airborne. We're well away now. How do you feel? Don't talk if you don't want to. Just enjoy the experience in your own way.

(*Sound and light effects to suggest speed and space.* MRS. VENNY *looks down. The noise softens a little.*)

Mrs. Venny.

Good-bye little earth . . . little school . . . little home. I've loved you such a long time . . . but just in case I'm not back soon . . . (*She blows kisses.* JOLYON *looks at her strangely.*)

Jolyon.

Are we—are you—going away for a long time then?

Mrs. Venny.

Who knows! Who knows how long? Or where? Or if? (*Much more noise now. Excitement whips up.* MRS. VENNY *shouts across at* JOLYON.) And all without tickets! No bother . . . no luggage. (*Pause.*) There's the sea . . . and there, look, the beautiful hills, the hills of Faraway. But—we're turning. Yes, we're turning back. Back soon, little home after all. We'll soon be coming in to land. There's the town—now the hill—and the thorny, thorny wood. (*Pause.*) It's home again! Hold tight!

> (*Bumping offstage. Dimming of lights. Tense pause. Stillness.*)

Home.
Jolyon.
(*With a sigh.*) Home. (*Pause.*) Are you all right?
Mrs. Venny.
(*Looking round.*) My dear little home. I've come back. After all.
Jolyon.
(*Surprised at her tone.*) After all?
Mrs. Venny.
One never quite knows if one will come back to the same place. (*Pause.*) One never quite knows if one will come back at all. (*Pause.*) One doesn't necessarily come back from every trip. (*Looks around briskly and changes voice.*) Not a thing out of place, you'll notice. Doesn't that show what a good little craft she is?
Jolyon.
I don't believe—

> (MRS. VENNY *takes off her cape.*)

Mrs. Venny.
You be careful of what you don't believe, young man. (*She goes to hang up her cape.*) The beauty of imagination is—
Jolyon.
So that's what it was!
Mrs. Venny.
Is—Instantaneous Transportation. No fuss, no passports, no money.
Jolyon.
As long as you realize it was only imagination—
Mrs. Venny.
Only! Only imagination! You'd better be careful where you put your "only's," young man. (*Yawns delicately.*) Hah! Hah! Hah! Traveling *is* rather tiring now, I must confess—but you—if you ever get the chance to trav-

el—the OTHER way, you know what I mean, promise
you will.

Jolyon.

Oh, I will. As a matter of fact, I intend to go abroad
as soon as I have the money. That's one of the reasons I'm selling this pl—

(MRS. VENNY *makes a sudden ejaculation and*
JOLYON *stops short, but she is only exclaiming because
she has noticed the tea things.*)

Mrs. Venny.

We never had tea! (*Going to the stove.*) And now the
kettle's boiled dry. (*She lifts up the kettle, tilts it, then
puts it down by the side of the stove.*) Never mind,
darling, I'll fill you up again tomorrow. (*She stands
surveying her belongings affectionately.*) I've a good
mind to give you a special polish tomorrow, my dears,
just to make sure you'll be tidy and trim for Christmas. Everything spick and span. That's always been
my way. But it's getting so dark. I must light the
candles.

(*She takes a box of matches from her pocket and
goes around lighting all the candles. Getting to those
in the window she looks outside and cries.*)

Mrs. Venny.

Look! It's snowing! (*Flakes of snow fall gently past
the window.*) While we've been away, winter has come!

(*She clasps her hands, entranced, looking out the
window, then she goes to the tree, takes down her
travel cape again and purposefully wraps herself in
it.*)

Jolyon.

Surely you're not going traveling again!

Mrs. Venny.

Only as far as Skinch's snares in the wood. He sets
them every night you know. (*Chuckles.*) And then I
unset them. (*Chuckles.*) He's furious every morning.

(*She goes out quickly through the back door into the wood.* JOLYON *quickly brings out pen and paper, goes to the desk and rapidly begins to write.*)

Jolyon.

Now for it. Now or never! (*Crossing out and rewriting, stopping and starting again.*) "Dear Mrs. Venny, I am sorry to have to tell you that I am going to sell your house." That's it. Keep it plain and simple. "I AM GOING TO SELL YOUR HOUSE." But it's not HER house . . . it's mine or I wouldn't be able to sell it. But it doesn't feel as if it's mine at all. (*Looking round.*) It feels as if it's hers. Quick. Short and simple. Get it all over at once. "I AM GOING TO SELL THIS HOUSE TO TOM SKINCH."

(MRS. VENNY *comes in at the words "Tom Skinch."* JOLYON *loses his courage and crumbles up the paper. She takes off her cloak, shaking the snow from it.* JOLYON *moves away from the desk, guiltily.* MRS. VENNY *hangs up her cloak, then takes off her wet shoes. There is a hole in the toe of each stocking. She goes to the side of the stove and picks up a slipper, puts it on. The other is missing, she hunts about for it while she talks to* JOLYON.)

Mrs. Venny.

Tom Skinch, did you say? Now *where*—don't talk to me about Tom Skinch—especially before I go to sleep. I don't want *him* in my dreams. What a troublesome boy he always was, to be sure. In this very school-room at that very desk—why you'll find his name BURNED into it. It's a wonder the place is still here. Still—all his traps are spoiled for tonight. That's one good thing. You should see the snow. It's so deep. (*Measures with her hand.*) What's the matter?

Jolyon.

I must go now. I've already stayed much longer than I meant to—

Mrs. Venny.

Go? You can't go now. (*Laughs.*) You wouldn't talk

about going if you knew these hills when the snow is deep. And you haven't even a coat. Bless my boots and bonnet, you can't go now. (*She darts to the truckle bed and drags it into view.*) There, you see. Just the right size.

(JOLYON *is in rebellion now.*)

Jolyon.

I can't. I won't. I shan't. Besides—what about you?

Mrs. Venny.

Oh, me! Don't worry about me. I often sit up in my chair to keep the fire company. (*She gives the bed a push with her foot.*) But *I* know what you're thinking ... (JOLYON *looks startled.*) Confess now ... You're thinking it's not a comfortable bed.

Jolyon.

It does look rather.

Mrs. Venny.

Try it. (JOLYON *sits on the edge of the bed. Boisterously.*) Not like that. (*Moves him out of the way.*) Like this! (*Surprisingly she jumps on to the middle of the bed, and bounces up and down into the air as if on a trampoline, her one slipper flying off. She stops, breathless.*) There you see. Solid as a rock. (*She gets off the bed—*JOLYON *is wearing a trapped look. She plumps up the pillow, shows him the blankets.*) Pillow—blankets, you see. Everything you want.

(*She goes after her slipper and puts it on.* JOLYON *sits on the bed. Then feeling as if he has lost the struggle he puts up his feet.*)

Mrs. Venny.

Surely one doesn't sleep in shoes, nowadays? (JOLYON *wearily takes off his shoes. His big toes show through his socks.* MRS. VENNY *notices these, murmurs.*) Honi Soit Qui Mal Y Pense.

(*And tactfully turns away but carries off his shoes. She pulls her chair into position by the fire, then goes about the room putting out all the lights. Finally she*

*settles her respectable hat more firmly on her head,
then sits in her chair.* JOLYON *sits in a defeated attitude
on the bed.*)

Mrs. Venny.
Pleasant dreams, dear boy, pleasant dreams.

(*Soon her head drops forward. There is a silence.*
JOLYON *is keeping watch, then carefully keeping his
eye on the dozing* MRS. VENNY *he sits up and looks
around. He gets up from the bed, remembering with
chagrin that his shoes are under* MRS. VENNY's *nose
by the fire. He quietly moves over to get them. Dar-
ingly he makes a grab for them.* MRS. VENNY *stirs. He
holds his breath. She gives no further sign so he
breathes again and begins to tiptoe across the room
to the back door, holding his shoes. Now he remembers
that he hasn't got his hat. Looks around, cannot see
it, feels in his pocket—finds it—puts it on, keeping an
eye on* MRS. VENNY *and waiting in agony at every
creak of the floorboards. Suddenly the small blue star
of light seen in the first scene appears again. It stays
only for an instant, leaving him not quite sure whether
he has seen it or not. He stands still, looking about for
it. It is not there. He moves again—and again it appears. He follows it with his eyes. He forgets to be quiet
and drops a shoe. He holds his breath. Now the light
hovers distractingly over* MRS. VENNY's *head. He holds
his hand to his mouth. At last it disappears. He waits.
It does not come again so he pulls himself together and
makes for the back door. Just as he is about to put his
hand on the latch to open it, the door opens by itself
with a great clatter, and a rush of wind swirls in.* MRS.
VENNY *stirs and calls over her shoulder in a fairy-tale
voice—*)

Mrs. Venny.
Is that the wind walking in the room?
Jolyon.
(*Answers in a similar tone.*) Yes, it is the wind walk-

ing in the room. (*Ordinary voice.*) I mean, the wind blew the door open.

Mrs. Venny.

(*In an ordinary voice.*) Then shut it again, but don't lock it—(*Sleepily.*) The door is never locked and everybody's welcome.

(*She settles again in her chair.* JOLYON *stands by the open door, undecidedly. The blue star of light catches his eye again. To look at it he stand facing the audience, his back to the door and the wood. The tiny blue light fixes itself in the middle of the stage and begins to grow until the whole stage is a pool of blue light. Now, faintly and far-off from the wood a strange cry is heard that has been heard once before. It is fearsome and yet sad.*)

Cry.

(*Offstage.*) Ahoo! Ahoo! Ahoo!

(JOLYON *quickly closes the door and stands with his back to it. Again the cry, louder this time.*)

Ahoo! Ahoo! Ahoooo!

Jolyon.

What is going to happen now, I wonder? WHAT IS GOING TO HAPPEN NOW?

CURTAIN

ACT II

The schoolroom several hours later. The curtain rises upon a dimly lighted stage. The stove glows red. The light in the storm lantern is out. The blue light is distilled over the scene and gradually clears away until the figures of MRS. VENNY *and* JOLYON *can be plainly seen.* MRS. VENNY *is still asleep in her chair, her head sunk further down so that her hat has slipped askew.* JOLYON *is lying at full length on the bed, which has been pulled further into view of the audience. His shoes are off and his big toes are shining out of his socks.*

There is silence, then a number of little sounds are heard, no more than little creakings and scratchings, soon stopped but enough to keep the ears alert. Suddenly the opened umbrella falls from the top of the stepladder. With a start, JOLYON *sits upright on the bed. He looks around, then relaxes a little, leaning on one elbow. Soon he is sitting up again to stare at the hole in the floor. Apparently of its own accord the cardboard cover jumps up—once, twice, then it is thrown clear.* JOLYON *watches intently. Is he awake or asleep? He presses his hands over his eyes; takes them away again and looks around cautiously. Everything is as before. He is off guard just at the moment that something is hurled out of the hole to rattle across the floor.* MRS. VENNY *now begins to move. She looks like the figure in a dream, as she slowly arises from her chair. She puts on her one slipper, straightens her hat and jacket, and walks to the center of the room looking about her with an air of expectancy. She picks up the fallen umbrella, folds it and props it aside. (It will be used later in the scene.) She notices with a smile that the hole in the floor is uncovered and she moves the lid out of the way. She stirs the fire in the stove, takes matches and lights the lantern, then moves it from the tree and puts it on top of the harmonium at which she seats herself and begins to play, a pensive old-fashioned tune.*

The blue star of light appears again and drops to focus upon the hole in the floor. Pause. Now to the sound of MRS. VENNY's *music the head of the* SQUIRREL *appears peeping about. Sleepy and yawning at first, he jumps out into the room. He hops about looking for the object which was thrown out. When he finds it he holds it up. It is a nut as big as an Easter egg. He half dances about the room,* MRS. VENNY *fitting the rhythm of the music to his movements. Then he perches on one of the benches, aside. Now the blue spot moves up to the hole in the roof. From it comes the* CAT, *the owner of the largest of the striped tails seen earlier. She walks watchfully down the ladder, stretching, pausing, taking her elegant time; sits on the step halfway down to wash herself, goes to rub round* MRS. VENNY's *skirts as she sits at the harmonium, goes to sit near the stove, where she yawns, then sits staring out at the audience. Now* MRS. VENNY *stands up, but the music goes on without her. There is a scratching outside.* MRS. VENNY *opens the side door and the* DOG *rushes in, bounding and fussing and carrying in his mouth her old slipper which she accepts from him and puts on her foot.*

DOG *goes up to greet* SQUIRREL *and* CAT. *All is perfect friendliness except for a brief spurt of warning from the* CAT *when he goes too close.* DOG *now sits aside. From above (as from the rafters) is heard a clucking and flapping.* HEN *comes down, carrying in a basket an egg which is at least as large as a duck egg. She gives it to* MRS. VENNY, *who receives it graciously and puts it in her pocket. The* HEN, *keeping the basket, goes to perch aside on one of the benches.*

MRS. VENNY *stands center stage. There is still an air of expectancy and waiting amongst the characters. The music is still going on. Now upon the back door are three portentous knocks. All look toward it. Slowly it swings open. At first nothing is seen outside but an intense blue light, then out of it comes a* WILD WHITE PONY *with a golden mane. He comes up to* MRS. VENNY *and bows his head to be caressed. She reaches up to the shelf to take down a wisp of hay from her stores. He nuzzles her hand, then bowing and tossing his head, he moves around in a circle, then goes away through the side door, which opens for him. He is too mysterious and magical a visitor to stay. His hooves are heard as he gallops away. No creature moves until this sound has died away.*

MRS. VENNY, *whose eyes have followed his depar-*

ture, now sees the door close again. She then turns to give her attention to the CAT, DOG, SQUIRREL, *and* HEN *who are all disposed before her somewhat in the manner of a class before the teacher.* JOLYON *is still sitting on the bed, watching. He must give the impression of being in the process of a dream. The music reaches a finale and stops. Silence.* MRS. VENNY *opens her mouth to speak, but before she can do so there is a sound outside.* "Baaa-aaaa!" *All look toward the back window. Pressed against the panes is a mournful* SHEEP's *face. All the animals in the room stir uneasily. Again the* SHEEP *bleats, a sad, long-drawn-out sound:* "Baaa-aa-aa!"

Mrs. Venny.
Come in! Come in! Just close the door behind you.

In spite of her invitation the SHEEP *stands still. The atmosphere in the room becomes charged. The animals are nervous, move closer together. Now there is a muffled sound like the beating of a drum, soft at first, but gathering force and speed. It is as if the disturbed beating of the animals' hearts is gathered into one sound that becomes more and more insistent.*

A red light glows in the doorway, and the SHEEP *stands in it. Now, with one hoof, he kicks the door closed behind him. The noise makes* MRS. VENNY *jump. The animals moan. She turns from them to rebuke the* SHEEP, *who takes a step forward. There is a flash and a roll of drums.* MRS. VENNY *cries out and recoils. The* SHEEP's *skin is thrown off and a loud bellowing laugh is heard which is reminiscent of laughter heard before in Act 1. The Unruly Creature is revealed.*

The animals flee to the corners of the room. The SQUIRREL *jumps into his hole. The stage is now filled with harsh glaring light. There is a silence in which* JOLYON *tries to move from the bed, but he cannot, nor can he speak, although he tries to call out. He is in*

*the grip of his dream and so must seem to be until the
end of this act.*

    MRS. VENNY *is the first to recover from this shock.
As the Unruly Creature takes his first step toward her,
she picks up the umbrella and quickly pokes the fer-
rule under his mask. It falls off backward like a hood
and reveals the face of* TOM SKINCH. *A mingled cry
from the animals.*

Mrs. Venny.

You, Tom Skinch! (*Pause.*) You don't frighten me,
whatever you think you are!

Skinch.

(*In a cringing voice.*) I don't want to frighten anyone, I'm sure. I only want to come in out of the cold.
You know, "Everybody's welcome."

Mrs. Venny.

So everybody is if—

Skinch.

I thought there'd be an "if" in it. There always is for
me. I'm just as cold and hungry as all the others. In
fact—(*He grins and looks around the company.*)
hungrier. *I'm* starving. (*The animals move further
away.*) I only want to be friendly.

Mrs. Venny.

Grinding your teeth isn't a very polite way of showing
it.

Skinch.

That's the way I always smile, when there's fresh meat
about . . . fresh meat.

    (*He rolls his eyes in the direction of the animals.
The* SQUIRREL, *who has been looking out of the hole,
dives into it again. Smiling,* SKINCH *steps forward.*)

Mrs. Venny.

Wait. (*He halts. She hesitates.*) I suppose you may
stay. (*He steps forward.*) Wait! (*He halts.*) No trouble,
mind.

Skinch.

(*Grumbling.*) I haven't done anything yet . . . not a thing. Always watching to see if I break out.

Mrs. Venny.

It's usually "when" not "if."

Skinch.

'Tisn't fair. (*Steps forward. Stops.*)

Mrs. Venny.

Very well, stay! (*He moves again.*) But if there's any fuss—(*He takes her up mockingly.*)

Skinch.

Outside I go. I know all about that. (*He moves forward mincingly.*) *I* know how to behave when the right time comes. You'll see. Move up, Feathers. (*He moves nearer to the* HEN.)

(*The* HEN *squawks.*)

Mrs. Venny.

(*Uneasily.*) Be careful, that's all. Or—or I'll know what to do.

Skinch.

Or? What?

Mrs. Venny.

Er—well—

Skinch.

Something different? Go on, tell us.

Mrs. Venny.

Never mind. Just be careful. Now—supper.

Skinch.

Didn't know I was going to be invited to supper . . . if I'd known, I'd have . . .

(*As* MRS. VENNY *turns to reach up to the shelf,* SKINCH *puts on the mask of the Unruly Creature again and frightens the animals. The* HEN *disappears. As she turns back holding a bag of seeds, his mask is off.* MRS. VENNY *sprinkles seeds.*)

Mrs. Venny.

(*Looking round.*) Where's my Hen? Tom Skinch if you have—

(HEN *squawks offstage.*)

Oh, I thought—
Skinch.

(*Sulkily.*) I wish I had . . . and I would've too if I'd had any sense. Seeds. (*He pulls the* CAT*'s tail. She yells and escapes up the ladder where she sits halfway up.*) I've seen *you* sniffing about in the wood and it wasn't seeds *you* were after!
Mrs. Venny.

(*Sonorously.*) Cat-a-puss. Cat-a-puss. You have been —where?
Skinch.

Into the thornwood to sniff round a snare!
Mrs. Venny.

(*Still addressing the* CAT.) You know what would happen if it tore your fine coat. Someone, I won't mention any names, would . . . oh, dear, the only word I can think of to rhyme with coat is too dreadful, I can't finish it . . .
Skinch.

I will. Coat . . . Throat . . . (*He laughs and gestures with his hand across his throat.*) That'd soon learn her some manners.
Mrs. Venny.

Teach her some manners.
Skinch.

All right. If you say so. I will.

(*He puts on his mask and snaps. The* DOG *has come up with a friendly gesture, and now retires yelping behind the bed where* JOLYON *is sitting and is not seen again until the end of the act. As* SKINCH *walks about in his mask the* CAT *unobtrusively disappears through the hole in the roof.* MRS. VENNY *turns angrily upon the Unruly Creature, who whips off his mask and becomes* SKINCH, *the schoolboy, shamming contrition.*)

Skinch.

Please don't trun me out and make me miss all my education like you did before.

Mrs. Venny.

I only meant you to go out for a few minutes. How was *I* to know you'd never come back . . . no wonder you're such an ignoramus.

Skinch.

So I never came back to your silly old school . . . and look at it now. Hurrah! Who cares? (*He begins to walk about restlessly.*) Just stretching me legs. No need to send for the fire engines—yet.

(MRS. VENNY *uneasily watches his movements. He begins to pick up things, examining them contemptuously and carelessly dropping them.*)

Mrs. Venny.

What are you doing? Be careful! Put that down.

(SKINCH *picks up the photographs.*)

Skinch.

Cricket team nineteen o'—something. Hey, I remember this one. I should've been on this . . . but you wouldn't let me play.

Mrs. Venny.

Wouldn't let you play? You'd just thrown a ball and broken the umpire's front teeth because he'd said you were out.

Skinch.

I wasn't Out.

Mrs. Venny.

You will be in a minute if you're not careful.

(*She takes the photograph from him and puts it on the shelf.*)

Skinch.

It might be somebody else who's out next time.

Mrs. Venny.

It MAY be somebody else.

Skinch.

I'm glad we agree about that. (*Moves about the room.*) I like this place. Just suit me it would—with a few alterations. (*Sweeping his arm along the shelf.*)

'Course, I'd clear all this rubbish out. (*He picks up the shell.*)

Mrs. Venny.

(*Much disturbed.*) Stop! Put that down. Give it to me.

Skinch.

Try and take it. (*Teasing, he holds it aloft. He shouts into it.*)

Ahoy, there, you silly old sea-snipe.

Raids, Rumpuses, and Rollickings a-going on
   Tonight!

(*He evades all* MRS. VENNY's *efforts to take the shell and dances the hornpipe with it, mockingly humming the tune. Then he kicks at the furniture, singing.*) I'll soon shove that outside—get rid of that. (*He arrives at the harmonium, laughs.*) Here's the old DOH ME SOH ME. (*He sings.*) DOH ME SOH DOH. (*Tries the notes on the harmonium. Nothing happens. He puts the shell down at random. Turns to* MRS. VENNY.) Come on. Make it play.

Mrs. Venny.

It doesn't play.

Skinch.

Doesn't IT? *It'd* better or it'll be the worse for *IT*. Wind it up.

Mrs. Venny.

One doesn't wind it up. One blows it up. (*She puts a foot on a pedal and presses.*)

Skinch.

That's what I will do soon if you don't get a tune out of it. (*She presses his hands on the bass notes and a groan comes out.*)

Mrs. Venny.

Wait! Wait! (*She sits down, pedals and produces a few chords.*)

Skinch.

Wait! Wait!

(*He opens the back door so that the wind blows into the room and the lights go out. Outside, darkness and the screech of an owl.*)

Mrs. Venny.

What are you doing?

Skinch.

Just letting 'em all see who's arrived. All the little furry 'uns and the ones with feathers too.

(*She begins to play the same melody which* JOLYON *sang earlier in the play.* SKINCH *sings to the same tune that* JOLYON *sang.*)

Skinch.

Deep in the thornwood the keen owl is hunting,
With saber and sword, she swoops on her prey,
Deep in the thornwood my snares are all waiting,
Their sharp teeth are waiting, my victims to slay.

(*This music captures the note of darkness in this play. When the verse is over, the wind blows violently.* MRS. VENNY *gets up to close the back door. The harmonium music continues for her verse. She takes matches and lights all the candles as she half-sings, half-says—*)

Mrs. Venny.

Out of the darkness, I'll call to the morning,
I'll call to the sun from the darkness of night
Soon its dark dreams and its fearful forebodings
Will all fade away, will fade with the light.

(*Now the scene is well lighted. Behind her back* SKINCH *has become the Unruly Creature again.*)

Skinch.

Call that singing! It's more like the thorn trees scraping together.

(MRS. VENNY *turns round. She accepts the fact of his ugly mask and merely says with a sigh—*)

Mrs. Venny.

You're putting on that ugly face again.

Skinch.

(*Fingering his mask.*) What if I am? (*Pause.*) So are you.

Mrs. Venny.

I? (*Surprised she touches her face.*) It's the same as usual. (*Pause.*) I can't help it.

Skinch.

More's the pity then, but you'd better not make remarks about other people's faces. (*Looking about.*) Where's all the livestock gone? (*No animals are in sight.* SKINCH, *the Unruly Creature, stamps his feet and grinds his teeth. He comes to the hole in the floor. Stops.*) Ha! What's this? There's something in here to be sure.

Mrs. Venny.

Keep away. (*She picks up the umbrella.*)

Skinch.

Very interesting.

(*He bends down to look closer.* MRS. VENNY *stands over him, slowly raising the umbrella above his head.*)

Mrs. Venny.

I'm very tempted! (*She half aims the blow.*) But I mustn't. (*She changes her mind again.*) But I WILL.

(*She brings her umbrella down just as* SKINCH *moves his head away. The umbrella falls on the floor.* SKINCH *quickly picks it up, laughing.*)

Skinch.

You'll have to be cleverer than that when you're aiming at me. (*He whirls the umbrella at her.* JOLYON *now emerges from his half hidden position at the side.* SKINCH *sees him.*) Hello! Look who's here.

Mrs. Venny.

Leave him alone. He's a visitor. Besides, he's sleeping.

Skinch.

Sleeping in school! You'd never allow that! He deserves a nightmare. (*He puts his masked face close to* JOLYON *who recoils.*) He'll remember that. (*Laughs.*) Tomorrow he'll be boring everybody about his bad dreams.

(*He teases* JOLYON *with the end of the umbrella.*
MRS. VENNY, *annoyed, goes to intervene.* SKINCH *turns
upon her and with a quick movement pokes off her
hat. There is a shocked silence. Even* SKINCH *is mo-
mentarily awestruck. Impressed.*)

Skinch.

I didn't think it'd come off. I thought it'd *grown* on.

(*He pokes it up from the floor on the end of the
umbrella, hesitates as if he is going to give it back,
then with a shout of laughter he begins to twirl it
around over his head, bawling.*)

> Who wants a ridiculous hat?
> Latest fashions for sale . . .
> Going cheap,
> Who wants a silly old hat?

(MRS. VENNY, *controlling her anger, goes to the
door, opens it and points outside. He looks at her
grinning, then ignores her gesture. She points more
vehemently.*)

Mrs. Venny.

I dare not trust myself to speak but . . .

Skinch.

Don't speak then.

Mrs. Venny.

I warned you Tom Skinch—

Skinch.

Sounds like speaking—don't it? (*Pause. She still stands
and points.*) Oh dear, she don't seem to realize that
times have changed. That's all over, ma'am. (*Speaking
slowly and clearly.*) It's not like that anymore dear.
(*Aside.*) She hasn't got the idea at all. You're the
one who's going, Mrs. A.B.C. Not me. I'm staying
here. (*Pause.*) Me—stay . . . You—go. Got it?

> Doh Me Soh Doh
> I Stay—You Go!

(*Changes manner, snapping suddenly.*) O-U-T spells

"out." (*He moves nearer to her, she nips away from the door.*)

Mrs. Venny.
I'm glad you can spell something.

(*Her brain is working furiously. Suddenly she skips up the ladder as if to escape through the hole.* SKINCH *hooks the handle of the umbrella around her ankle and stops her. She turns, shrugs, as if accepting defeat, moves as if to come down, but she suddenly brings out of her pocket the outsize egg the* HEN *gave her earlier on, and she holds it over* SKINCH'S *head, threatening to break it over him. He puts up the umbrella to protect himself, leaving her free. She puts the egg back in her pocket, and considers her next move. Now from outside there is a loud cat-cry. Pause.*)

Skinch.
What's that? (*Pause.*) I've caught something in one of my snares. Hurrah!

(JOLYON *makes a tremendous effort and breaks the bonds of his silence.*)

Jolyon.
C-Cat . . . a . . . puss. Where's the Cat-a-puss?

(MRS. VENNY *looks around and sees that the* CAT *has gone.*)

Skinch.
(*Laughing.*) I've always fancied a Cat-a-puss Skin.

(MRS. VENNY *forgets her struggle with him. She gives up the fight and rushes out through the open back door, the* DOG *comes out from behind the bed and racing pell-mell after her.*)

Mrs. Venny.
Cat—a-puss. Oh—Cat—a-puss.

(*She disappears through the back door.* SKINCH *laughs and mimics her cry.*)

Skinch.

Cat—a-puss! Oh—Cat—a-puss! (*He strides quickly to the back door and locks it.*) I didn't think it was going to be as easy as that. That's settled her . . . and maybe I've got a cat-a-puss as well . . . I've always wanted to catch one o' them. (*His mask falls off and he begins to laugh. He laughs and laughs, sliding down to the floor with his back against the door.* JOLYON *is still watching, helpless and tongue-tied.*) Did you ever see anything so funny . . . as . . . her . . . as the way she went. Easy as pie it was in the end . . . Oh, my sides. They'll split. Got her out at last . . . and so easy . . . (*He begins to struggle to his feet, laughing until he wheezes.*) Give us a hand, old chap. (*Grabs hold of* JOLYON *and pulls himself up. Digs him in the ribs, slyly.*) You're a clever 'un. That about the Cat— in the trap. She'd never've gone . . . Did the trick straight away. She *flew* out . . . couldn't get out quick enough. Door never locked, she says. Well, it is now. (*There is no key so he puts a chair in front of it. Moves to the side door.*) Don't want her creeping in here with her silly old ideas. Oh, Lor'—never-laughed -so-much-in-all-me life. Can't you laugh . . . no sense of humor, eh . . . ? (*He loses his breath on the word "humor" and fumbles in his pockets for a small phial from which he drinks.*) That's better. Never fails. (*Calms down.*) Acts like magic. Very old recipe. Strength and cunning, that's the mixture. That's the stuff that makes the world go round. Try a drop. (JOLYON *shakes his head.*) I don't care. (SKINCH, *still without his mask, goes to the window and looks out. He beckons* JOLYON *to come over.*) Come and see a sight for sore eyes. (JOLYON *joins him.*) You're frightened of me, aren't you? (*Puts the mask on.*) I'm a nightmare you're having. Grrrr— (*He growls. He digs* JOLYON *in the ribs and laughs. They look out the window.*) There she is! Poor old Mrs. A.B.C.— under a tree in the middle of the night with the snow falling onto her old gray head. (*Raised voice.*) What about lessons now? Better learn how to keep dry sit-

ting in the snow . . . or better still, how to like getting
wet. (*He opens the window and in a loud voice—the
voice of the Unruly Creature—he addresses the night
outside.*) Creep up, you little furry things . . . to keep
her warm tonight. I'll have your skins in the morning.
Her benevolent spell is at an end. I shall be king of the
wood tomorrow. (*He is going to shut the window.*
JOLYON *has picked up* MRS. VENNY'S *hat.*) Here you
are, Ma'am—keep your ears warm. (*He throws the hat
outside.* JOLYON *runs for* MRS. VENNY'S *shoes and
throws them out too.*) And your toes . . . if you can.
(*He closes the window and moves back into the room,
stretching luxuriously.*) Just what I've always wanted,
this nice little den. Got it at last. (JOLYON *makes a
strangled sound.*) What's that? Still dreaming? Wish-
ing you could wake up, eh?

(JOLYON *begins to break free of his dream.*)

Jolyon.
(*With an effort.*) Worse . . . worse for you.
Skinch.
What?
Jolyon.
When—I do wake up.
Skinch.
Eh?
Jolyon.
For *you*'ll fade away and be gone.
Skinch.
Oh, shall I? What do *I* care about you? Whether *you*
wake or dream doesn't matter to me. I shall always be
around somewhere in one shape or another—SO
LOOK OUT!

(*With the last words he arrogantly pushes* JOLYON
*away so that he stumbles and falls into the easy chair.
Now* SKINCH *begins to enjoy his conquest of the room.
Sometimes during what follows he is the Unruly Creature in his mask, sometimes* SKINCH *the schoolboy. He
kicks the hamper of apples, bites one and throws it*

away. He rattles pens, rulers. Going to the teacher's desk, he hits behind it, rummages in the drawers, brings out a pair of pince-nez and puts them on so that he can take off MRS. VENNY.)

Skinch.

You boy! Work harder! And you—over there, 500 black marks for talking . . . and—Hey, you—Sleepy! (*To* JOLYON.) Stay in after school . . . for a week . . . for a year . . . forever. (*He goes to* JOLYON *and pulls him up, pushes him down, pulls him up again.*) And answer these question. (*He gabbles quickly.*)

How does the horse-fly?
What does the house-hold?
How many dreams make a nightmare?

Answer all of 'em at once and in one breath. (JOLYON *is silent.* SKINCH *drops him back in the chair.*) Thought you were stupid. Now I know. Watch me and you'll learn a thing or two.

(*Now begins* SKINCH's *orgy of destruction which must work up to a climax. He kicks furniture, sees the shell again and gives a warning shout into it.*)

What-o—you slippy old Sea Slug. Watch out for Batterings, and Breakages and Bangings and Burnings!

(*He drops the shell. Knocks books from shelves, sees a pile of exercise books, throws them on the floor and jumps on them. He takes a pile of papers and tears them up, throwing the pieces about like a snowstorm. Finally he gathers up in his hands* MRS. VENNY's *papers which are lying about and rushes to and from the stove, in a crisis of excitement, pushing as many as he can into it, and chanting.*)

> Curse pen and ink
> That make me think
> And every kind of learning,
> The printed page,
> Fills me with rage,
> It's only fit for BURNING.

(*The last burst of demoniac energy is too much for* JOLYON's *dream. He rises from his chair.*)

Jolyon.
Shut—up!

Skinch.
(*Pausing.*) Who dares to speak?

Jolyon.
(*More firmly.*) Shut up . . . and stop that!

Skinch.
Oh—very brave—(*He grinds his teeth and pushes his masked face at* JOLYON *who is now quite calm.*)

Jolyon.
I'm waking—really waking . . . so . . . look . . . out.

(SKINCH *looms up center stage and cries in a loud voice, being very terrible, and behind his voice is a faint throbbing like the beat of a drum—or a heart. Perhaps it is* JOLYON's *heart.*)

Skinch.
What do I care for you? I? I am everywhere, always.
When the earth rumbles and shakes, when the
mountains breathe flame, I am there.
When Oceans rage—when cities vanish overnight,
I am there.
When thunder rolls, and lightening burns,
When guns boom, when the bomb bursts—
I am there. I shall always be there.

(*The drum beat rises to a crescendo until* JOLYON *shouts out above it.*)

Jolyon.
I am waking. (*Shouting.*) I AM AWAKE.

(*The stage fills with a red glare.* JOLYON *moves toward the Unruly Creature, who moves backward to the door. He is laughing and booming, but his voice grows fainter. He seems to disappear through the door mysteriously as if it is made of mist, and is swallowed up. Silence in the room. Suddenly there is a wild rush of hooves outside, the deafening uproar of confusion, then the cry, heard before.*)

Cry.

(*Offstage.*) Ahooo! Ahooo! Ahooo!

(*The sound of the cry, and the sound of the galloping hooves die away.* JOLYON *leans against the open door, exhausted but fully awake. The red light dissipates. A pale white light gradually grows. It is morning.* JOLYON *suddenly remembers* MRS. VENNY. *He steps outside.*)

Jolyon.

MRS. VENNY. Mrs. Venny! Where are you?

(*Pause.* MRS. VENNY *comes up, her hat firmly on her head. She and* JOLYON *come into the room together, he fussing about her.*)

Jolyon.

Are you safe, dear Mrs. Venny? Are you all right?

Mrs. Venny.

Bless my boots and bonnet, of course I am. What's all the fuss about?

Jolyon.

All that snow! So cold . . . out in the wood all night.

Mrs. Venny.

All night? I've only been out a few minutes. It's five minutes to morning, the time I always get up and go round the snares. And as for the snow, it's all gone . . . not a sign of it. It didn't come to stay. (*She takes her slippers out of her pocket, and puts them on the shelf out of reach, turning to him, and says.*) The Dog takes them out, you know! Oh—and look what else I found . . . (*She holds up the pair of spectacles which he lost.*)

Jolyon.

(*Taking them, pleased.*) Oh, good! Thank you very ter. (*Suddenly remembers.*) That Cat. Your Cat-a-much. (*Polishes them and puts them on.*) That's bet-puss, where is she? Is *she* safe?

Mrs. Venny.
Of course she's safe.
Jolyon.
How did you manage to get her out of Skinch's snare?
Mrs. Venny.
Skinch's snare? She's much too clever for Tom Skinch
and his snares.
Jolyon.
So she wasn't caught.
Mrs. Venny.
Not she. (*She takes a saucer and puts it down on the
back door step.*) Puss, Puss, Cat-a-puss! Here's your
breakfast.

(JOLYON *stands at the back door and looks outside. There is a loud "meow" and an ordinary-sized
striped tail waves round the door post.*)

Jolyon.
She seems just an ordinary-sized cat this morning,
quite different from last night . . .
Mrs. Venny.
Things often seem different in the morning, haven't
you noticed? (*She looks round the room becoming
aware of the state it is in.*) Bless me! This room! What
a mess . . . whatever . . . ?

(*Before* JOLYON *can speak, three shots are heard
outside.*)

Mrs. Venny.
There he is! That's Tom Skinch. He comes every
morning. He's trying to catch that pretty white pony
but he won't. He'll blow his silly head off first, rattling
about with that gun of his. (*She turns to tidy up the
room.*) Whatever's been happening in here? A tor-
nado I should think or a typhoon—or at the very least
a tantrum—everything looking so tattered and tossed.
I suppose I left the door open and the wind's been in.
The winds up here, you know, are quite—

(*Her sentence is never finished for loud groans and piteous cries are heard outside. Then there is a rap at the window.* JOLYON *and* MRS. VENNY *turn to look. Pressed close to the windowpanes is the ravaged face of* TOM SKINCH.)

Skinch.
(*Moaning.*) Help me! Help!
Mrs. Venny.
There! He's done it! I knew he would.

(SKINCH *disappears from their sight. There is the sound of a thud outside.* MRS. VENNY *hurries through the back door followed by* JOLYON. *In a few seconds they reappear dragging in the body of the wounded* SKINCH. *They place him center stage, and kneel one at each side of him, looking down. Silence.*)

Jolyon.
(*In a hushed voice.*) Is he . . . do you think . . . do you think he is dead?

(MRS. VENNY *bends over* SKINCH's *body.*)

CURTAIN

ACT III

Scene One

The curtain goes up to reveal JOLYON *and* MRS. VENNY *bending over* TOM SKINCH's *body as at the end of the last scene.* MRS. VENNY *is listening for the beat of his heart.*

Jolyon.
Is he . . . alive?

(MRS. VENNY *raises her head then puts it down to* SKINCH's *chest.*)

Mrs. Venny.

I can hear something. (*Raises her head.*) Quick! Water, bandages, ointment, medicine!

(JOLYON *begins to fly this way and that, distractedly.*)

Jolyon.

Where? Where?

Mrs. Venny.

Up there on the shelf. Don't delay.

(JOLYON *moves things about on the shelf.*)

Jolyon.

There's salt up here ... and seeds up here ... and hay ...

Mrs. Venny.

I don't need a list. There's *everything* up there. Here, you hold his head. I'll get what I need myself.

(JOLYON *changes places with her at* SKINCH's *side. She goes to the shelf and comes back with a bottle marked "wine."*)

Jolyon.

That's wine.

Mrs. Venny.

I know what it is. *I* made it. (*She uncorks the bottle, smells, sighs.*) It seems a pity but—(*She flings a generous splash into* SKINCH's *face.*)

Skinch.

(*Sitting bolt upright.*) Ouch! Help! Save me, I'm drowning. (*He makes a brief struggle, scrabbling about with his hands, then relapses with a deep groan, a spectacular collapse.*)

Jolyon

He looks dreadfully bad, now. What can we do? We must get help.

(*Another deep groan from* SKINCH. MRS. VENNY's *suspicious looks have given way to an expression of anxiety. She shakes her head over him, full of regret.*)

Mrs. Venny.

Poor Tom Skinch! P'raps I could have been more patient—sometimes. (SKINCH *warily opens an eye, rolls it around impudently, and quickly closes it again.* MRS. VENNY *purses her lips and turns to* JOLYON.) Will you be so kind—(*Pause.*)—as to pass me—(*Pause.*)—that long—(Pause.) sharp—(*Pause.*)—PIN—(*Quickly words all in a rush.*) and I'll jab it into him to see if he's alive.

Skinch.

Oh! Oh! I'm coming to. Oh my head!

Mrs. Venny.

H'm. (*To* JOLYON.) You see. No need to worry about *him.* (*To* SKINCH.) You're lucky you've still got a head. It's a wonder you haven't blown it right off, playing about with guns. (*To* JOLYON.) Bandages now. (*To* SKINCH.) Sit up.

Jolyon.

Bandages? Bandages?

Skinch.

Sit . . . up?

Mrs. Venny.

That's what I said. Heave ho!

(*She pulls him up to a sitting posture, props him up behind with a chair.*)

Jolyon.

I don't see any bandages.

Mrs. Venny.

Never mind. (*She sees that* SKINCH's *shirt has come out of his waistband. Without more ado she tears off a generous strip and proceeds to wind it round his head.*) Keep still, or I can't put the bandage on.

Skinch.

Bandage? Is it as bad as that? (*She continues to do up his head.*) Are there many bones broken?

Mrs. Venny.

Not more than 99. (*Pours wine.*) Here, drink this.

(SKINCH *drinks, shudders but begins to recuperate.*

She feels his arm and begins to work it around in a circle vigorously.)

Skinch.

(*Wincing and wriggling, trying to escape.*) Ow! Ouch!

Mrs. Venny.

Don't fidget so. Your bandage will fall off.

Skinch.

My arm'll fall off if you keep on pulling it like that. (*He rescues his arm from her, and nurses it miserably.*) It's my shooting arm too. I bet it's done for.

Mrs. Venny.

Serve you right. (*To* JOLYON.) He's better now.

(*She begins to gather up her impediments.* SKINCH *appears to notice* JOLYON *for the first time.*)

Skinch.

You! Still here. (*Laughs.*) So you couldn't get away. Well, I warned you. Told you not to come in the first place—Ouch! (MRS. VENNY *has tweaked him again.*)

Jolyon.

Have some more wine. (*Offers the bottle.*)

Skinch.

Wine, d'you call it? Wine! (*He waves the bottle away with a shudder.*)

Mrs. Venny.

Now you're recovered you can tell us what happened.

Skinch.

Happened? When? Where? What d'you mean? Everything's going round again. (*He puts on an act.*)

Mrs. Venny.

We're all going round—but in twenty-four hours we'll be back in the same place, more or less. If you'd listened to your lessons, you wouldn't find it so surprising. Now, get on with your tale—or your taradiddle, for that's what it will be, I'm sure. (*Pause.*) What were you *UP* to, out there?

Skinch.

Up to? I wasn't up to anything. I was just having my early morning walk as usual—

Mrs. Venny.

H'm. I know all about that.

Skinch.

—Morning walk, looking—

Mrs. Venny.

For trouble, I suppose.

Skinch.

If you're not going to listen—

Mrs. Venny.

Go on.

Skinch.

I was just looking—(*He stops.*)

Mrs. Venny.

You were looking at those wicked traps of yours and spying for my beautiful wild one, but you shan't have him, Tom Skinch.

Skinch.

I don't know what you mean.

Mrs. Venny.

You'll never catch him. He's too quick for you, and too clever.

Jolyon

(*Looking* SKINCH *over.*) There don't seem to be any bullet holes in him anywhere.

Skinch.

What d'you mean, bullet holes? I tell you I was just walking around and enjoying the fresh air when all of a sudden—(*Pause.*)—there was a thunderbolt, or a flying torpedo. I remember falling—and it was all black.

Mrs. Venny.

All white you mean. The white pony. I knew he was too smart for you and your silly bit of rope. Let that teach you a lesson. Get on your feet now.

Skinch.

I don't know if I—

(*But* MRS. VENNY *gives him a heave.* SKINCH *gets up with much wincing and exclaiming,* JOLYON *helping.*)

Jolyon.
How's that?
Skinch.
A bit dizzy. Oops! Fierce little brute, that dratted pony.

(MRS. VENNY *gives a very expressive ironical laugh
and begins to gather up the wine, etc.* SKINCH *nods and
winks at* JOLYON *when her back is turned and whispers
at the first opportunity.*)

Skinch.
Does she know? Did you tell her? When's she leaving?

(JOLYON *shakes his head looking embarrassed.* MRS.
VENNY *turns and sees them close together.* SKINCH
hastily changes his face.)

Skinch.
I was just saying . . . must be leaving. I've got an appointment this morning with my lawyer. (*To* JOLYON.)
You haven't forgotten about those important papers
we've got to sign.

(JOLYON *looks at* MRS. VENNY *to see if she has
heard, but she is busy around the room and gives no
sign.* SKINCH *looks curiously around the room and
gleefully rubs his hands together.*)

Jolyon.
Ssh. No, I haven't forgotten—but—Ssh.
Skinch.
(*Turning to* MRS. VENNY.) No hard feelings, ma'am.
I'm sure you'll soon find somewhere—another little
place—much more comfort. (JOLYON *kicks him in
the shin.*) Oooh! (*Hobbles.* MRS. VENNY *holds out her
hand to* SKINCH.)
Mrs. Venny.
We've been at cross purposes for a long time now,
Tom Skinch.

(*They shake hands.*)

Skinch.
Aye. We've had some right old rows. Ever since I

was—(*Measures with his hand.*)—and used to sit—
(*Indicates the school benches.*)—in your school.

Mrs. Venny.

Since . . . long before that . . . (*He looks at her.*)
Since creation, if you'll excuse the hyperbole. (*He is
bewildered.*) But never mind. Imagination was never
one of your strong points.

Skinch.

(*Heartily.*) That's right. That's the spirit. (*For the
want of something to do he holds out his hand again.*)

Mrs. Venny.

It'll be but an uneasy friendship between you and me,
but I don't mind trying. (*They shake hands again.*)
We must make the best of it we can—and—(*Pause.*)
—I tell you what I'll do. (*Pause. She considers. They
look at her.*) I'll—yes I *will*—I'll invite you to breakfast. Both of you! (*They both stare at her and then
both refuse at once.*)

Jolyon.

Very kind, but, impossible—kind hospitality.

Skinch.

Thank you kindly, but, pressing engagement . . .
lawyer's office.

Both.

Thank you, all the same.

(MRS. VENNY *smiling a coaxing smile and with her
conjurer's flourish produces the egg out of her pocket
and holds it aloft.*)

Mrs. Venny.

Et voilà. (*Pause.*) It'd be a *good* breakfast, you know.
(*Flourishes the egg.*) It's quite big enough for three.

(JOLYON *stares at the egg, which is an ordinary
hen's egg now, then at* MRS. VENNY *and* SKINCH *to
see if they remember any of the incidents of the night.
Neither make any sign.*)

Mrs. Venny.

Fresh from my little hen this very morning.

Skinch.
Must be going. Kindly, all the same.
Jolyon.
So must I.
Skinch.
(*To* JOLYON.) If you're going now, I'll wait for you outside. I'll just go and pick up my gun and things.

(*He goes to the door. As he passes through it and is lost to view,* MRS. VENNY *laughs.*)

Mrs. Venny.
Pick up his gun, indeed. Did you ever? (*She calls out, with a twitter of laughter.*) Throw it down the well, my boy, and be well rid of it. (JOLYON *closes the door and turns to* MRS. VENNY.) P'raps I'd miss him if he went away.

(*She suddenly looks very tired. She walks over to the tree, and taking down her traveling cape, she slowly, and with deliberation, puts it on.* JOLYON *watches her in surprise. She takes down her carpetbag from one of the branches and goes about the room picking up her most treasured objects. She takes down the photograph of the cricket team, for instance, and the photograph of Captain Venny and his bride. She looks at this long and closely before putting it in the bag. She takes up the kettle and puts the handle over her arm like a handbag's. Lastly, she takes the shell and holds it to her ear. She listens, then with a sigh as if there is no message from it, she puts it in the bag. At last she stands center stage looking steadily at* JOLYON. *He looks at her, completely at a loss. As if to give herself something to do, she takes a pair of gloves from one of the pockets in the cape and patiently begins to work them onto her hands. There is a hole in one finger.*)

Jolyon.
But—you're not going away again?

Mrs. Venny.

(*Surprised.*) I'm going with you. (*Pause.*) Isn't that why you came?

Jolyon.

Me? I?

Mrs. Venny.

Didn't you come to tell me that I—that I must leave my dear little home? (*She turns, picks up* JOLYON's *hat and hands it to him.*) Shall we go?

Jolyon.

No. I mean—perhaps I did—but—

Mrs. Venny.

I'm ready. (*Looks around.*) Quite ready.

Skinch.

(*Shouting offstage.*) Come on if you're coming. Don't be all day about it.

(MRS. VENNY *takes a step toward the door.*)

Jolyon

No, Mrs. Venny. (*Passionately.*) Why should you leave your dear little home?

Mrs. Venny.

It isn't mine. It's yours . . . until . . . it's . . . (*Nods her head in the direction of the noise outside.*) Tom Skinch's.

Jolyon.

You know? You know what I—meant to do?

Mrs. Venny.

It's quite natural that you'd rather sell it. Money means more to a young man than a tumbledown place like this, and a thorny old wood and a bit of ground that grows nothing but stones. I knew the day would come . . . I've been expecting it. And yet—I hoped, perhaps . . . (*She breaks off, looks all around, then says.*) I'm ready now. I'd rather go quickly.

Jolyon.

But you're not going at all, Mrs. Venny. (MRS. VENNY *seems not to hear him.*)

Mrs. Venny.

One to be ready, two to be steady, three—to be off.

(*Looks round.*) Good-bye, my dears. (*Some link between her and her house is already broken. She steps toward the door.*) Come along!

Jolyon.

You don't understand. (*He tries to take her carpet-bag from her hand. She resists.*) There's no need for you to go away. (*He tugs, and takes the bag.*) You can put all these back again now. Look.

(*He moves quickly about the room putting things back on the shelves at random.* MRS. VENNY *is coming back to herself now. She suddenly notices that things are being put in their wrong places, and she cries out sharply in her usual voice.*)

Mrs. Venny.

Not there! Not like that. (*She takes the bag and begins to place things in their right order.*) There! That's better. (*She hangs up the toasting fork and puts the kettle back again on the stove saying as she does so.*) We're not going yet, dear. You can boil for breakfast.

Jolyon.

(*Smiling.*) Huff-uff-uff-uff-uff.

Mrs. Venny.

Whatever can I be thinking of? It won't sing until there's water in it.

(*She picks up the kettle and goes out through one door.* SKINCH *appears at the other. He looks more like himself, but disheveled, the bandage drooping askew.*)

Skinch.

Come on! What's keeping you? Let's be off.

Jolyon.

I'm not coming, Mr. Skinch. (*His manner is nervous but he gains firmness.*)

Skinch.

What? (*Blustering.*)

Jolyon.

I'm not going to keep that appointment.

Skinch.

Not *what?*

Jolyon.

I'm not going to sell—all this. I'm not going to sell any of it.

Skinch.

You can't say that . . . it's as good as sold, it's as good as mine—you can't—

Jolyon.

I'm sorry, Mr. Skinch.

Skinch.

Sorry! What's the good of that to me! I know what it is! It's her fault. She's at it again—she's trying to spoil things for me like she always does . . . well, she shan't, I'm not having—(JOLYON *cuts into his words.*)

Jolyon.

And another thing, Mr. Skinch. Perhaps you won't go around in the woods so much now—after the pheasants.

Skinch.

What?

Jolyon.

And please—leave the white pony alone, will you? I intend to keep an eye on things around here myself, now . . . so no shooting, Mr. Skinch, and no snares.

Skinch.

No shooting? No snares? No sport? No Skinch's wood —Oh, it's too much . . . it's her—she's at the bottom of it but she won't . . .

(MRS. VENNY *comes in with the kettle.*)

Jolyon.

Ssh.

Mrs. Venny.

Still here, Tom Skinch? (*She puts the kettle on the stove.*)

Jolyon.

He's just going. (*To* SKINCH.) I'll try to explain— someday . . . but you see . . . I can't really explain quite clearly to myself yet—but—there it is.

Skinch.

We'll see about that—oh yes—we'll see.

(*He disappears, grumbling.* JOLYON *begins to pick up apples from the floor.* MRS. VENNY *looks around taking everything in. She takes off her gloves, then her cape. Then she walks to the tree to hang it up, seeing the overturned basket of apples.*)

Mrs. Venny.

What a state everything's in. It'll take a week of sweeping. (*Begins to help* JOLYON *pick up the apples.*) Apples all over the place. (*Drops them one by one into the hamper.*) All my Special Selecteds. They won't keep if they're bruised, you know. I don't know what I'd do this winter for my apple pies and apple puddings and—(*She stops, holding an apple over the hamper before dropping it in.*)

Jolyon.

(*Tosses one into the hamper.*) Apple Charlotte.

(*In excitement and delight* MRS. VENNY *drops her apple.*)

Mrs. Venny.

That's it! At last! Oh, say it again.

Jolyon.

What? Apple Charlotte?

Mrs. Venny.

Charlotte. That's it. My name . . . the one I've been trying to remember. I knew it had something to do with puddings—and apples. Now I feel as if I knew myself properly again. Annie Beatrice Charlotte!

Jolyon.

Mrs. A.B.C.

Mrs. Venny.

(*With great formality.*) Now we can introduce ourselves correctly. How do you do, Jolyon? (*They shake hands.*) You are so very much like your grandfather. Yes. I knew you at once. He loved this place, these hills, the thornwood. This . . . this was the school he built, you know—(*Moves about.*)—all his own idea for the children who lived around here. And now . . . and now . . . (*Her eyes travel around the scene.*) But no matter. It served its purpose well. And I—(*She stops, and smiles more to herself than to him.*) I, too.

(JOLYON *moves and nearly puts his foot into the* SQUIRREL's *hole.*)

Jolyon.
(*Rubbing his ankle.*) What *is* in there?
Mrs. Venny.
Just a little nuttykin asleep for the winter. Look for yourself if you like.

(JOLYON *peers inside the hole. He puts his hand inside.*)

Jolyon.
Just a squirrel. An ordinary-sized one.
Mrs. Venny.
What did you expect?
Jolyon.
(*Slowly.*) I don't know. I don't know.
Skinch.
(*Banging about and calling outside.*) 'Tisn't fair. But we'll see about that—
Mrs. Venny.
A noisy boy. He always was.
Jolyon.
(*Still pursuing his thought.*) I only know—
Mrs. Venny.
Yes, what is it that you know?
Jolyon.
I only know that I feel so glad. So glad that you're going to stay here, that you're never going to leave (*Pause.*)
Mrs. Venny.
Never, my dear? *Never*? (*She smiles mysteriously.*)
Jolyon.
And I'll plant trees. If only they'll grow! And I'll call the wood Vennswood—after you.

Mrs. Venny.

A wood named after me. Why it may grow into a forest someday and I'll be a part of it. Vennswood! Now that's a tale to tell!

(*She ceases to think of* JOLYON. *She moves to pick up the shell.* JOLYON *goes to the side door where he pauses and looks back.*)

Jolyon.

Good-bye, Mrs. Venny. Good-bye.

(*He waits a second, but she seems to have forgotten him already. She is holding up the shell and saying softly.*)

Mrs. Venny.

Captain Venny, Captain Venny, the storm's blown over —the dark clouds gone. I'll soon have everything tidy and shipshape, just as you'd like it and . . . All's well.

(JOLYON *watches, then turns away and goes off. Pause.*)

Scene Two

TABLEAU

Very softly there is the sound of the musical theme again. MRS. VENNY *sits amongst her possessions, holding the shell. The animals move in slowly to the music in the same order as before in Act II. The blue light comes and spreads over the scene. The back door opens as before and in a haze of blue light the white pony can just be seen.*

CURTAIN

BETTY JEAN LIFTON, a graduate of Barnard College, has spent many years in the Far East gathering folklore for her children's books and plays and traveling as a journalist in Korea and Vietnam. In 1970 she was artistic director for the Second Celebration of the Arts for Children at City Center where her play *Moonwalk* was performed. Her other plays are *The Many Lives of Adam and Eve, Joji and the Dragon,* and *The Dolphin Dreamer.* She has her own experimental troupe, The Jugglers, which performs in New York City, and is one of the founders of the newly formed Playwrights Theater for Children. She is married to Robert Jay Lifton, Yale psychiatrist and writer, and has two children.

JACK STOKES received his Ph.D. in theater at Southern Illinois University, Carbondale. He is presently teaching speech and oral interpretation at Belleville Area College where he is also the director of the children's theater and the Dramachoir. His *Wiley and the Hairy Man* was published by Macrae Smith Co. Other plays for children include: *The Honkybird, Nobody Likes Mordacious, The Day the Plottypo Danced,* and *The Last Days of Good Old Bill.* He is married and has four children.

JAMES REANEY was born in 1926, near Stratford, Ontario. He took his doctoral studies in English at the University of Toronto, and, since 1960, has lectured in English at the University of Western Ontario, London. A well-known poet, as well as a playwright, Dr. Reaney has received many awards for his work in poetry and theater. His latest play, *Donnelly,* was produced at Tarragon Theatre, Toronto, 1973. His best-known plays for adults are: *The Killdeer; Colours in the Dark,* produced at Festival Theatre, Stratford, Ontario, 1967; *The Easter Egg*; and *Listen to the Wind.* As well as *Names and Nicknames,* his plays for children include: *Apple Butter, Geography Match,* and *Ignoramus.* His latest work for children, "All the Bees and All the Keys," was commissioned by the (Junior) Toronto Symphony

Orchestra, with music by John Beckwith, Dean of the School of Music, the University of Toronto.

AURAND HARRIS has an M.A. in drama from Northwestern University. He taught college drama and worked as director, designer, and actor in various summer theaters before settling into the Grace Church school in New York where he has been teaching for twenty-seven years while continuing to turn out plays—twenty-five published, some in German and Hebrew translations. His awards include ones from Johns Hopkins University, Stanford University, Seattle Junior Programs, as well as the Horatio Alger Award for a dramatization of an Alger novel, and the first American Educational Theater Playwrighting Award. Most of his works are adaptations of old tales and juvenile fiction, the best known of which is *Androcles and the Lion* which has had over four thousand productions in the past ten years. He is a bachelor and lives in Greenwich Village, New York City.

JONATHAN LEVY was born in New York and educated at Harvard (A.B.) and Columbia (M.A., Ph.D.). He taught at Columbia, The University of California at Berkeley, and The Juilliard School of Music. His plays, for both children and adults, have been done Off and Off-Off-Broadway, and in Canada and England. His English version of Carlo Gozzi's *Turandot* is included in Eric Bentley's *The Genius of the Italian Theater* (New American Library). He is one of the founders of the newly formed Playwrights Theater for Children.

DOUGLAS L. LIEBERMAN was born at the end of the war, attended prep school, considers himself a "rescued pre-med" (Columbia), having "crossed the tracks to theater for a Master's degree" (the Goodman Theater). He has held "the fashionable assortment of odd-jobs" and taught steadily, first at Cranbrook in Michigan, then the Art Institute of Chicago. His adaptation of *Starman Jones* won the 1972 National Society of Arts and Letters Award as one of the two best new children's plays in the country.

BETH LAMBERT was born in Calgary, Alberta, and began to write poetry at about thirteen. Besides short stories and radio and TV plays, she has written three stage plays for children, a stage play for "grown-ups," and two novels—"both rejected." Now in her thirties, she works as an assistant professor of English at Simon Fraser University and lives on a hill over the sea with her daughter, Ruth Anne, eight years old, and her cat, Lolly, sixteen. She is presently working on a series of plays on the "growing pains" of the liberated woman.

MARY MELWOOD was born in Carlton-in-Lindrick, a north Nottinghamshire village "while it was a truly rural community." Her first play was produced there when she was twelve with the encouragement of her mother who had written plays for the community. She married in 1939, lived in London for a year, and then settled in Nottingham where her husband was in business. She stopped writing until her two sons were in their teens, and began again while teaching school. Her *Tingalary Bird* was produced in 1964 by the Arts Theater in London (published in *All the World's a Stage*, Delacorte) and received an Arts Council Award, as did her next play, *Five Minutes to Morning*. In 1971 she left Nottingham to live at Rottingdean near Sussex Downs, outside Brighton. She has just completed her first full-length book *Nettlewood*, a novel for "growing ups."